TESTIMONIALS

"This book breathes new life into every gay mans journey to self acceptance, love and the difficult, yet liberating, process of "Coming Out." Rick does an excellent job of mixing his personal experiences with humor to tell an honest and candid story that anyone coming out can appreciate. This book is a must read for anyone who is questioning their sexuality or for friends of anyone who has recently come out."

David Cruz, III Founder of Finding-Cupid.com and

Matchmaker on Bravo TV's The Millionaire Matchmaker"

It takes courage to practice radical transparency, especially when sharing the awkward and often painful coming-of-age experiences that can pave the way to coming out. Rick's authentic, sweet and comedic voice makes it safe to walk with him through the messy parts of his life and inspires you to celebrate when he discovers his path to self-acceptance and love. Easily relatable and full of heart, "Frankly my dear I'm gay" is a fun read for anyone who's been there and great companion guide for those who are ready Come Out to play.

Jesse Brune-Horan

Spiritual Director/Co-Founder, Inspire Spiritual Community

Frankly My Dear I'm Gay is a heartfelt, and witty look at a controversial topic - coming out late after living in a traditionally heterosexual marriage. This is a rare find in a book where the story of the journey is shared, accompanied by practical tools for navigating the transformation from who you've thought you've always been to who you've always been in your sexual energy. Spoken from the heart with directness, care, love and humor, Clemons provides an arms wide open approach to help those struggling with living their sexual truth.

Joe Kort, PhD, MSW, MA
Author of "Is My Husband Gay, Straight, or Bi?

Frankly My Dear, I'm Gay is irreverent, funny, witty and remarkably real, Clemons is a master at sharing what it is like to find out your normal isn't so normal. Written with the same power, skill, blunt honesty and humor of David Sedaris, we ride as spectators in the front seat of the pink coming out bus – to see first hand its challenges and turn ons, its difficulties and discoveries. Clemons hilariously trashes the myth that being gay means you are somehow flawed, and in a masterful way, replaces it with wise, practical and profound life success wisdom of embracing who we are and appreciating our differentness. You'll blush. You'll laugh. You'll understand what stepping into your true, gay, different, unique, amazing and awesome self really means. A winner.

Jay Forte Author of The Greatness Zone –
Know Yourself, Find Your Fit, Transform the World.

If you are looking for practical guidance wrapped in a truly humanistic approach, Rick Clemons is the guide you are looking for. He presents his insightful advice in way that real people in the real world can apply to their lives. As a therapist that specializes in helping people come out and live their true lives, I highly recommend Rick for his compassionate and honest approach to finding your own truth.

Elliott Kronenfeld, LICSW

For every person who has struggled to come to terms with the true person inside of themselves, this book is a must read. The potential to live the life that your highest power intends for you, requires that you get honest about who you are. Rick gives gay men and women permission to break down their walls, resistance and fears so they can live with passion and truth. Rick does this with humor and insights from walking his own path and helping hundreds of people along their own journey. If you are a individual contemplating your sexuality, this book truly cuts to the chase and offers timeless insights so you can get on with LIVING your life instead of just thinking about living it.

Melanie Gorman, Sr. VP YourTango Experts

With sharp wit and unabashed transparency Rick not only shares his colorful story but also includes a roadmap of self-discovery to assist the reader with their own journey. It is an entertaining and provocative read!

Joel Barrett, Joel Speaks Out

FRANKLY MY DEAR
I'M GAY

Rick Clemons

MOtivational PRESS®
LEADERS IN GLOBAL PUBLISHING

Published by Motivational Press, Inc.
1777 Aurora Road
Melbourne, Florida, 32935

www.MotivationalPress.com

Manufactured in the United States of America.

ISBN: 978-1-62865-268-0

CONTENTS

This book is dedicated to my daughters Shelby & Riley, my husband George, to the mother of my children, and to all the people who are forced by society to hide the truth of who they are by pretending to be someone they're not.

—Namaste

INTRODUCTION

I'm a bottom. No, that's not true. I'm a bottom-line type of guy. I'm also transparent. As well as a parent. I visited heterosexual land for 38 years, did the white picket fence thing with a wonderful woman (and no, the sex didn't gross me out, but it wasn't my preference), and I got bitch slapped by a handsome British guy into my truth. The truth that I was a gay man. (But, more about that later.)

Now, back to the part about me being transparent. I'm not going to blow smoke up your Andrew Christians, or ruffle your Victoria Secret panties either. *Coming out* late in life wasn't easy, fun, joyful, a cakewalk, or a mind-blowing orgasm. Well, actually, it was all of those things and then some. My experience was more like a drag queen; I played a straight guy, who was really a gay guy, pretending not to be gay, all without makeup, or costumes to make the illusion work for a long, long, time. Precisely, the reason IT finally unraveled, IT being my less than Oscar winning performance of living the heterosexual life.

Like many of you who are brave enough to have purchased this book (make sure you have a good hiding place for it, or get the Kindle version), I couldn't keep track of whether I was coming, or going. Wasn't sure I'd covered my tracks, kept my stories in order, or even slipped up. Stress, worry, lying, pretending, and sleepless nights were all tightly packed into the Louis Vuitton of my life. Those bags had become so damn heavy and there wasn't a hot bellboy in sight. Well, there were a few bellboys, but I'm not one to kiss and tell.

So why the damn hell am I sharing all this with you? Because I want you to know that I feel your pain. I don't understand you because I can't fully understand you, your journey, or even your challenges. However, I do get a whole heck of a lot of what you're going through and that's the gospel truth of why I wrote this book. I wanted to provide as many people as possible, with a sassy, serious, light-hearted, heartfelt, perspective and guide for *coming out* of the closet, after having been married, possibly with children, and attempting to live the white picket fence societal dream. I'm determined to virtually hold your hand as you bravely take a stand and utter the words, "Frankly My Dear, I'm Gay!" You will survive. You will thrive. You too will have a happy, peaceful, and productive life after closet dwelling... if you choose to do so. You just gotta slip into your rainbow super hero cape, click your Dorothy heels, and start to trust, believe, and let go. Oh, and you gotta finish reading this book. Starting with, the next paragraph that explains from whence I came into this world to write this book!

❅

Unfortunately, or fortunately, depending on how you look at it, wires got crossed. My D, to the N, to the A, ended up being pre-wired with a penchant for Broadway shows, evenings engrossed verbally slapping down the designers on *Project Runway*, and of course, a deep admiration for furry chested men with nether region packages stuffed into Andrew Christian underwear.

As much as my attention-starved inner diva (Lemon-Odd Pop) would like to imagine that we are better than you, it just wasn't so. Our life began in our Mother's frickin' womb, just like you. It was a short-term, 9-month lease, replete with heated swimming pool, dark, meditation room, and with of course, an umbilical cord featuring curbside delivered meals on demand. Compared to the stresses of adulthood, Momma's Mom-cave was a cushy space to hang out while the Divas of the universe and the Big Guy upstairs worked tirelessly on the construction zone that was me, using Dad's little swimmers and Mom's egg. They did their best to make me in the likeness of the parent's image, except for one little flaw, but we will get to that!

Of course, nine months passed in the blink of an eye. The years zoomed by. Before I knew it, I'm 38, Mom's 55, and about to experience labor pains again. Pains so severe, even Dad will be begging for ice chips laced with Bourbon! But, I'm getting ahead of myself.

For 9 months/270 days/388,880 minutes, Lemon-Odd Pop (remember her, my alter ego diva) and I hung out in Chateau' de Mommasita, practicing water ballet and fabulously pre-designing my future life. Boyhood Tonka Trucks, Matchbox cars, and dirt bike racing with an occasional detour into Barbie dolls and Easy Bake Ovens all made for a damn good kick-start to life. What we didn't factor into our plans were the early boyhood explorations of, "Is your pee pee bigger than mine?" and a confused, raging, sex drive smitten with both genders. At least, that's the line of bullshit I tried to sell myself even though I leaned towards the gender that sported a penis. Along about the teen years, Lemon-Odd Pop and I tired off script writing my life the way we saw it, and took a hiatus. Excess fogginess on the horizon of adulthood, made it easy for us to dismiss the work of planning my future life. Or were we in denial? Yes, that was it. Denial with a capital D. A pattern that would become a fixture in my life for years to come.

Some might blame the way I turned out on one too many high heel kicks to my own head and impersonating Fred Astaire dance moves in *The Gay Divorce* while squirming around in Mom's cave. Others would say it was due to the suffocating tightness of Mom's ever tightening hot pants she insisted on wearing until I came full term. And then there's the theory that because my parents were groovy hippies who frequented

Haight Ashbury and Golden Gate Park, that might have inhaled a little too much of the little green weed, thus screwing up my genes. As far as I know, they neither partook nor inhaled. Even if they had, there's no scientific proof that smoking pot screws up one's sexual orientation. I'm sure someone, somewhere would love to make that correlation and use it as a means to rid the planet of us deviant homosexuals. Fact is, with or without hallucinogens, I was destined to take a sexual orientation detour. Even in my Mother's womb, I felt a magnetic pull towards doing and being what I desired, even if it meant saying, "No, no, no" to others expectations. YUCK! Conflict and confusion were already taking up permanent residence in my cerebral cortex before I'd even learned to say "Momma" and "Da Da!" This sucked, and not in the pleasurable way I would come to enjoy years later.

Fact is, I was and always would be a man marching to a different drumbeat. Of course, the truth wouldn't come to light until my gay adolescent age of 38.

Here's the bottom-line, and dammit you better listen up! During my development, an X Chromosome met a Y Chromosome that led to a uniquely, non-hetero courtship, meaning one thing: "I was destined to be gay!" It had nothing to do with my Fairy Godfather visiting me in the womb, my desire to coquettishly announce, "I'm ready for my close up, Mom and Pops" as I exited the birth canal, nor the slap on the ass from the hunky doctor who delivered me (at least I fantasize that a Dr. McDreamy delivered me) . Although, I must admit, that slap on the ass did awaken a yearning to play, "Me master, you slave!" But, I digress. I am gay and there's nothing that could change that.

Heck, the moment I sprang to life, swaddled in baby boy blue blankie, I began cruising. No, not like hooking up on Grindr, Scruff, or Growlr, "Was sup" cruising. I couldn't even get a non-urine driven stiffie at that point in my life. Instead, I curiously cruised the little rug varmint next to me. That little bitch was styling a hot pink onesie with yellow butterflies!

Damn … just three hours after slip sliding down the birth canal and she's already got a stylist working for her! Nice going! Where was mine, Mom and Dad? I wanted a costume change right then and there. Alas, I would have to wait to learn the life lesson: "patience is a virtue." Oh, screw that! Patience is for the birds. Darn it, I'm an impatient Leo, with no tolerance for waiting. Why should I have to wait for my sexual orientation to catch up to my maturity? I wanted to be me right then and there. It seemed utterly insane, at such a young age, to watch my life turn into repeating tapes of someday. Did I truly have to let my boyhood dreams get lost in the abyss of manhood obligations: for instance, mortgages, marriage, career, and parenthood? Yes. It was part of the master plan. A plan that would derail me from loving me, and being myself. A plan that would kick my ass into learning the art of patience. A plan that would teach me the fine art of letting it go, and letting it flow. Ok, whatever! All hail to the plan. It still sucked until it didn't, 38 years later.

There I was. 3 hours, 17 minutes and 24 seconds old. Me, a controlling, hungry Leo, whose balls had not yet dropped, lacking the balls to say, "Damn it, listen up, and listen now, so no one gets hurt in the future. I'm gay." Instead, I relinquished full trust to Father, Son, Holy Ghost, Mother Earth, Buddha, The Universe, and Higher Power into the principles of The Secret. I choose to let my sexual orientation take its own course from that moment on.

To be perfectly clear, not that I have to make it clear to anyone but myself, my homosexual desires were not purely driven by my consuming fascination with Henry, my pet name for my penis. Nor were, or are they, the mischievous doings of my divaesque essence Lemon-Odd Pop, pushing and prodding me to discover my fabulous sexual self. Instead, my voracious desire to be at peace with just me, without damning judgments or need of others approval is what drove me to the delicious sweetness of self-acceptance, self-love, and embracing the beautiful gay man I am.

I stepped forward. Henry (my penis) and Lemon-Odd Pop (my inner diva), bravely standing by my side, supporting my quest to live my truth. Funny how my penis, alter ego diva, and my muddy conscious, guided me to look deeply into my soul. Examining a truth that has always been and always will reside within me. How do I know this to be true? Ironically because I paused, gave myself permission to question, go still, find my answers, let go, and free fall into the brave, bold, honest, raw truth of me, myself, and I. I'd finally grew weary of listening to my disasterbating thoughts, questioning "Am I, or am I not gay?"

The constant struggle and endless nights hoping for a miracle to wipe away the gay were futile. Rather than fight myself any longer, I finally went still. I let go. I descend into the truth of who I'd always been. No more denying my sexual orientation. I was finished being a ringside observer, watching as others forced me to shred the rainbow colored fabric of my truth to pieces. Deep within, my soul sistah, Lemon-Odd Pop, cried one last apology, "I'm sorry, but I am no longer responsible for making you feel comfortable with me by denying my gay self." No more apologies regarding my Gay DNA.

My sexual orientation is simply a part of me. Me, a powerful gay man with an alter ego diva who'll kick your ass, if you can't handle my truth. I'm a man who appreciates all people, regardless of gender, race, and sexual orientation. UmmHumm! I'm a man whose truth emanates from the stirrings of his heart and heads: the one above his shoulders and the one between his legs. I'm a sexual energy with simple, raw, animal attraction to men, the male body, and the appendage we affectionately call penis, dick, schlong, erection, and of course in rare instances, more than a mouth and handful!

That's who I am and how I roll, in my life and in the hay. For those of you of the lesbian varietal, I'm sure you too can identify. Nothing beats the TaTa's, Va-jay-jay, and sweet surrender as you utter the words: "She's my type of girl!" That's how you roll. So, let's roll!

Are we on the same page? If not, then you better catch up. This book is about getting you on your own gay page, in your own gay way, in your gay sexuality. I want you to feel pulled towards the light of your truth in a loving, amusing, and heartfelt way. I wrote these words to inspire you to bravely grasp the handle of your closet door, twist it open with unbridled confidence, cast fear and shame to the wind, and declare in the light of your rainbow: "Frankly my dear, I'm gay!" Damn it, it's not just my mere musings about womb water ballets, treks through the birth canal with a diva in tow, or holding lovely male appendages in my hands, or a 38-year detour of playing with TaTa's. Truth be told, there's a powerful purpose from whence this story emanated.

I'm challenging you to trust, have faith, and be open to taking the vulnerable detour of finding yourself – whether you want to, or not! Of course, I encourage you to take a light-hearted sense of sensibility on your journey. Don't make fun of your journey, that's insulting to the universe from whence you came. Simply realize that humor and love are the kick ass elixirs that will prepare you to stand bravely in front of those you love – parents, a spouse, a child, friends, co-workers – and say with a rainbow colored brave heart, "I'm gay."

Swan diving into the heart of your homosexual journey, one question you may want to explore is, "Did the 9-month lease in your Momma's womb, perfecting your own water ballet, or dreaming of being a girl on a Harley, lead you to be (GASP) gay?" An even more ludicrous question would be, "Could they have tested for gayness during the ultra sound and prevented gayness somehow?" Neither of these ridiculous questions hold a candle to the most important question you'll pose to yourself. It doesn't matter if you're 15, 30, 55, or 80. The question remains the same: "Why do you believe and know that you're gay?" No amount of wicked humor, blaming tweaked DNA, or magical insights from your whimsical Fairy Godmothers and Godfathers, confirming your sexual orientation, will replace the deep serenity of knowing your spiritual soul. In the depths of your soul is where the raw truth of your inner Diva or Butch voice lies. It's where your life is talking to YOU! Trust me! The deep soulful place is what gives you the brave, bold, insight and kick in the butt you'll need to proudly declare, when you're ready, "Frankly my dear, I'm gay," to whomever you need to in your life!.

However, let's call a spade a spade, shall we? From the wisdom of those who've travelled before you, listen as they share about the detours lurking just past the snipping of your umbilical cord. Trust their stories about the chills and challenges that await you on the outskirts of the post-birth heat lamp, ready to throw you off course of being your most authentic gay self. Yet, calm down and be not afraid. No need to get your Calvin's and Vicky's Secrets in a bunch! Ain't nothing that lies ahead in your forthcoming gay life that a little Cosmo can't cure...provided you're of drinking age, of course! Otherwise, Godiva Chocolate works just as powerfully to heal the scars of others crying in dismay: "Frankly My Dear, You Can't Be Gay!

I'm curious. Have you accepted who you are? The purest essence of you without any stressful guilt and shame? If not, for the sake of yourself and your sanity, it's time to take a stand. Shed the rose-colored glasses that taint your view and that aren't really that great of a fashion statement. Brothers and sistahs, there's a beautiful art in seeing thine self. Find your butchest or most divaesque, ever-loving voice, and your deepest truth. Ignite your brave, bold, raw fire within and declare, "Frankly My Dear, I'm Gay!" Now let's have a Cosmo and a little chocolate, and get started unraveling the truth of who you're meant to be. Can I get an "Amen?"

CHAPTER 1

Denied For Now, But Not Forgotten

The blissful age of my first *coming out* was 19. It wasn't that I shoveled heaps of blame for my sexuality on my gypsy-esque childhood (we moved a lot), the fact that my parents had a fair share of rocky roads in their relationship (they're still at it after 50+ years), or that I spent my early years in fundamental church schools (denomination respectfully unnamed). If I was bitchily compelled to sling mud in that manner to justify my "gayness," I'd...

a) end up with dirt under my nails (not pretty),

b) probably miss my target (I'm not that good of an aim), and

c) feel slimy for jumping on a stereotypical band wagon of, "I'm gay because..."

My logical mind and joyful heart know that I'm gay because I'm gay. No need to lug around a fine piece of Samsonite luggage, filled with excuses regarding my sexual orientation. However, truth be told, "not making excuses" wasn't always the case for me. In fact, for years, I hefted steamer trunks filled with beliefs about being gay that did nothing for building up my biceps, popping out my pecs, or ripping my abs. Oh contraire. Instead, I schlepped those trunks with me from Loveland,

Colorado (my birthplace) to Orange County, California (the location where I finally kicked open the closet door), and everywhere in between. I stacked those trunks neatly around me, my own little mobile fortress, to ensure my truth never would be unpacked. I realize now, a career as a bellmen at The Four Seasons would have be a more prudent choice given the amount of baggage I was carrying. Yet, I don't think a Bellman's job description requires "the keen ability to lift heavy false assumptions, stack hair brained interpretations upon hair brained interpretation, heft limiting beliefs that require you to pretend to be happy for the sake of others, nor holding the door open for the 'not good enough' voices to take up residence in the hotel room of your life." Yes, I confess, I masterfully bought into the bullshit that said, "You're gay and that's just not right!" Overbearing and powerful as those thoughts were, I never fully deterred from my quest to strip the naked truth of my sexuality to its core.

Early boyhood explorations of penis and testicles fascinated me (including my own, of course). Oh please! You know you did it, too. You explored your privates that you'd been told were off limits, so quit being a prude! Like any young person, male or female, SEXUALITY was a big word that created a 5,000 piece puzzle in my mind that had yet to be put together. SEX, on the other hand (because one-handed sex makes you tired), was a little word that caused me to blush. The sight of a naked body, male or female, caused Henry to pop awake at the most inopportune times. Of course, my sexplorations became more exciting, and hand-challenging once I discovered the world of *Playboy* and *Playgirl*; "Shhh, no one needs to know we have these magazines;" - the ones that were hidden away in spots my parents and uncle cleverly thought were undiscoverable, unreachable, and completely perplexing to a curious boy in Superman undies with an even more inquisitive mind. It's truly amazing, the super powers that exist within the groin of a 9-year old on a mission.

The most vivid first memory I have of being fixated on a man happened after my parents made a very curious stop at our local Safeway. A stop where only Mom was allowed to pop into the store. Why was this so curious, you ask? Well even if you didn't ask, I'm going to tell you because it's part of the damn story - Ok? It was a rare occasion for our family that anyone was left out of a shopping spree at Safeway. For crying out loud, Safeway was worth the price of admission (FREE), and was a night on the town for our little family of four. Yet, off Mom went without explanation. How rude! Even though Dad stayed with my brother and me in our 1969 Impala (Dad's joy...well not really, but it sounds so much more dramatic), this entire WTF moment was completely unorthodox to me. It was as if Mom had suddenly transformed into a Bond Girl (not really a stretch of the imagination given my mother's an effervescent, Spanish beauty), who was on a secret mission to discover the elusive ingredient that was making Tuna Helper, the standard dinner fare, beating out Rice 'A Roni, the San Francisco Treat. Boy was I wrong, and glad that I was about her secret mission.

Returning quickly from her expedition, strutting her faux-suede hot pants, patent leather white belt, and white floral embroidered daisy duke halter-top, I noticed one thing was missing – the standard issue brown paper grocery bag emblazoned with the circular red "S" logo of Safeway. Instead, squeezed discretely (or so Mom thought) between her arm, hand-tooled leather clutch, and her breast forced into her halter-top, was a plain brown paper bag that wouldn't even hold a Cragmont Cream soda! What the hell could that bag hold that would magically feed a family of four for less than $.84 per serving? Little did I know then, that brown bags of that size would someday conceal and satisfy a different type of hunger I had yet to discover: gay porn magazines.

Even then, not one to let my curiosity hide in a dark corner, I blurted out, "What's in the bag?" Quicker than a drag queen's ferocious snap, my

Mother replied, "Nothing!" Seriously, I thought? You're going to tell me that we stopped at Safeway, left trapped in the car with Dad, and you come back carrying a bag barely large enough to hold my *Highlights For Kids* activity book, and you have the frickin' audacity to say, "Nothing!" I know, I'm as shocked as you that at 9 years old I could say "audacity," and of course "frickin" hadn't even show up yet in the great American slang dictionary. But, back to the story. Either Mom a) bought us some comic books as a surprise for us sitting in the car with Dad; b) held up the cashier, requesting small bills only, to pay the rent; or c) bought the latest issue of *Cosmopolitan* with Burt Reynolds laying naked on a bear rug as the centerfold.

I personally hoped option "a" was the answer. Prayed that "b" wasn't on the radar because I was too young to be raised by Dad, only having weekend visits with Mom while she did 15 years (well, maybe 5 years for good behavior, and 1 year if the judge liked her hot pants). But, secretly I placed bets that "c" would be the answer and begin to shed light on whether little Ricky liked Dick, more than Jane. Not that I'd really come to terms, by any stretch of the imagination, with my 9-year old "What do I do with this boner?" reality! However, I have to say, the hubbub being made about sexy Mr. Reynolds within the covers of Cosmo even had me curious to see what the "au natural" superstar would do to my desires and stiffy. Yes, I once overheard Mom, Aunty, and of course, others in their ladies circle chatting it up about "How big do you think it is?" with regard to Mr. Reynolds, and I knew they weren't talking about his bear-skin rug!

Unable to wait for the privacy of her own bedroom to enjoy said package and its contents, Mom instructed my Dad to drive, keeping his eyes on the road, and for us boys to, "go ahead and aggravate each other, just don't break any bones because we can't afford to go to the doctors." Even though my sight line was blocked by Mom's shag hairstyle, and, the fact that I was seated directly behind her, I intuitively knew at some point in the not so distant future I would be donning my own 007 persona to sleuth through the house in search of the mystery Safeway package and its contents. What I didn't realize was that wouldn't be necessary because I was about to discover the hidden truth about what was hidden in the little brown bag minus the Safeway Logo.

Even though my forward vision was blocked, I obeyed my mother for once and started horsing around with my brother in the back seat of Dad's precious Impala. Tactfully, I positioned myself on top of my brother to tickle him (remember these were the days before "click it or ticket" seatbelt laws). I then pretended to try to get away from him, bounced up, cast my eyes forward, to the right, and downward at my mother's lap. Mission accomplished! Mr. Burt Reynolds lay naked in my Mom's lap, so to speak. The controversial *Cosmo* had been acquired, although soon it would be hidden out of sight in our home. The hiding place was no mystery. I knew that as soon as we got home, Mom would hide the magazine on the top shelf, of the linen closet, under Grandma's hand-sewn doilies. Bet Granny never saw that one coming...her doilies covering Burt Reynolds' package!

Memory doesn't serve me well, nor does it have to, as to the exact number of days that crept by before I rendezvoused with Mr. Reynolds, one-on-one. What I do remember is the thrill of setting my eyes on his silken hairy chest. A gasp escaped my mouth as I took in his dark nipples, rubbing my upper lip as a I stared at his smirky mustached mouth, and licked my lips as I followed the pleasure trail down his chest and chiseled stomach to his package, wedged gracefully behind his left arm and purposefully between his legs in a taunting, "Wouldn't you really like to see what's behind door #1?" It was the first time my stiffy and my secret had come out to play (no pun intended) in such a bold manner. I was fixated, heart racing, head spinning, and my 9-year old crotch was stretching the fabric of my Jantzen running shorts. I really didn't know what I was experiencing; I only knew I liked it! Looking back 40+ years later, I'm now seeing clearly how that moment defined my fondness for scruffy men with facial hair, furry chests, trim builds, and of course my own hungry desire to play an adult version of "Let's Make A Deal" with guys, so that I could see what was behind their Door #1 (aka zippered crotch). Alas, I was too young to know that it would take one failed attempt at *coming out* at age 19, a 13 year marriage to a woman I loved for all the wrong reasons, and fathering two beautiful daughters, and 38 years of living, before I would stumble intentionally into my honest truth as a gay man.

✄

As the years progressed, things began to stir in many other areas besides the crotch of my Levi's 501 button flys. Living on a farm in Western Colorado, attending a one-room, multi-grade elementary school, there were few options for male bonding with guys my age. On the things to do front, it pretty much came down to, "you ranch hand, me farmer, let's plow," literally plowing, changing sprinklers, stacking hay, picking apricots, and etc. On top of my already dismal California Kid meet Colorado lifestyle, my family wasn't really all that welcome in the community, for a variety of reasons that will go unprinted. Let's just suffice it to say lots of drama emanated out from us, adding another nail in the coffin of my unhappiness. Stack it all up with typical pre-teen angst and it's not surprising that I started having regular visits from Mr. Not Worthy, Mistress of Self-Doubt, and Madame Insecurity. Of course as anticipated, kids being kids, one day I would be the Queen of the Crop, the next "Queer Eye for the Country Guy," even though my sexual orientation had yet to come out of its cocoon. Teasing, name calling, not feeling "boy enough" lead to frequent trips to "cowboy down," as I kept trying to avoid my truth.

Solace and some glimmers of happiness came in performing. Not in a sexual exploration way of performing, so get your minds out of the gutter. Like many individuals, who, at this pre-pubescent age become confused about their feelings, I hid my true feelings in activities that led the naïve observer astray and off course. I learned to play the piano with fervor. Partially because my parents insisted I learn to play; however, I was willing to play because I found my piano teachers husband to be very hot. While Julie, my piano teacher, was cool and a dead ringer for Barbara Streisand (hello, that should have also rang some bells that my Gay DNA was alive and thriving), I simply couldn't wait to show up for my lesson and have even one minute looking at her handsome, rugged, furry chested husband. No, he didn't walk around with his shirt off (trust me, I wish). However, I'd learned the thrill of his little bit of fur cropping out the top of a t-shirt or visible above the top button of his shirt would make my heart go pitter patter. To feed my solitude of "farm boy with no toys and very few boys to call my posse," my days were spent creating theatrical show stoppers in my head that from time to time landed on the little farm community fellowship hall stage. One production in particular, I must have channeled from the future. Ironically, this Tricky Ricky Production, had dark shades of the future Broadway hit "RENT" interwoven into the plot, even though there weren't gay characters around for miles (except for me and my friend Johnny). Plus, "RENT" was still in the womb, waiting to be birthed on the Broadway stage, years into the future. Internally, I began acknowledging my own "shades of gay," continuing to hide in the darkness of "it's just a phase," and chalking it up to my raging adolescent hormones.

On rare occasions, a trek from the farm to the local swimming pool, found myself once again squarely bobbing in the ripples of confusion. Surrounded by my farm and townie buddies of all shapes and sizes, each blossoming in their own state of adolescence, more often than I liked, I had to deal with the anchor between my legs (aka pre-pubescent boy penis) protruding straight out from my Ocean Pacific swimming trunks, just as the life guard would blow the whistle for a "all-hands-on-deck" pool time out. Embarrassed by Henry standing at attention, I did my best to race out of the pool ahead of everyone, clambering over innocent duck and horse floaties, walking/not running, to quickly squat cross-legged Indian style on my towel, before anyone would notice Henry

attempting to escape the confines of my swimsuit. Inevitability, as I ran/
walked for cover, the lifeguard would blow his whistle at me, instructing
me to "slow down farmer boy with the pitch fork standing out of your
crotch," causing all eyes to fall on me and my non-dysfunctional erection.
As expected, laughter ensued, my buddies ribbing on me. This led me
to a dysfunctional belief that something was physically wrong with me
sprouting boners...until one day. It was a sunny summer day. The kind
that caused sweat to bead up on our skin and trickle down our hairy
treasure trails...sorry, wrong book. Anyhow, it was the day I noticed,
other guys copying my WNRIS (Walk Not Run Indian Squat) move that
I'd perfected.

Finally, I realized I wasn't abnormal nor the only one with a penis
jutting from a hairless groin every time the Lifeguard blew the whistle
for time out! I was so over joyed with my discovery that I memorized
the "time out" breaks, so that I could be out of the water, resting on my
towel, before the husky, hot, privileged townie lifeguard could wrap his
sweaty lips around the whistle and blow. Not only did I wish my stiffy
was his whistle, I learned how to fulfill my wanton desire and curiosity
about other boys and their penis toy. I became a spectator of the "stiffies
on parade," as guys ran for safety of the squat at each time out break.

One particularly wretched 100+ degree day, you would have thought
there was Mutiny On The Bounty; whines, and muttering arising from
everyone in the pool, when the moment the whistle shattered the summer
air. It was simply too damn hot to leave the cool pool for the rest break.
Yet, break they did. I say "they," because I was already in position to count
full-mast crotches. Even as my innermost thoughts scolded me, telling
me, "This isn't what normal boys do," I gleefully counted more than 20
protruding swim trunks emerging from the pool. Might I remind you
that these were the days before board shorts had even been conceived;
therefore, Speedos with built-in flagpoles only added to my voyeuristic
delight, a delight that was short-lived as every one of my buddies, as well
as strangers had perfected my WNRIS move. DAMMIT. Luckily for all

of us, due to the extreme heat, the break was short lived as the concrete was too hot to sit on; it was blistering our precious little boy and girl buns. Unluckily for the boys suffering from erectile function, they had to "walk, not run" back to the pool, speedo, trunks, and cut-off jeans, flying at full mast. For me, it was like seeing a double feature at the cinema, without having to pay extra, and getting popcorn for free.

After I'd watched the double-feature and allowed my Henry to come to rest, I joined my gang in the pool. I noticed my good friend Johnnie hovering near the ladder, masthead and chest turned towards the pool wall. The rest of the "boys will be boys" gang wasted no time getting back to horse play, dunking each other in the water, hand-standing to impress, and checking out the mostly flat chested girls who'd become less than interested in the boys now that they'd seen the size of their mastheads. I made my way to Johnnie's side in the hopes that he would hang with me. For some reason, he wasn't much into chatting, and continued to keep his back to the pool, hands firmly grasping the ladder, chest glued to the wall. Not wanting to join in the masculine hoopla overtaking the pool, I settled in next to Johnnie quietly observing the young male bodies within my grasp. Holding onto the edge of the pool with one hand, my back turned towards Johnnie, I felt the ripples of water as someone pushed by us, using the ladder to exit the pool. In that moment, Johnnie had to let go of the ladder or have his fingers crushed by a strapping, muscle bugging, ranch hand that in reality was probably all of 16. Before I knew it, Johnnie's hands were latched onto my shoulders, chest to my back, and, as you probably guessed, his protruding penis was poking me in my yet undeveloped bubble butt. No wonder he was facing the wall. Yippee! I had found a comrade in arms who understood what it was like to "stand at attention without being asked!"

Being somewhat sun burnt, I used my condition as an excuse for Johnnie to remove his hands from my shoulders. Freed from his grip, I pivoted to face the pool, and instead ended up face-to-face with Johnnie. To say that time stood still would be too theatrical. However, what did stand still were both of our crotches; still, at attention, pre-pubescent masthead to pre-pubescent masthead, rubbing up against one another. Egads, it was my first "close encounter of the crotch kind," and also another reminder to "put that thought away, it's not right!" Yes, I'd already begun to firmly set the stage for denial, shame, and guilt of being who I was to require a complete mindset reset 30 years in the future.

⚜

By the time I reached my high-school years, I'd created an unconscious habit of wash, rinse, and repeat about my feelings towards who I was as a young man, and the feelings and desires I harbored towards other guys. I'd be lying if I didn't admit it. Like many adolescents – males and females – I was red-faced embarrassed to drop my drawers in locker room, found sexual innuendos about girls and crotch sizes laughable, yet discomforting, and froze at the thought of describing which base I'd got to on a date, even as few and far between as dates were.

My high school was small, not as small as my farm community elementary school. Though large by comparison, at 400 students my high school was still TINY. It was a boarding school of lovely Christian teens from all over the Southwestern U.S., where each of us came to the halls of academia from varying socio-economic backgrounds, and of course our own hierarchy of who's cool! Though I didn't live on campus, I somehow seemed to be at least on the fringes of the "in crowd." Mostly because I

a) was an easy going guy (not easy sleazy),

b) wasn't one to make too many waves (except when jumping in a pool),

c) strategically made friends with the best looking guys on campus (surprise?)

Being a Christian boarding school, boys' dorms were on one side of campus, girls' dorms on the opposite side of campus, and hell hath no fury like a pink slip to the principal's office for crossing that line without permission. However, teen hormones are teen hormones, so from time to time they allowed "date-approved" social events, which basically meant happy hour at the hormone bar. Everyone scrambled to get dates for the talent shows, choir performances, or intramural basketball games. I referred to these events as "PGPSRPA Dating" (Parental Guidance, Permission Slip Required, and Principal Authorized Dating). Yes, it was that strict. In fact, so strict that even if it had existed in that decade, uttering the words "Gay, Straight Alliance," would have gotten you expelled and prayed for at church for weeks on end, unless there was a funeral. Funerals trump praying the gay away, any day of the week!

Feeling obligated to play along, I dated, felt a few girls up (ughh), pushed a few boundaries by making out during "school approved" rated films (mostly Disney stuff), and came frighteningly close to a couple of third base moments. Even then, the little gay voices cried, "This isn't you, but it's what you think you're supposed to be!" In some weird twisted way, I often wanted to blame the constricted environment and rules for brainwashing me into playing the role of "boy meets girl, boy dates girl, boy touches girl," and avoiding my truth. After all, everyone on campus was trapped in the belief bubble of "sex for procreation" – NOT! Ok, maybe a few; however, the rest of us were just horny teens with hormones out of control. Co-ed activities were limited to classrooms, cafeteria, and the occasional social event with, (gasp) "GIRLS." This made it very easy for me, and others, whom I suspected shared my same proclivity of same-sex attraction, to fly stealthily around campus, under everyone's radar while we perfected our gaydar. Socially forced to hang mostly with the same sex, provided the perfect cover for our secret, "I'm gay, are you, and let's not admit, it or tell anyone, ok?" society to be seeded, but not to blossom fully.

From time to time, I stayed on campus with my buddies in the boys' dorm. Manning it up, I'd hang with my most masculine friends, in hopes that their testosterone would rub off on me or at least pool around my feet in the cavernous 10-head community shower with no privacy stalls, and miraculously seep into my skin, curing me of "hot guy you make me hot" disease. Of course it didn't, but at least the thought of it kept me feeling protected in the company of more macho guys than I ever thought possible! Alas, every so often my truest self, Lemon-Odd Pop (although she hadn't yet been named) would strap on her Diva heels, ready to taunt and test me as only the little bitch could. Whether it was stolen glances at someone's family jewels in the steaming shower, having my towel ripped from my hips that caused me to scream like a drag queen who just got sent home from Rupal's Drag Race, spontaneous erection of Henry my penis, or pretending to be a heterosexual would be tested more and more frequently. While my masculinity did battle with my femininity, I kept my external cool, never letting anyone see me sweat...until one fateful night.

Rowdy and hyper undercurrents of energy filled the cinderblock structure of the dorm that fateful evening. I'd stayed over, hoping our study group would finalize our preparations for the semester history project and presentation. Needless to say, the never-ending racket emanating through the halls was annoying Lemon-Odd Pop and me, so we went in search of the Hall Monitor to let him know, "We'd had enough and weren't not putting up with this, no how, no way!" The second floor of the dorm, where I was staying with my best friend, was usually the quietest at it was reserved for the more mature Juniors and Seniors. As Lemon-Odd and I continued our search, it became obvious that the rumble was coming from down under, on a lower hall to be exact. Unable to find my best friend, or the Hall Monitor for that matter, I descended to the 1st floor, also finding it quiet. Realizing the racquet and masculine man snorts were coming from Freshman quarters in the basement, I almost retreated back upstairs versus deal with nimrods of the Freshman kind, even though there were a few tasty morsels I'd eyed and remembered from the Freshman orientation that I helped organize. However, like a magnet my inner self drew me towards the sounds that had invaded what was supposed to be quiet study hours.

Rounding the corner at the base of the stairs, I was greeted by a crowd of guys, in varying forms of disrobe, most only in their "tighty whities," nothing else adorning or covering their beautiful masculine bodies. You'd have thought I'd stumbled into a "G-Rated" version of a "Broke Straight Boys" porn shoot. As usual, my inner logical voice started shouting at me, "Run! You shouldn't be here," while Lemon-Odd Pop giggled, "It's raining boys. Hallelujah!" Before I could retreat, unidentified hands grabbed me, willingly and yet unwillingly dragging me into the mass of shirtless, boy/man bodies.

Taller than most, and still fully clothed, I was at an advantage and disadvantage. Advantage because most the guys had to jump to up to grab me around the neck or get on my back, thus losing their footing. Disadvantage because my clothes made it easy for a multitude of hands to grab hold and pull me into the fray of sweaty bodies. Without my consent, my shirt and pants were ripped off my body as taunting voices cried, "Too many clothes, too many clothes." Scared and vulnerable, I was caught in a in a myriad of emotions. From the depths of my masculinity, I was inspired to join in the dog pile and wrestle – man-to-man. This thought was a stranger from a foreign land in my subconscious mind. I, Rick, was not ready to rumble and wrestle...but I did.

Jockeying into position amongst the sweaty chests, Fruit of the Loom covered butts, and straining quads, pecs and abs, I grabbed a shorter guy (still one of my turn-ons – short guys). He was a guy I'd always secretly crushed on – blonde hair, boy next-door type, crooked smile, stocky tight body - the epitome of the "lover boy on campus" with all the girls. Here we stood face-to-face, my hands gripping his bulging biceps, his hands grasping my shoulders. Beginning the dance of the youthful warriors, I heard the warrior taunts around me, "Take the wus down Todd! Show him how a real man wrestles." Normally, words of this caliber would've sliced through me like shards of broken glass and ripped at my face as I flew through a windshield in a head-on collision. Little did these boy men, with insignificant minds, know this time they were about to meet a new Rick. By blatantly showcasing their packages, abs, and round bubble butts, they'd ignited a fire within that wasn't going to be doused. Me, my manhood, my perception of self were ablaze and I wasn't backing down – even though I was half-naked and sporting a rather impressive hard-on!

Slightly lifting Todd off the ground, I quickly kicked his feet out from under him, leaned into him with pleasure and victorious determination, chest-to-chest, eye-to-eye, sweaty breath to sweaty breath. Forward momentum slippery footing catapulted us to the ground, I was on top of Todd – my first unconscious indication of my desired role in forthcoming man-on-man conquests to come – I was a dominant top! Struggling to free himself from underneath me, driven by the beating chant of the man boys, veins popping out on his neck, Todd wiggled and squirmed beneath me to my conscious and unconscious delight. Physical exertion, and animal thrashing about had turned his face from the pallor of winter white snow to beet red. Surprisingly, yet not surprisingly, sweaty faces, deep breathing, and pained faces weren't the only things that had responded to the friction between us. Hidden away, safely out of sight, tightly pressed against my right quad was a stiffness most teen men our age awakened to every morning – a hard penis. Ironically, it wasn't morning. It was late in the afternoon, in the basement hallway of the dorm, as sweating, masculine, testosterone-pumping boy-men, shouted, "Don't surrender to the Faggot," and Todd laid flat on his back experiencing a blood pumping erection. Of course, what was I to do with that other than spring forth my own to rest safely out of sight on his thigh, less than a half an inch from his low hanging balls?

Without missing a beat our eyes met, fear and embarrassment creating an intoxicating cocktail that neither of us had tasted before. I knew, my teenage angst was finally face-to-face with the essence of my sexual self. I was a homosexual, and it appeared short, stocky, boy next-door, blonde hottie Todd was either...

a) experiencing the same confusing feelings as I

b) embarrassed that he'd sprung a woodie, or

c) didn't know how he was going to face the ribbing of being pinned by the guy that most people loved to call "light in the pants."

Forgetting about Todd, I basked in the euphoria of having mounted, pinned, and conquered the hot short guy that made the campus girls swoon, while I on the other hand, no hand job required, provoked a reaction out of him that he and I least expected. Caught up in my own reality, I subconsciously accepted my attraction to short, boy next-door types, and my desire to be the dominant, from time-to-time, behind bedroom doors, or where ever my sexual exploits would take me. While my brush with Todd was a liberating experience, for the remainder of high school (however), I put same sex attraction thoughts to bed, in a deep slumber, and to not be awakened. Until a handsome Brit, and a big bitch slap of reality would ignite the fire within to have the courageous confidence to step out and be the gay man I was meant to be 20+ years later.

✂

Like many who've marched before me, and those who will follow after me, I wandered, ran, and played the masculine role of dating girls in high school and college, living to please, and consistently using my own version of Cover Girl Makeup to hide the real me; the me with blemishes that no make-up could ever hide. Contrary to the stereotypes placed on gay men by society, I was never overly effeminate, or fabulous to a fault. I was simply a gentle soul, versus your average "Macho, Macho Man!"

Embarking into my college life, a private Christian one, things really didn't change until they did. Stealing glances at guys in the showers became a more overt past time. I continued to purposefully make friends with guys I found attractive, ensuring they only saw and got to know the masculine side of me that played the role of a "man's man!" Ironically in Tennessee, the legal drinking age was 18, and drink I did without getting caught drunk on campus. I didn't drink in excess, but I did enjoy my cocktails, even though I had to be extremely careful to not get caught by the undercover faculty sent to various restaurants and bars to spy on and catch those of us who weren't obeying the school rules. Cunningly, my circle and me discovered ways to circumvent the stalkers, making our way to various fine establishments of ill repute like Ruby Tuesdays, and TGI Friday's, so we could enjoy our libations of choice.

During this period, I also found an escape from my false reality by participating in dance classes and performing in theatrical productions. Same script as the farm and high school years, just different stage location! I experienced deeper, self-guided, sexual orientation, mining excavations. Whether it was the cutie from our school production of "Fiddler on the Roof," sitting on my lap during a rehearsal break suggestively wiggling his tushy on my crotch, or the Mikhail Baryshnikov look alike from dance class who always conveniently never had a ride back to his college after our rehearsals, I was having my fantasy, just not eating it too.

More and more, in these moments my heart ached, as did my restrained crotch, each time I experienced the touch of another undercover college guy hiding his own similar frame of mind and desire. Shackled by my own inability to shake free from false assumptions and limiting beliefs about being gay, I remained imprisoned in my mind, only enjoying the fantasized world of what might be, if I was to break free to be myself. Self-satisfaction only in the stolen moments of masturbation, a practice that suspended me between hetero and homo worlds, which in reality, was a twisted avoidance to be "gay!" It also alleviated any risk of actually going further with Mr. Fiddler on the Roof, or "I need a Ride (I bet you do)" dancer guy. Needless to say as the college years progressed and to the deep disappointment of my inner Diva, Lemon-Odd Pop and me played the "straight-gay role," and stuffed my honest truth deeper into the "It's Not True" folder, I completed my degree in Nutrition and Hotel Restaurant Management. However, as bland as my college years may sound, they were much more vivid than the picture I just painted.

Two significant situations finally presented themselves that firmly laid the foundation that shifted my beliefs, almost 20 years later. First, I finally "came out" to my parents at age 19. Did it over the phone and was immediately shut down. "Not acceptable, no how, no way, this is not what

God intended you to be." Thanks Mom and Dad for being inconveniently non-supportive and pulling religious house of cards when I needed you most. I was and wasn't surprised, nor was I capable of standing up to their position, so I crumpled and retreated. Just like I crumpled and retreated to spend thousands of dollars to go to a Christian college, so that I could be in debt because they thought it was best. Honestly, in a very alternative universe sort of way it was for the best. It saved my life...so to speak.

I immediately started counseling with the College Pastor after I came out to them, which I now realize served two purposes. First, it planted the seed that nourished my desire to do the work I do now, enabling me to listen and provide perspectives, so that individuals can discover their truth for themselves and live it without guilt and shame. And second, (this seems sacrilegious to share, but it is true), I developed my attraction for lean guys, with glasses who are kind of nerdy. I confess...YES, I thought the pastor was hot. Wise in his words, and handsome to look at, a winning combination in and of itself, his counseling provided a perspective, which made me realize that I wasn't ready. I was in no shape to step into living the life of a gay man in the early 80's because I was not mature enough to do so. Nor was I ready, willing or able to stand up to my parents and their beliefs, no matter how contradictory they were to my own. I now realize, my decision to stay in the closet was a life-saving moment. Had I *come out* at that stage of my life, I wouldn't be writing this book and sharing my ideas for "coming out without coming unglued" with you. It was the early 80's, and the confusion about "something's killing gay men and we don't know what" was running rampant. I know that I have a tendency to jump before I think; thusly, I would have jumped and potentially ended my ability to think clearly or stay alive. At one moment I almost said, "Fuck you," to my parents and the pastor. I didn't and not two years later I learned why, which leads us to the second significant event in my college life that changed everything.

My Dad's oldest brother was one of the early casualties of the HIV/AIDS virus. He was a San Francisco resident, well known in the community, and my favorite uncle. Even when I wasn't capable of seeing my gay self, he showed me what a loving gay couple could look like, during a time where gay couples were considered FREAKS! After moving away from California, I still knew what was going on with my uncle and his partner, and I know now that subconsciously their life represented the out of focus blueprint of what I wouldn't allow myself to believe would one day be my life. Once again, truth got buried in the back of the closet behind Lemon-Odd Pop's stilettos.

Caught in the throes of unanswered questions and diagnoses, we all stood on the sidelines wondering what was next for my uncle. Like many a family faced with this ravaging beast of a disease, all we could do was to watch him deteriorate from a handsome man into a skeletal being held together by drawn skin. Provoked by familial duties and out of pure love for my uncle, I flew from my new college, Oklahoma State University, to California for what would become my last visit with him before his passing.

I vividly remember arriving at the hospital and finding my dad hunched over this man he called brother. Gone were the days of fancy dinners, hosted in the restaurants owned by my uncle and his lover. The lackluster view from his hospital room, in no way resembled the breath-taking cityscapes we all enjoyed from his home nestled above the Castro and right below Twin Peaks. Wrapped in the thin fabric of a less than stylish hospital gown, my uncle struggled to be present, aware, and awake in his surroundings, purple blotches covering his skin. During brief moments of rare clarity he'd speak, only to drift away, one step closer to his calling on the other side.

In an awakened state of clarity, in the stillness of his hospital room, he and I were shared a moment; a moment that is forever etched in my mind. Rolling his head painfully towards me he uttered, "I had a choice. A choice to be faithful, and to play safe." That's all he said. A strange stirring in my heart caught me off guard. I was not prepared to embrace the wisdom of those words because I had yet to release myself into my own truth.

Within a matter of weeks, my uncle transitioned from his human experience. The moment I received the word of his passing, a new fire kindled within me. I was inspired to follow a path of undefined direction, in order to in some way honor the life of my uncle Wil. What that path was, remained a mystery.

College life continued at a rapid pace. I toyed with a few gay guys in my dorm without truly admitting I was gay, or doing anything sexual. I even embarked on an ménage a trois with my roommate and his girlfriend. That experience, opened my eyes to the touch of another man, me touching him more than him touching me. Thank God, we were drunk and I was able to play it off as being more turned on by his girlfriend than his horse-sized penis (hello, size queen alert). Awakening from that drunken experience, I stepped even deeper into exploring the reality of "This is not me and this is just a bad dream?"

On trips home from Stillwater to Tulsa and Oklahoma City, I often found myself sitting outside of gay bars, shaking like a leaf, afraid to enter, fear masterfully preventing me from pushing through those forbidden doors of mystery. More and more often, I found myself checking out guys at the gym, sharing mutual jerk-off sessions from afar, leaving the locker room, filled with guilt and shame, which became a pattern that would become my life for many years to come. Fear of being caught became a prescription that I thought would rescue me from acting on my desires. To heal the wounds I'd created by settling into a routine life of denial, I'd permit myself the occasional, mutual jerk-off session with a stranger I'd meet in the most unorthodox places. In some weird demented way, these encounters masterfully helped me pull the wool over everyone's eyes, including my own. I'd become a closeted homosexual man, hiding in the pretend heterosexual body; in addition, creating and living within beliefs that ironically got me through the day, which enabled me to build a life, pretending to be something, and someone I'm wasn't, all the while racking up gold stars from everyone around me whom I needed to please. I wasn't just pleasing them, I was also being who they wanted me to be, in order to make them feel comfortable with me!

Unbeknownst to me, my own confused hidden agenda, placed me on a yet undetectable gay journey where I had the innate ability to disconnect from reality. This confusion was the ironic start to my healing, to resetting my mind-set, so that by the age of 38, I'd finally retreat from the dark madness to stand in my own power, staring down the demons of other's expectations of me and look them in the eye and say, "This is me and I am worthy of being my own authentic self." And so I did! Me, the hidden homosexual, along with my alter ego diva Lemon-Odd Pop, I finally had the balls and make-up remover to wash away the mask to say, "Frankly My Dear, I'm Gay!"

CHAPTER 2

Flushing The Toilet Works Wonders

Regardless of which side of the bed you wake up on, the Zodiac sign you're born under, or the tragic childhood you may have endured, everyone has the ability to take a "thought dump." Take the idea of who or what you should be, flush it down the toilet, and let the toilet bowl cleaner of your life help your "new truths" become crystal clear. **No toilet brush required.

Parents, society, and even friends are telling us *who we should be,* and *what we are to believe,* which is setting a ridiculously fast pace for buying into bullshit on a regular basis! If that works for you, then great, it works for you. Please take no offense, none intended. Rarer than finding delicious fruit cake, it's hard to be human, let alone gay, and then to be stung by the "Should Bee's" of life put upon us by others! Don't roll your eyes and look away, or jump in with a fake hand to chest shriek of, "Not Me!" I'm not buying it honey! Admit you've been stung more than once by the "Should Bee's." If you don't, I'll just have to bitch slap you. And I'm really not in the mood for that, given we've only just met!

Reality is reality, and as a gay parent (not that being gay has a darn thing to do with it) there've been more than one "Daddy Dearest

Moments," where I've said to my daughters, "You should..." It's pre-wired in our parental, societal, and human DNA! Fresh out of the womb, we're introduced to our first "Should Bee's." While not intentionally directed at us, grandparents, doctors, nurses, and experienced parents, hustle and bustle around our temporary plastic condo murmuring...

"You should make sure he's swaddled tightly!"

"Shouldn't her cap be pulled down tighter over her ears?"

"You should ride in the back seat with him on the way home!"

Fantastical advice and insights. They're the first precarious steps that plant those seeds, which grow into a whimsical garden of fauna and flora that attract "Should Bee's" for our lifetime. Buzzing with frenetic activity in the grey matter of our mind, "Should Bee's" are repeatedly planted, cultivated, blossomed, harvested, and exquisitely arranged into bouquets of our lives. Being wee peoples with free minds and spirits, we enter this big, exciting, scary, interesting world. Stripped free from any belief structure, we're free to create our views as we please, provided we adopt others viewpoints without question. It's questioning and challenging what we've been told to believe that sets us free, and allows us to find ourselves.

And, that, my friend, is exactly what I did with my rainbow colored bouquet of beliefs. I finally looked myself in the mirror after 38 years, and said, "Frankly my dear, Rick, you're gay and you have full permission to decide what that really means for you." In that moment, and in the many seconds, minutes, hours, days, weeks, months, and years to come, I sorted through a myriad of "Should Bee's" – stale, rotted, dead beliefs that had been shoveled, and dumped, into the compost heap of my life. I replanted new thoughts, fearlessly embraced my core beliefs that I chose to live by.

✄

Sigh! It's common for those of us who haven't blossomed fully into a heterosexual to believe there's something dangerously and hideously wrong with us. Could it be that dear Mom's sweet hot pants, had put on too much pressure on our DNA ladder while lying on her side as we were nestled in the condo of her womb? Of course, it's always possible Dad dropped us one to many times off the changing table while he tried to master the art of diaper duty. Or, God forbid the DNA fairies were too busy mixing Cosmos while they worked and accidently forgot to match "X" with "Y" in the appropriate order, and voilà: another homosexual was mistakenly, yet purposefully, born into this world! After all, THERE ARE NO MISTAKES!

Can I be candid? Of course, I can. Like many of you, I constantly questioned, "Why me?" which lead those lovely adornments of shame hanged over my head. At times, it felt like I had a migraine the size of the Grand Canyon filled to the brim with Sarah Palin worshippers. Thankfully, I came to my senses – as did Ms. Palin's PR folks – realizing no good would come from rationalizing and fitting myself into a place where I didn't belong. I was not intended to be a heterosexual any more than gun toting, bubba loving, talking-out-of-both-sides-of-her-mouth Sarah Palin was meant to be co-pilot of the United States of America. Although, I do have to say, "That gurl sure does know how to pick a good-looking husband." Woof! And, for a straight, confused republican, possible tea party thrower, her fashion sense ranks about an 8! But, enough about Ms. Palin, she's taken up more words in this book than she deserves. Now, just as I did, it's time for you to dump your quirky thoughts into the toilet and flush them!

My first awareness that my false perceptions about my "gayness" were beginning to slip away was in my late twenties. Yes, I was a late bloomer, so get over it. And don't be so damn judgmental. There's wisdom from whence I come late to this party we call being gay. I, like many of you will, finally realized...

1. Gay isn't gross and I'm not gross
2. Admiring men doesn't mean you lack masculinity. If you're of the Lesbian persuasion, admiring women doesn't rip the femininity out of you either.

3. Effeminate, soft spoken, swishy, and fabulous isn't the only recipe for being gay

4. Lack of interest in sports, working on cars, and smoking cigars (the gross smelling kind) didn't make me less of a man

5. Going to Gentlemen's Clubs isn't my cup of tea, and I find it demeaning to women. Although, some of those male bartenders in those joints sure can make you holler!

As fresh crops of thoughts and insights began to flourish, I realized I had a right to grow my own garden of genuine thoughts, intimate feelings, and mindful behaviors that would kick my booty closer to my true self. Admittedly, family, friends, and societies expectations continued to influence me. Yet, I didn't have to buy into anything unless I chose to, and neither do you. Really, you don't! I swear you upon a stack of *Advocate* magazines, you don't!

I learned that respecting my own thoughts, feelings, and behaviors helped me respect others thoughts, feelings, and behaviors without being a flaming, sadistic, bitter queen. During that revelation, I also found that loving myself first opened up a brand new South Wing in my heart making room to love others more. Getting caught in the hamster wheel of "others first," while wearing high heels, may seem the best way to keep the world going round. To that I cry, "No, no, no, no" to the beat of Amy Winehouse's "Rehab!" (God rest her soul!) If you don't know how to do loving for yourself first, then you don't know how to do loving for others any better. I admit, there's a fine line between selfishness and selflessness. No one likes selfish, all-about-me people like the "K" family (Kardashians). No offense, ladies, you're just not my cup of tea. It becomes really simple when we discover how to make room for ourselves in a deliciously healthy manner, which in turn un-fogs our Dolce & Gabbana sunglasses, so we can see the brilliance of seeing others without being blinded by the light of our own ego!

I also started to realize I wasn't broken, weird, a freak of nature, or gross for wanting to touch, hold, kiss, be intimate, or have a lifetime relationship with a man. Quicker than I could run to a 31% Off Sale at the Kenneth Cole Outlet Store, my self-perception dramatically began an upward spiral on the ladder of self-esteem. Step by powerful step, I realized I was as much responsible for my own self-image and negative beliefs regarding my "gayness," as was anyone else. Sharp as a bitch slap between Alexis and Crystal on *Dynasty*, I comprehended it was time for the blame game to stop, and my truth be set free. I lifted the lid off the treasure trove of the false beliefs I'd created without breaking a nail, and started smashing each little, semi-precious, no longer needed belief jewels, one by one! For the first time in my life, I acknowledged and stood for what I believed. I encourage you to do the same, in your own way, in your own time, so that you can fill your own treasure chest to the brim with beliefs that have you shouting from the rooftops, "Hallelujah, I'm FREE!"

✄

I'd always held a conflicted belief that being gay meant I had to be girly, effeminate, and somewhat weak. Granted, I wasn't a ball-scratching, sports-head, man's man. Nor, was I walking around wishing I had a hunk of a man to protect and take care of me like a damsel in distress. I was a guy who was emotionally and physically attracted to guys: plain, and simple! I just happened to like guys! I remember the first time the International Male underwear catalogue arrived in our (mine and my wife's) mailbox. I was...

a) surprised how it got there,

b) intrigued by the bodies and crotches on the front and back cover and every page in between, and

c) afraid I was going to spring a woodie that would rip a hole in my freshly pressed Dockers!

Try as I might to act uninterested, a delusional state of being one foot in one life and one foot in the other life, I couldn't wait to look through the catalogue once my wife went to sleep. I even made a grand production out of throwing the catalogue in the trash can, although I was careful to place a layer of paper towels between it and the leftover scrapes from dinner to protect grease from blotching up those perfectly chiseled male bodies. Yes, I knew then that I was, you know, on a deeply quiet subconscious level, a man attracted to other men, but not gay. Sound familiar? Of course, it does. Your annoying little voices are whispering, taunting you to the edge, and inviting you to come out to explore and play. Yet, you brush them off, ignoring them, and say, "That's not me!" I know. I was there once too. So why do we ignore the obvious? Because we choose not to believe that we are what we are – gay!

Here's an interesting insight that Lemon-Odd Pop wants to share with you. In your moments of utter disbelief is where clarity can and will prevail. It shines a glimmering light on your truth, provided you give yourself permission to be lucid in your thoughts, emotions, and behaviors. Yep, you have to stamp that hall pass, "permission granted," and bravely step forward to reset your mindset about what you believe to be true, so that you can discover that some beliefs aren't true at all. Here's another little secret gem of truth. For each of us, this journey towards our truth will be uniquely different, and yet in so many ways, similar. Based on your values, family/societal brainwashing influences, perceptions of the world, and the way in which you put yourself in a pretty little petri dish to be examined under the microscope of your critical mind, you'll either thrive through the *coming out* journey (Yay), or remain in a conflicted state of feeling hopeless, until you don't (Nay).

In order to step over the "woe is me" ya gotta don your overalls, grab your intellectual tool box, and retool your mindset about what gay means for you and only you! Every crazy perception and blindsided belief you have about your sexuality starts with a thought. Each of your thoughts leads to a "You're messed up" or "You're cool" feelings, which ignites the "WTF" or "It's all good" behaviors. I'm not sharing with you anything you don't already know, but just reminding ya the simple truth! How we behave has a positive or negative impact on us, as well as the peeps around us. Just like choosing between a Kenneth Cole and Calvin Klein, we can "Wash, rinse, and repeat," producing the same negative results over and over again, or "Stop, reset, choose a different setting, wash, rinse, and evaluate!" Personally, I like being the master (um hum), which is embracing the reality that everything in my life begins with a thought. The more I adopt this powerful principle, the easier it became to have a joyful *coming out* journey that continues today.

My ***Masterful Mindset Reset*** formula is simple, and works as good as a CrossFit training session with Ryan Reynolds barking at you. Oops, sorry got off track with that little fantasy. Here's the formula:

I Think → I Feel → I Behave

Of course, to create massive biceps, abs of steel, and a booty you could bounce a half-dollar on, you have to add a little more weight each time and invite another Ryan, the Gosling one, to be your training mate for extra motivation. The same goes for the ***Masterful Mindset Reset*** formula. At each step we add the simple twist:

I *Choose To* Think → I *Choose To* Feel → I *Choose To* Behave

That's it! The **Masterful Mindset Reset** formula. Wait that sounds too clinical, so we're going to call it the **"Shift Ya Shit (SYS) System."** It reduces stress, gets rid of muddy thoughts, helps you get real with your values and beliefs, and fills up a big martini glass of relaxed, authentic you being yourself.

Let's not mince words. There are lots of messed up crossroads we're going to travel while *coming out* of the closet. Honestly, at times you're going to be overwhelmed with a trunkful of conflicted thoughts, out-of-control feelings, and beliefs that will confuse and derail you; therefore, making it virtually impossible to navigate any direction, even with your newly found Gay GPS – you know the SYS System. No worries! Just put the pedal to the metal and engage your new SYS System to help you efficiently undress the false beliefs and instead choose to think, feel, and behave as the powerful and free you. The you that you've been and always deserved to be. Before you can shift gears and use your SYS System for living, you need to address some annoying little obstacles that will crop up on the road of your *coming out* journey. Once you identify these little buggers (not boogers, that's just, so not gay to talk about boogers), you'll apply the SYS System to each bump in the road, so you can enjoy the ride without paying costly tolls as you journey down the freeway of loving yourself on the other side of the closet doors.

Obstacle #1

"There's Gotta Be Something Wrong With Me!"

Unless you've grown antennae out of the top of your head, started wearing outfits made of meat like Lady Gaga, or been diagnosed with chronic sleep disorder due to watching to many "Ex-gay YouTube Videos," there's absolutely nothing wrong with you, nor the feelings you're experiencing. Your burning attraction towards the same-sex might feel weird because the majority of the population surrounding you is wired differently. The reality is that THIS IS YOU. PERIOD! END OF DISCUSSION.

I'm not going to debate whether the medical or psychological findings that support same-sex attractions are fake or real. If you need that type of validation to get solid in yourself, then Google until your hearts content in search of, "Why are people homosexual?" Instead, I'm calling forth my Diva, Lemon-Odd Pop, to hold up her sassy hand with a fresh new perspective and holla, "Been there, done that honey!" If you follow our lead, and before you know it, you'll be cutting yourself free from the closet of perpetual conflict of "I'm weird and being gay just isn't right!" So, let's get started with some "Duh" moment questions, shall we?

1. When did you choose be right or left-handed?

2. At what point when your Daddy's sperm met your Mommy's egg, did you choose your sexual orientation?

3. Do you remember the name of the hair-follicle salon where you chose your hair color?

4. Ditto for when did you choose your eye-color?

I rest my case for now!

Interesting how perspective always flushes out the best in us. In order to determine for you, and only you, what is **RIGHT** and **WRONG**, you gotta let go, let it be, and start thinking for yourself. The world, your friends, and family provide you with a ton of good, bad, and ugly information to process. Of course, depending on the source of reference, we humans have between 50,000 and 70,000 thoughts per day. I'd sure love to know who is counting and how they do that! No matter! At that pace, which is enough to wear you out and muss up ya'lls makeup, that's slightly over 4,000 thoughts per hour for the 12 hours you're awake. Now factor in, trying to figure out which thoughts are **RIGHT** or **WRONG**. That's enough to make Mother Earth pull up roots and leave this planet and for Lemon-Odd Pop to drop her dreams of being the next Diana Ross.

However, there's another way to keep the peace and stop the insanity. Choose your thoughts rather than being at your thoughts' disposal. Following this train of thought, pun intended. You invite Sistah Clarity to the dinner table of your human experience. Life is a banquet of rights and wrongs, good and bad, lucky and unfortunate, beauties and ugly ducklings, jumps and falls! While you graze through this buffet of thoughts, you'll discover the power of choice. Some, as you probably have discovered, attempt to argue that being gay is a choice. Good for them, that's one of the entrees of their beliefs they'd chosen to and piled on their plate of life. (I hope they choke without someone who knows the Heimlich Maneuver in sight, or get perpetual diarrhea eating that belief. Wait! That's not being understanding nor hospitable, so just erase that last sentence from your mind.) Ok, back to you! What do you choose to put on your belief plate? A belief based on what everyone else has told you? Or, a deep understanding of how you feel in your essence? Butterflies in the tummy and hearts beating with desire typically don't point to "Danger Will Robinson. Something's wrong!" Go ahead! Turn up the volume on your authentic inner voice, take a delectable taste of everything you've experienced throughout your life up to this point, and savor the truth. Listening to the truth that dwells deep within leaves no room for anything to be **WRONG** with you!

Obstacle #2

"God Hates Me and Has Given Me a One-Way Ticket to Hell!"

No road has been more travelled, bridge crossed more frequently, argument more heatedly debated than the tired old cassette tape playing, that "Homosexuality is a sin!" Now, for good measure let's throw the bisexuals, gender non-conforming, and transgenders on that same train to keep the damn, sinful homosexuals company in hell. Now that we know where we stand, and where were going, let's take a big Muscle Daddy, Butch Lesbian step towards uncovering the real truth.

For myself, (and millions of other "sinful gays") the obstacle of religious strife regarding our sexual orientation is probably the largest hurdle (other than family acceptance) to get past, both internally and externally. Why? For many of us, faith and church, from a very young age, with or without our consent to participate, represented community, acceptance, love, hope, joy, belonging, and (on more than one occasion) a chance to take a much-needed nap. Regardless of said faith, practicing religion made us a part of something bigger than ourselves. Amen to that. And no, I'm not being sarcastic. Some power greater and bigger than me brought my beautiful gay self into this world, and it wasn't just Mom and Dad's ba da bing, ba da boom, bedtime antics.

I'm sure you've heard the saying, "Bigger is better." If not, now you have. For me, this phrase helped me pull up my britches, skip past the potholes of my confused religious beliefs, leap forward into a renewed peaceful state of being, and be at peace with my higher power beliefs. I unlocked the naked truth about my maker, discovered he/she was "Bigger and better" than any "HELL" I was headed towards just because I happened to fancy having sex (and a relationship) with a man. I deconstructed my faith, and reconstructed an enlightened sense that my maker was the *biggest and bestest* power in the universe, who created a full spectrum of feelings and emotions for us wee mortal humans to experience. I also realized because my maker was a *bigger and better* higher power that there's no way he/she could have screwed up designing me. For me, it's as simple as the reason 1 + 1 doesn't equal 3! Someone *bigger and better* doesn't screw up simple math. So, why would he/she screw up making millions of homosexuals throughout history and beyond?

Don't think for one minute how I came to reconcile my faith with my sexual orientation is how you should go about doing it! How you choose come to terms with your own religious thoughts and forks in your spiritual road is entirely up to you. You know better than anyone else, the depth of your faith and relationship with your maker. Nevertheless, I encourage you to explore the following questions:

1. Why do you believe in a higher power?
2. What answers does your higher power give you when you ask, "Am I a sinner because I'm gay?"
3. What do you want most from your religion?
4. Where do your beliefs come from regarding homosexuality?
5. Who holds the answers about your sexuality for you?
6. When you feel most content, is your spiritual guide still at your side?

As you contemplate these and other questions in an effort to bring balance between religious beliefs and your sexuality, please consider embracing your *coming out* as one of the deepest spiritual journeys you'll embark upon in your lifetime! Residing at the core of your being is a harmonious, spirited, Tango dance of your spirituality and sexuality. Your logical mind holds tightly to old beliefs, while your inner spirit steps gracefully and powerfully forward in the new rhythm of your life. The quick-footed dance, calculated steps, and drive to be your truth should and will catapult you center stage into the spotlight of authentic living. I envision our maker smiling proudly; leading a standing ovation that assures you that this is your moment, your truth, and your destiny. So, by GOD, kick up your heels and bask in the limelight!

✄

Obstacle #3

"Gay Sex Is Kind of...Yucky?"

Overcoming thoughts that gay sex is gross may or may not show up on your list of thoughts as you embark upon your adventure out of the closet. However, for many gays and lesbians, their illusions of how gay sex is done stems from a screwed up sense of over indulgence of porn or teenage locker room talk. Crazy right? Not if you're one of those petrified about their first same-sex sexual encounter.

Slightly beyond our toddler years, many of us were harshly told, "Child, it's not appropriate to touch your privates in public." To avoid the confusion, "Privates" in the armed forces and "Privates" between your legs are two different things...of course you know that! We've been clinically trained to address our privates as penis and vagina. That's just appropriate and politically correct. Of course, already being a rebel with a cause to be my own unique person at the age of 3 or 4, I threw caution to the wind, touching my penis, wee-wee, pee-pee, Mr. Happy in public, whenever I desired because it felt good! It wasn't my parents who were the sexual prudes, it was the others in my life who deviously attempted to brainwash me into believing my privates were "Dirty, yucky, and purely for the purpose of procreating, not sexual pleasure!" Greatly confused, I struggled to grasp the concept of "No touch penis." Yet, I was supposed to fully understand the definition of procreation! Sound familiar?

At this juncture of my young life, the curiosity years - elementary through middle school - were in full swing. I was equally fascinated and perplexed by my little boy body, as well as other little boy bodies and of course the admiration of fully developed adult male bodies. Unfortunately, the only answers to my questions typically came from equally confused classmates, bullies who didn't know as much as they thought about the male anatomy, or from state mandated "Shhhh...Sexuality for Dummies" classes. Of course, none of those sources satisfied my questions nor doused the fire of my imagination about sex, either homo or hetero!

I fantasized constantly about touching, kissing, being with someone sexually of the same gender, and hoped my fantasy would become a reality. Due to a lack of proper education about sexual fantasy vs. reality, I suddenly found myself, drawers down, hard-on up, wondering, "What's next?" You know what I mean, don't you? Every day, in bedrooms, on living room sofas, under high school stadium bleachers, and in overgrown woods (regardless of your sexual orientation or age) at some point in your hormone driven life, whether it's a solo flight, or a "Sexploration, party of two," you venture forth timidly, not knowing exactly what to do. Of course, the lucky ones, with open-minded, cool parents like my friends Todd and Brian, kick off family dinner conversation by saying "Tonight, we're going teach you boys about cunnilingus and fellatio. Now, Todd, please slow down, or you'll gag yourself on your wiener. Also Brian, take your time, savoring each tasty morsel of that raw Tuna!"

All kidding aside, it's normal to feel frozen, stiff, and petrified during your first homosexual experience. For crying out loud, even big mouthed, small penis, heterosexual jocks suffer from performance anxiety. For some insane reason, we're a race who's intent on "award-winning porn performances when we have sex – gay or the other varieties". Regardless of which way you play, and depending on your point of sexual reference, first sexual experiences might make you feel dirty – even if only in the 30 seconds it takes to rip your clothes off. Quite honestly, dirty is in the mind of the beholder and is nothing a little wash, rinse, and repeat won't clean it up.

Getting your sexual groove on as a member of alternative sexualities, doesn't take practice because you're "not the norm." It simply takes practice because like heterosexual sex, "until you've ridden the joy stick or glided into the Tunnel of Love," it's simply a brand new experience. You just have to try, try again until you're good at it. Like riding a bike or learning to walk, gay sex requires patience, letting go, and being vulnerable to go where you haven't gone before. Allowing yourself to be hung up, conflicted, and obsessed about doing it right, snatches the enjoyment away from the moment. Why waste all the energy you've spent coming to terms with being "born this way," so that you could kill the pure enjoyment of your first time?

To scrub away the dirty, yucky feelings I was having about gay sex, I had to get out of my own way and develop the sense and sensibility to overcome my fears.

1. **Created a new normal.** I embraced my desire to be intimate with another man in a gentle, loving way that was "normal" for me. I accepted the fact that what really mattered was what I thought, wasn't what others thought. In fact, this was one of the very first steps I took towards caring for myself, so that I was more capable of caring for others.

2. **Hit the bookstores.** No I didn't start cruising the adult video arcades and bookstores. I literally started reading everything I could find about gay sex. Books like *The Joy of Gay Sex, The Ins and Outs of Gay Sex, and Tantra for Gay Men* were my lifesavers! I sucked down every bit of information I could swallow...no pun intended!

3. **Got educated.** In addition to reading about sex between men, I became highly educated about safe sex. I'm not referring to "The

Art Of Safe Sex On A High Wire Over NYC Pride!" Rather than buy into all the hype and misinformation that "Gay sex is deadly," I decided to find out how and when gay sex would kill me, so I could fully enjoy life. In all seriousness, by taking the invaluable time to understand the potential risks of contracting STD's, and how to enjoy a healthy gay sex life, I built confidence and maintained control of how I showed up and played in my sexual encounters.

4. **Permission Granted.** I wasn't a serial dater during high school and never really had "sex" (yes, I know that sounds very Bill Clinton/ Monica Lewinskyish) until I was an adult. Even though I was a lying, chatting bastard while I was married, it wasn't until I "came out," that I truly gave myself full permission to fully experience rich, no-shame and guilt-free gay sex. This is a big step for many people – relinquishing guilt and shame. Why? We often "have sex," yet don't "experience sex." Giving yourself the hall pass to experience sex makes you vulnerable, curious, spontaneous, and in control. By granting yourself permission to "experience sex," you take control and allow yourself to be in pleasure, based on your rules and your rules only.

5. **Explored the full spectrum of sex.** Notice I said explored, not dropped your drawers, and became a big "Ho." One of the things that makes us feel yucky, insecure, afraid, or judgmental about sex and sexuality is operating from a lack of knowledge. Once I decided I no longer wanted to live in fear of being who I was, I realized I needed stop judging others. The stereotypical gay lifestyle is viewed as a "sex free-for-all." I hate to be brutally honest, but it is same in the "hetero-normative world," it's just not talked about and is kept as a dirty little secret. It's the heteronormative version of "Don't Ask, Don't Tell!" Rather than becoming a judgmental asshole about other people's sexual desires, I started exploring the full spectrum of sexual practices. I found that the more comfortable I became in my own sexual skin, the more I could truly appreciate at a deep level

the many flavors we sexual beings taste and experience — even if cross-dressing doesn't cause Henry (my penis) to stand at attention!

True fulfillment and pleasure as a sexual being comes from being unabashedly who you are as a sexual being! Wrap yourself in the warm embrace of this idea and you'll soon realize, just as I did, there's nothing yucky, or dirty about gay sex … unless you're rolling around in the mud. Even that can be one more fantasy to get checked off your "sex adventures bucket list!" Anyone who attempts to persuade you differently about gay sex deserves to be handcuffed, whipped with a riding crop, and told not to touch themselves. You'll then have to threaten them with 30 days of missionary-position sex as a punishment. To become fully at peace with sex and what others do in this arena, you only have to step into the space knowing you and others are doing the best with what knowledge you've be given to work with. And finally, let it go!

Obstacle #4
"I'll Lose (Fill in the blank) If I Come Out!"

By now, I'm quite sure you've entertained thoughts about losing friends, feeling the sting of family rejection, and maybe even losing your job if you come out of the closet. Check, check, and checkmate. All of these things are possibilities, but aren't true, until they happen. Take a deep breath, get out of your head, drop your shoulders, and relax.

Like you, I got caught up in fears I believed to be true, instead of honoring my authentic self and allowing life to unfold naturally. Of course, it's easier said than done. The fear of the unknown is similar to stepping into a cavernous dark room — scary, until you flip on the light switch. In the light is when truth reveals itself. Until then, all those over-exaggerated, silicone implants of misguided logic and "true-isms" aren't real…unless you buy into them. Granted, situations, circumstances, and the influence of others often lead us to believe, "If I do 'x' then 'y' will happen." Sometimes true, other times (probably more than we want to admit) not true!

The ability to let life unfold naturally cuts the false fears loose of "what may be," and releases us to be in the moment. Sure, uncertainty is always there. That bitch is always just around the corner. However, the more in the moment we are, the more likely we are to see our screwed-up, over-indulged thoughts **PROVEN WRONG**. For instance...

» I feared losing my children and never seeing them again, if I came out of the closet. I'd witnessed horror story after horror story of ugly divorces with children being caught in the middle. That is what I *ASSUMED* would happen once I said, "Frankly My Dear, I'm Gay." – *I WAS WRONG!*

» My inclinations led me to believe my family would disown me, never having anything to do with me once I said, "Mom, Dad, I'm gay, and this time I'm sticking with my story!" I had a good basis for buying into this screwed-up, self-limiting type of belief! Remember, I came out at 19 and was sent to work with the hot, hunky, handsome pastor to rid me of sinful sexuality. It didn't work. It also led me to stay in the closet until I was 38. Yet, even in my strongest moment, as I dialed that phone to confess my truth for the second time to my parents, I was still convinced my relationship with my parents was about to come to an end. – *I WAS WRONG!*

» Given my limited experience of gay life – growing up with a "Don't Ask, Don't Tell" mentality concerning my uncle and his lover; my own cowardly infidelity, sneaking out to have anonymous sex with men; working and socializing with a handful of gay men at my office, pretending to be a cool metrosexual male — I also believed I'd never find love with a man. Up until that point, my gay role models had been my uncle and his lover, other single gay men, or gay men in long-term open relationships. Oh, and of course married men like me who "weren't gay" and liked having SEX with other married men! Thus, I interpreted this is the way I was to do gay life, alone, having one nightstands, being miserable, or in relationship being made fun of by others – *I WAS WRONG!*

Every time I considered *coming out*, cavalcades of *loser*-thoughts formed into mighty armies. Thousands of taunting, crazy-making gremlin voices haunted me. I retreated into the darkest corners of hopelessness, where the Generals of my false beliefs ordered me to stand down from my authentic self. I'd bought into a false truth that *"gays and lesbians"* are losers, freaks, and the bane of human existence. *I WAS WRONG.* Actually strike that thought: *I WAS HIGHLY UNEDUCATED, GRAVELY MISINFORMED, AND RECKLESSLY LED ASTRAY BY OTHERS' EXPECTATIONS – NOW I'M NOT!*

Don't be frightened if you find yourself caught in the clutches of "loser" at some point in the not so distant future of your *coming out* journey. Once you realize you're not a loser, whatever you thought you might lose by embracing your authenticity will be replaced by the kick-ass power of being authentically you. Allowing yourself to *Shift Your Shit* about our sexuality is the first step towards having your own Rhett Butler, Scarlett O'Hara moment when you calmly say, "Frankly My Dear, I'm Gay." The next Step, *Creating Courageous Confidence*, lays the fierce, powerful foundation to love and trust yourself to be yourself – no more shame, guilt, or lack of self-worth. Are you ready?

❧

Mindset Reset (aka Shift Your Shit) Check-In

Answer these questions and complete these exercises before moving forward to the next chapter, My Dear!

1. What beliefs do have about being gay, that is keeping you from being authentic?

2. Which of these beliefs are actually **TRUTHS** undisputable, undeniable facts?

3. What situations or individuals taught you these beliefs?

4. Which of these beliefs would you like to change?

5. Why do you wish to change these beliefs?

6. What will you gain by changing your beliefs?

7. What might you lose by changing your beliefs?

8. Who do you have to forgive for causing you to buy into these beliefs?

9. What might get in the way of you being able to reset your mindset and build more loving and accepting beliefs about yourself and your sexuality?

10. Who, or what resources might you enlist for support during this transformation?

�֍

Mindset Reset (aka Shift Your Shit)
Putting Motion In Your Ocean Challenges

1. Based on the belief work you've done, pick three beliefs that you would like to change about yourself as a homosexual and take the necessary steps to begin changing them in the next week.

2. After examining your beliefs, identify at least 3 people responsible for helping you formulate false beliefs about life and yourself. With your eyes closed, envision these people one at a time and say the following words: "I forgive you for doing what you thought was best for me, my values, and beliefs. I now know it's time for me to do what's best for ME, my values, and beliefs. You are now released from that responsibility. I love you and always will in my best way possible to love you. And so it is!

3. Now that you've identified resources to enlist for support as you transition into your most genuine homosexual self, pick three people from that resource list and reach out to them in the next two weeks

and enlist their support. It's important to tell them specifically what kind of support you require, why they've been chosen to provide that support, and how much you appreciate them for being in your life.

Now you're ready to move into the world of Creating, Courageous, Confidence, so you can say "Frankly My Dear, I'm Gay!"

CHAPTER 3

Curious, Conflicted, Confidence

I've come to an enlightened realization that just about every darn thing we set out to do in life requires five "C" ingredients – curiosity, conflict, confidence, commitment, oh, and one other "C" word, ~~COCK~~ (NO!) courage. These "C"s play significant roles in our journey to achieve our desires. Of course, courage would be much easier to come by if it was delivered by a hunky super hero, clad in a skin tight outfit that shows off the goods in all the right places. But, I digress. However, courage can be a stinker to muster up, depending on the situation. I also found that *courage* and *confidence* flip flop (not like sexual position flipping). Think of it like the chicken before the egg scenario – does courage come before confidence or does confidence come before courage? Doesn't really matter? The truth is all five "c" words, plus a few more, are must have accessories to don before you *come out of the closet.* For simplicity sake, let's turn to a little eastern Zen philosophy and bring a 3-some into play (no, not that kind). It's a three-way process for becoming more you in your own skin.

Curious → Conflicted → Courageous Confidence

Write those down, arrows and all, and we'll jump back to them later in this chapter. Do it. Do it now, or endure the wrath of Lemon-Odd Pop!

❈

Beyond my initial *coming out* at the age of 19 and despite the "chat the gay away" sessions with the hunky pastor, my curiosity got the best of me regarding my sexuality. Raging harder than a sailor's crotch in a pair of 2xist briefs after 6 months of no shore leave, my curiosity taunted me into the game of *catch me if you can!* A super, sneaky thrill-seeker awakened both my conscious and subconscious during my first two years of college.

Conversations with the studly pastor (have I mentioned that he was a WOOF?) only teased my hunger for "M2M" intimacy. I felt mind-numbingly different. It wasn't the few taunting brushes of sexual electricity passing stealthily between ripped guys at dance school, or the intimate dressing rooms I shared with fellow male cast members during various college theater productions that awoke a new desire within me that is alive and well, even to this day.

It happened when I finally said, "enough is enough" paying for higher education at a ridiculously high cost. I took a year off, started working for Dad in his construction business, and found myself even more confused on the "Who the heck am I sexually attracted to?" front. I continued to hide my sexuality, as I slipped closer and closer to my virgin M2M sexual experience. Curiosity drove me towards the edge of insanity, while my 20-something hormones created more wet stains in my Jockey's than a drunken bride-to-be's panties at a Chippendales Show. Drenched in uncertainty, I talked daily with my maker and inner self, begging for magical insights. I begged and explored, "Why am I battling these feelings?" If I wasn't pre-occupied with my bromance crush on Gary at the gym, a short dark-haired, preppy, OU grad with chest hairs that crept just above his shirt collar to drive me crazy, then I was figuratively and literally stroking one out, fantasizing about the homeowner's son on the job site. He was a blond-haired, blue-eyed, pecs, abs, bicep and triceps to die for, captain of the football team type of guy. Naturally, being on a construction site, day-in, day-out, also provided a non-stop parade of electricians, plumbers, and lumber yard delivery guys to fuel my sexual flames. Daily a slew of rugged, muscled-manly men, helped me hone my skills at the sly check-out without being caught. Don't be shocked. Yes, even a not-yet-out gay guy knows how to nail a stud, screw a hole, and caulk a gap! To this day, I can still make a square peg fit in a round hole – shave, trim, sand, and pound it in until it fits.

During my sabbatical, I came to terms with God, my spirituality, and self-awareness, long before "present moment thinking" had made its mark on the world. This new state of open honesty with myself caused me to spend more time in the gym, sharpening my gaydar, making a few gay friends, who by no fault of theirs, scared me into hiding because I was venturing a wee bit too close to my truth. I was frequently invited for a "gay" evening out, only to graciously, as any good gay man in hiding should do, bow out using excuse #27: "Got to be up and on the job site early." Settling once again behind the mask of pretending not to be gay and into the fantasyland, letting Henry (my penis) and my right-hand further solidify their friendship. All was well in little white lies land, until one day, in the shower at the gym, I spied a lean, nicely built in all the right places, African American man checking me out. Or was he? Yes, there it was again. He stole a glance, longingly, lustfully, looking at me again. Parting the curtain, ever so slightly on his shower stall, he was beckoning me to enjoy the show. Shocked and curious, I was mesmerized by what was unfolding, all 10" of it. I was even more embarrassed by my reaction. In that moment, I realized the bonus benefits of gym membership. Enthralled by his performance, I suddenly felt dirty, excited, scared, and ready to explore further. But, how was I do to that or should I even do it? Hell no! I'm not gay!

Vulnerability and fear caused me to fling my shower curtain closed, practically ripping the rod off the wall in an attempt to protect my privacy. Shaken, chilled, and frozen in place, I stood, heated pellets of water raining down on me for what seemed an eternity. Finally, noticing goose bumps had overtaken my skin as the water temperature dropped, fearing hypothermia was close at hand, I toweled off behind the curtain, tightly wrapped the towel around my waist, and headed back to the locker room, retreating into the safe harbor of my clothes. Unfortunately, I haphazardly put my shirt on inside out and my shoes on the wrong feet, left my fly open for all to see, with no underwear insight! Suddenly, everything was wrong with me and everyone was watching me...or so I thought. In this madness, I found myself asking my maker once again, "Have I done something heinously wrong?" Yet, no answer came. Not only had curiosity thrown me into deep inner conflict, I somehow mustered up the courage to face my God, the one whom my beliefs of honesty, integrity, and eternal life had grown from, and asked him blatantly, "Is what I just did in the shower with that strange man wrong?" I know, it's kind of weird to ask the Big Guy upstairs if watching a peep show in the shower is right, or wrong. Then, logic and my answer entered stage right. There wasn't anything "sexual" that happened in the gym shower. I watched a handsome African American man pleasure himself, while I did the same before I flipped out. So, why did I feel like I committed a "burn in hell, you queer" sin? At that moment, the darkness became light, and I realized I was sorting out my definition of sex vs. lust. I was finally confronting a deep-seeded denial of my sexuality that I'd placed on the back burner of my life that wasn't going to just burn away without being addressed.

Deep in contemplation, dazed and caught in my own screwed-up internal conflict, my thoughts came to a screeching halt as I exited the gym. There he sat on the bench outside the exit doors of the gym: Mr. Shower Show. Quickly dropping my eyes, as if I was hunting for my keys in my gym bag, even though they jangled in plain sight from my pinkie finger, I avoided his gaze, marching intently towards my car. My heart was racing. I assumed he'd jumped up, was right on my heels, about to painfully grab me by the arm and slam me against my car, face first in a police hold, and shout in my ear, "What the #$%*, do you think you were looking at back there in the showers white boy?" My own naïveté had lost all sense of logic. Why would some guy, any guy, approach another guy, and ask him, "Why were you watching me rub one out in the shower?" Who in their right mind would do that? I'd lost control, and needed to get home and let Dad bore me to death about all the work we had to do, as a means of clearing my head.

As the flesh of my fingertips met the semi-cool touch of the door handle on my car, I heard this deep southern, sexy male voice, directly over my shoulder say, "Hey there, can we chat for a minute?" Barely able to move, and even more incapable of verbalizing an answer, I nodded yes as I shakily turned to face what I feared might be a fist in my face. Less than 4 feet away, *Mr. Let Me Show You What I Got* stood there, pearly whites smiling, glistening against the dark chocolate tone of his skin. Heart racing, toes curling in my Converse, I felt the intense heat, and heard the "Um hum honey, he's gay," voice of Lemon-Odd Pop, as my gaydar went off louder than I'd ever experienced it in the short time I'd even realized I was equipped with gaydar. Without making this chance encounter sound like $.99 porn novel, suffice it to say, he introduced himself, we chatted about random things for a few minutes, where he left me horny and salivating with a casual, "Hope to see you again soon!" Awash in amazed wonder, I stood there mouth agape as if I'd just swallowed his 10" chocolate candy bar!

Some random guy, not just any guy, a frickin' hot-chocolate Hercules, just told me he looked forward to seeing me again. What do you do with a comment like that when you're a 21-year old, virgin, who's not sure if you're driving in the homo or hetero lane of life? Do I assume he's a nice guy who'd like to be gym buds? Or do I need to become initiated, go through my gay "rite of passage," and be bestowed my "rainbow decoder" before I'd really understand what he just meant? Needless to say, I was so flummoxed by the entire experience, so I went straight home, skipped dinner, holed up in my room, and fervently asked for answers from the Big Guy upstairs; and I don't mean some gay guru living above us. We lived in a single story tract home. I'm referring to the big guy upstairs that created wizards like Steve Jobs! If he was creative enough to inspire a guy to build an empire using the letter "i," then he could help me sort out my attraction to chocolate!

Searching for some sense of Holy Grail regarding my sexuality, I laid awake most of that night, and attempted numerous times to get off fantasizing about "Hot Chocolate with a hint of cream." I stumbled to the job site in a zombie-like state and, once again, failed miserably at work, which isn't cool when you're the boss's son. By the end of the sweltering 100-degree summer day, after smashing my fingers twice with a hammer and almost slicing my right big toe off with a power saw, I left the job site, lost in thought, and headed home. I was placing myself on a gym detox after only having the membership for less than a month. I needed time to figure out the madness that was screwing with me, and not in a good screwing way. After a blissful recovery night of deep sleep, things were just as damn dismal as they'd been the day before. However, work flew by, and before I knew it, I'd shifted into auto-pilot, headed to the gym – detox be damned. Reeking of man sweat and covered with a day's worth of construction dust, I decided not to annoy other gym members with my stench and hit the shower, before I headed into the workout room. I had no sooner dropped my drawers and wrapped a towel around my waist, when I saw the black stallion headed towards the showers. Panicked, I decided a quick sink bath was sufficient to get me through my workout, screw offending anyone else. Of course now, I know that some gay men would find my stench a turn on. Yet another note to self ... never assume anything!

Distracted by the sight of my "strange encounter of the African American kind," I was unable to find my workout rhythm. Too many muscle jocks were hogging the free weights. My favorite machines were either occupied by some of Oklahoma's finest rump roasts, or out of order. Wandering around aimlessly like a lost school boy in a carnival maze, I kept watch on the entrance to the men's locker room, hoping beyond hope that I'd see tall, dark, and handsome leave before he spotted me, so I could get into the locker room, grab my smelly garb, and leave. Finally frustrated to the point of "Are you going to cruise around the gym all evening, looking like your blatantly cruising or get a workout in?" I finally resigned myself to a bench press machine, grunting my way through 5 reps of 10, until I was jolted out of my thoughts by a cute, short, stout cowboy with cute pecs, biceps you could chew on for days, brown eyes, and curly shoulder length locks, who tapped me on the shoulder and asked, "When you going to be done riding that pony?" Obviously my puzzled look indicated I hadn't heard him, or I lacked the ability to decipher his words amongst his Oklahoma twang. Disgustedly repeating himself, he slowly mouthed each word, "When-you-going-to-be-done-with-that-machine?" I knew it was time for me to get out of there before I became the center of attention in a cowboy gang bang, and I'm not talking about one I would enjoy! I was hallucinating about what people were saying to me, and if I wasn't careful I'd misinterpret, "Could you spot me?" for "Could you blow me?"

I immediately jumped off the machine, grabbed my sweat towel and said, "I'm all yours. I mean it's all yours!" Dazedly walking away, I swore I heard cowboy say, "I'd be all yours too," but logic and Lemon-Odd Pop screamed at me to go home, get a good night's sleep, and try to quiet the Gay Men's Choir singing, "If you're gay and you know it, slap your ass!" Without bothering to change clothes, I ripped my stuff out from the locker, practically taking the door off its hinges (a $50 replacement fee I couldn't have afforded), and determinedly strode out of the gym, intent on clearing my head. Rounding the corner of the building, I felt my body say "Yay," and mind say "Oh Shit!" The black stallion stood, next to my car, a gleaming smile on his face, taunting me to make a run for it in the opposite direction. Dammit. With nowhere to go, I walked less determinedly towards my car. But why? Why was I suddenly becoming Timothy the Timid? After all, it was my car and I had every right to claim what was mine, open the door, climb in and drive away, making sure not to run over the black Adonis. With newly ignited determination, I walked straight to my car, not flinching, trying not to let him see me sweat, an oxymoronic impossibility given it was July in Oklahoma. I smiled at him, hoping that was enough of an acknowledgement for him to say, "Good to see you again," which he did. Not quite knowing what to do, I swooned like a schoolgirl in heat, meekly venturing into a conversation with him again. Learning he was nice, not a freak and a recent graduate of the University of Oklahoma, who'd just landed a job in Oklahoma City. He also shyly shared he had a hard time making new friends, and wondered if I might be interested in hanging out sometime. Young and naïve, I had no concept that black stallion, three years my senior, was mesmerizing me with "Pick-up Line #22!" The courting signs were there: suggestive words, gentle touches stroking on my shoulders and arms as he spoke, and more obvious than ever he was closing the physical distance between us. I ignored all the signs, lost in the abyss of a handsome black man hunting me.

As our conversation wound down, out of left field, the expected unexpected, finally happened. Hitting me like a Quarterback sneak in the final play of the Orange Bowl with two seconds left on the clock, he said, "I'd really like to take you out sometime, if you're interested?" Stammering and gulping for a sensible breath of fresh air, I didn't know what to do. I'd just been asked out on a date by a guy. A beautiful, rock my world, African American guy. I didn't even think this sort of thing really happened, especially in Oklahoma City. That's how blinded by my own bullshit I was. I was at a loss for words. I didn't know his name or had forgotten. Scratch that. I was having a sensually, erotic, school-boy crush, and wasn't in tune with the reality of the situation. A feeling that would replay and plague me for the next 18 years.

I immediately sank into the deepest depths of fear; allowing my internal "I can't be gay" tapes to play at an ear-splitting decibel. Staring at him with a dumbfounded face in utter disbelief, I breathlessly said, "I have to go." Little did I know those words would become my shield of denial, protecting my authentic self and true sexuality for years to come, as I went through a parade of guys – sexually and non-sexually.

Diving deep once again into the abyss of trying to reconcile my confusion, I'd missed an important message; loving and being yourself first, teaches you how to love and accept others just as they are too. No, I wasn't ready to fall in love with Jared the black stud. See, I do remember his name. By no stretch of my virginal imagination was I ready for love on any level, no matter how I tried to convince myself otherwise. Though fairy tale romances danced through my head of one day meeting my prince charming, those visions weren't strong enough to prevent me from sculpting an intricate mask that would masterfully hide my truth, cover up my authentic identity, suppressing my sexual orientation. This mask was created purely because being gay was not who Rick was supposed to be according to Mom and Dad, my faith, and a majority of residents in the state of Oklahoma. In retrospect, I realize that shame, denial, and loss of self-identity led to my penchant for the *undercover sexcapades* that slowly began to take root my last two years in college. The locker room shower show led me deeper into a continuing saga of conflicted curiosity that would haunt me. It caused me to question my ability to be a confident man, let alone a confident gay man. Waning self-confidence combined with overt sexual hunger of either the homo- or heterosexual variety, ripped away any potential I possessed to be myself. I was swiftly constructing a mask, layer by beautiful layer, becoming someone I was expected be...a pretend me. It was simply much less painful. At least that's what I had hypnotized myself into believing.

After my year long detour into the world of Construction Hand 101, I realized it was time to get back to college, or break all my nails building houses! I feared returning to college in Tennessee as I might be labeled a big "HO," because I'd slept my way through the ranks of all the other *closeted homosexuals* in the dorm (oh so not true, but a nice fantasy). Instead, I chose not to return to the financial vacuum in Tennessee, and explored higher learning closer to home. My sojourn across the grand dust bowl of Oklahoma Universities, quickly opened my eyes to the positive possibility of going to school where the cowboy's roam free. Talk about creating fantasies! I'd already begun dreaming of landing me a brawny cowboy who's daddy owned a butt load of oil wells, that would grandly support us in the southern life style we deserved – a well-appointed ranch, surrounded by plenty of sexy, studly, ranch hands ready to drop ~~to their knees~~ everything to take care of us. A guy can dream, can't he? Even if that dream is confused by, "Do I want cowgirls or cowboys?"

I'd define my last two years of college from a sexual exploration perspective as "sexually asexual, laden with a heaping spoonful of voyeuristic desires, and the occasional *make-it-work experience.*" I sat on the fence. I was neither admittedly gay nor adamantly straight, and had become a master in the art of *now you know me, now you don't.* Other than my best girl friend, who wasn't my "girlfriend" in the traditional sense, which I now realize now, she was my beard, fag hag, cover, I didn't date anyone while I finished college. Instead, I put on my "not gay face" with the guys in my dorm and called forth my macho guy persona. Needless to say, much to her chagrin, I put Lemon-Odd Pop into a deep sleep, and more often than I like to admit, I slid into my shy shell of a wallflower...sort of.

Football, beer parties, hangovers, hangover recovery parties, working, and making the grades became my undercover routine for keeping my true identity hidden from myself, as well as keeping everyone within arm's reach. I only entrusted one other, "I'll keep your secret if you keep mine," guy on my floor. I wore my disguise so brilliantly that even my first roommate was incapable of infiltrating my hidden reality, mostly because

a) he didn't turn me on at all, which prevented spontaneous woodies when he walked in the room;

b) he and I lived and worked on opposite schedules; and

c) thankfully, we only lasted as my roommates for one annoying semester.

Roll forward to second semester. In a weak drunken moment, for all intents and purposes, I should have been outed. Luckily, roommate number two and I kept our drunken ménage a trios with his girlfriend a secret. Ironically, I know she knew my secret, and if she didn't, even though she wasn't a rocket scientist, she figured it out that night. You'd be pretty hard pressed, even in a drunken state, not to notice your boyfriend's roommate has his hands more on your boyfriend's ass and cock than on or in you. That's what you get, you little tease for coercing us into the *three-way* of love.

I'm interrupting this story for a brief check-in. Without assuming too much, I'm positive some of you have found yourself in similar state of "WTF did I just do?" Maybe you didn't find yourself in a ménage a trios, but possibly in some other ill-fated sexually awkward situation. If so, welcome to the club! Of course, given the fact that Lemon-Odd Pop was alive and well, just not conscious to me, I guess I should say I had an ménage a quad that night. Sorry, got off track. I'm actually referring to finding yourself in an alcohol or drug induced state that led you into the arms of someone of the same-sex, or unchartered state of sexual exploration. Some argue that finding yourself in this type of awkward state indicates an unconscious "choice" to become a *homosexual or bi-sexual.* Though I'm not a therapist or a psychologist, I am a certified life coach and experienced gay man, who would argue, you simply allowed yourself to explore a facet of your sexuality, so don't be so damn hard on yourself. Neither one drunken penis sword fight nor bouncing booby-to-booby dance on the bed by any rational means drives the hetero out of you. Shit happens ... and then you wake up sober wondering, "What happened and why is another guys/gals underwear in my bed?"

That ménage a trios was my last (only) college sexual exploration. Playing it *straight* in college became a top priority. I wanted to ensure I landed a great job, and kicked my career aspirations into high gear. Manning it up as much as possible over the summer between my junior and senior year, I returned in the fall and took on the job of RA, Resident

Assistant. My role was to ensure the boys/men behaved themselves as best as college guys could without trashing the dorm, killing each other, and impregnating the entire college female population. I discovered there was no better way to hide your true self than to let a whole dorm of over 400 (18 – 22 year old) guys think you're the coolest RA because you let them sneak girls in late at night and don't bust them for drinking in the dorm. Once again, I'd created the perfect cover, which allowed me to live out *undercover sexcapades* in my mind, being a wanna-be gay man in one fantasy and then a stud muffin heterosexual in another, without anyone suspecting. Plus, getting to walk those 10 floors every night, did feed my fantasies and make masturbating in the privacy of my RA suite sweet!

I'd actually begun to believe that pretending to be one of the guys, acting like I too was banging chicks on the down low in the privacy of my suite, was a sure bet for keeping my secret a secret. In reality, I was in a state of *conflicted determination.* I was deeply conflicted in my own sexuality, which I was equally resolute that no one, no how, be allowed to figure out how screwed up I was...ever! If this in some way sounds familiar than you too may be suffering from *conflicted determination.* Don't worry. It's not a chronic illness unless you allow it to be – which is exactly what I found myself doing. I graduated from college, jumped enthusiastically into my first big boy job in the hospitality industry (again surrounded by horny college guys) as a foodservice manager at a university, completely avoiding any prescription or remedy for healing my illness from *conflicted determination.* I'd brainwashed myself that it wouldn't be prudent as a young graduate, making $21K per year to throw it all away to be the authentically gay me. Plus, there were bridges of curiosity, conflict, courage, and confidence I'd yet to cross, before I'd be capable of embracing and facing my yet elusive truth.

Conversations I'd had with my soul during college, had sent me on a journey towards revealing and accepting the real me. Yet, even the comfort of the almighty wasn't powerful enough to rid me of my mistaken identity, nor guide me fearlessly into courageously confident space to admit, "I'm a proud gay man!" I still couldn't buy into that belief fully, even with overarching, wanton, college desires running amuck!

Haunted by, and swallowing hook, line, and sinker ingrained beliefs that I was "simply confused," I refused to accept my sexuality, yet blindly and freely acted upon my sexual desires, as if the two were mutually exclusive. Or so I thought! I, like so many others who'd gone before me, had created an alternate persona who was capable of engaging in safe sex with strange men, yet in my mind it wasn't me who was actually present during those moments. I hovered, outside of my own physical body, above the experience, looking both ways to ensure I didn't get caught in my web of lies. My body was the soldier fighting the physical battle of sexual exploration; while my mind was the sentry on duty, ensuring the enemy – my real self and everyone around me – never infiltrated my own little fucked-up country. I'd become masterful and naïve about how I was living simultaneously. I'd sharpened my *straight man's attraction to other straight men radar* so precisely, that all I needed was a hungry look from another guy to find myself engaging in sex with him. Of course, neither he nor I was gay. We were just straight guys who loved having sex with other straight guys! Look it up on Craigslist, they're all over that online "let's hook-up" and pretend we're not gay "meet-up!"

My *conflicted determination* had grown so strong that I blindly propelled myself into a "heart and good intentions" marriage to a wonderful young woman. Out of fear of not living up to others' expectations, I crossed over into my own twisted twilight zone, and pretending with all sincerity to be a happily married man, with the occasional bi-sexual wandering eye. I engaged in disengaged sex with my wife, brought two beautiful daughters into the world, and from all outward appearances was living the "hetero-normative dream by my 30's. I owned a home I couldn't afford, wallowed in credit card debt that precariously led me to the edge of bankruptcy, and hid my inner sexuality behind stolen moments, watching online gay porn and sneaking into AOL Gay Chat rooms, making sure to clear the cache at the end of each excursion on the computer that my wife and I shared.

I buried any proof that I was gay, deep into the ethers of mistaken identity. After all, how could I be gay?

» I'd married, had a traditional church wedding, fought over whose parents' faith would preside over the ceremony (not that either one of us cared), and I called forth Lemon-Odd Pop and my hidden gay energy to style and cater the whole event to everyone's delight. Hello! How'd everyone miss this "Isn't he gay?" moment.

» The circle of friends my wife and I shared were predominantly young, married couples, who were embarking on their own unique routes towards home ownership, popping out babies, and creating success with one exception – I secretly had man crushes of the gay kind on most of the husbands.

» My wife and I regularly engaged in sex as most young, married, couples do - passionate, exploratory, fulfilling, and sensual – provided I kept my fantasies alive envisioning I was Michael Ontkean in the arms of Harry Hamlin in *Making Love*. Rather ironic, how my life was going to replicate art just a few years down the road.

» Fatherhood became my reality, two times over – a reality I believed no gay man could ever experience. How wrong I would later find this belief to be. Thousands and millions of gays and lesbians can have kids. Who'd of thunk?

» I carried on the tradition, creating family ties to hold us all together, even though relationships with my family were always a disjointed mess of "I don't get you. No, you don't get me." I gave my parents the badge of grandparenting, leaving them to rejoice and believe that I'd finally rid myself of the gay plague to become a married with children kind of guy, as all eldest sons should do. Of course, I'd never burst their bubble by admitting I was having a relationship with this woman out of forced necessity to be someone I wasn't. It wasn't time for them to know and understand that yet (and maybe not ever!)

» I was simply a straight man, having sex with other straight men, as a means for dodging the bullet that had taken my uncle's life – AIDS. Married men could never contract that disease because we're married. Unless of course, he was stupid enough to believe because he's straight he didn't need to protect himself. (A thought many married men still buy into because they don't see themselves as gay. They're just having sex with other straight married men!)

In the twisted labyrinth of my thoughts, I'd created a screwed up concept of what it meant for me to be a gay straight, straight gay man. I was lost, confused, and curiously conflicted. However, I was confidently and masterfully hiding my cheating ways, inner stress, and self-hate behind masks of material possessions, outward display of *happy-happy-joy-joy,* and an extra 100 pounds of body fat that on any day could have led to a heart attack. The moment Lemon-Odd Pop bitch-slapped me with the realization that I was playing Russian Roulette with my life from the stress of living a dual life, I realized this wasn't just a *gay thing;* it was a *love yourself enough to be yourself thing* before you die trying to live a false best life*!*

❈

I felt crushed, as if a piano dropped down on me as I walked past a four-story New York City walk-up. Simultaneously compressed by the reality of my life and the fantasies in my head, I started to unravel quicker than a way to skin tight skirt on Kim Kardashians booty! Wait, they're all to skin tight, but you get the drift! I admit, I was living the good life that would make most men envious. Lovely wife, adorable daughters; 4-bedroom, 3-bath home in Orange County, California; sweet, young, nanny/housekeeper to make our life simpler; and leading the life of an executive warrior, traveling the globe, all expenses paid. What more could a guy want? A lot. I wanted to live a real life with real passion, go beyond quickie "I'm not gay" sex with men. I once and for all wanted to kick the guilt, shame, and *cheater, cheater, cheater* voices from my life.

My time had come to confront four very powerful "C" words that had lovingly guided me to this critical, life-changing moment.

» Curiosity had gotten the best of me, as I became consumed with thoughts and feelings of how freeing it would be to live with another man – loving, intimately sharing, and sexually enjoying one another.

» Conflict reigned supreme as I desperately struggled to keep track of all the characters and stories I'd created to mask my truth and fearing at any given moment I'd get caught in the snare of my lying, cheating ways.

» Courage tauntingly drove me to become brave, bold, raw, more out, and authentically me in trusted inner circles, concurrently empowering and scaring me to death.

» Confidence became second nature to me, as I began to peel back layer upon layer of deception I'd keenly decoupaged into the mask I hid behind.

Realizing, yet not fully comprehending, a spiritual transformation was underway, I began to listen deeply to others comments about my behaviors. "You never smile. What's wrong? Are you ok? You look unhappy!" Scraping like fingernails on a chalkboard, those types of words and inquires began to haunt me. How dare anyone accuse me of being anything other than this gilded, perfection of what everyone wanted me to be? I'd spent that last 38 years building a balanced, unbalanced life for all of you who now constantly accuse me of being unhappy. Rather than ruffle feathers I'd respond, "There's nothing wrong. I'm OK. I'm happy." All the while saying under my breath, "I'll smile when I damn well get the opportunity to rock the sheets and hold a guy in my arms on a daily basis. That's when I'll be happy, and you won't because it'll make you uncomfortable!" More and more regularly, I started exploding. Not like orgasm exploding. I erupted with verbal diarrhea, moodiness, and sullenness; in addition, I left my innocent unprepared friends and family members with no other recourse than to say, "What an asshole!" Spot on, no denying it, I'd become a curious, courageous, confident ASSHOLE, incapable of seeing straight – figuratively and literally. I'd do anything to make people believe I was the perfect father, husband, son, friend, and employee. My self-misrepresentations started to unravel, and the demise of *pretending to be heterosexual Rick* was close at hand! The time had finally come for me to acknowledge I was far beyond a conflicted gay vs. straight frame of mind. Little did I know a sexy, handsome Brit was about to ignite the curious fire within, leading me to muster up the courageous confidence to cast conflict to the wind in order to finally step into my own gay skin, once and for all.

Business travel to Europe had become a somewhat regular occurrence in my life. I was Director of Marketing for a hospitality software company with offices in London and Amsterdam, with satellite offices and distributor relationships throughout Europe, South Africa, and Asia Pacific. Our global reach led many of our team, myself included, into the dreaded and enjoyable world of being international road warriors.

My globetrotting revolved around tradeshows, product roll-outs, and maintaining a firm leash on branding and marketing initiatives in order to solidify our market leader position. I typically travelled with an extensive team, of co-workers, leaving me little time to wallow in the solitude of loneliness. I preferred traveling with co-workers provided I liked them, and that, of course; at least a couple of my companions were of the gay or lesbian breed – gay preferred. In these circles, I could be *quasi-gay* for a day or a week, and then quietly retreat into the *heterosexual Rick* as easily as changing my sexy underwear from the Undergear catalogue. By no means did my gay and lesbian co-workers cover my ass, or create alibis for my whereabouts. Without judgment, they gave me space to disconnect from *Reality Rick,* no harm, no foul, and no kiss and tell!

I didn't intentionally intend to be out in this circle; it simply evolved. In comparison to other corporate environments, there was a higher than average concentration of gay men, and lesbians in our ranks compared to the average corporate America environment. We even had a lovely Transgender employee named Cherise. The supportive manner in which this organization-embraced diversity was a rather ground breaking approach, not often found the workplace in the mid-90s. It made me feel comfortable enough to slowly slide the closet door open a crack, a surreal experience that only compounded my dual existence. Everyone knew my wife, and they even helped us celebrate the birth of our first daughter. They, each in their own way played supporting roles in the stage play of my life, helped me to finally summon up the courageous confidence to say, "Frankly My Dear, I'm Gay."

The prelude to that moment culminated in yet another business trip to London; my final visit to the land of the Brits before I'd kick my way out of the closet. Before I lead you to jump to any conclusions, let's clear the air. First, London doesn't turn you gay or instantly cause you to acquire an alter Diva Ego named Lemon-Odd Pop. That bitch/love of my life has been inside me since I was conceived. Second, working in a gay-friendly company, surrounded by gay men, in no way forces you to switch-hit your sexuality. And finally, the lovely Brit, who was the catalyst for my decision to finally come clean and come out, can in no way be blamed for anything other than being in a London gay bar at the right time, so my destiny could play out. He was nothing more than the catalyst that would enable me to finally reconcile my cheating ways, get real with my gay spirit, and once and for all stop pretending to be a happy heterosexual.

Contrary to any assumptions you might have about my previous visits to London or the evening that was about to unfold...

1. I'd never ventured out to the gay London scene, prior to the night of said adventure, even though my curiosity was more than intrigued

by the thought of what it would be like to be in the midst of a sea of British gay men. Often pondered, never acted upon.

2. While I'd always fantasized about it, I'd never diddled secretly, or otherwise with an English sausage, even though the desire was overtly available, each time I visited jolly old London town.

3. I honestly had no intentions of going out for the evening other than to attend an awards ceremony, which I was obligated to attend. Honest to goodness, I was intent on being a good boy.

4. Most trips, including this one, I was always keenly focused on tradeshow activities, ensuring the brand was well represented, and that I kept close track of our sales guys, so they didn't do something offensive in a Gentlemen's Club that would cause the queen to ban us from Great Britain forever.

My goal this trip was to get the job done, grab a couple of souvenirs for the wife and kids, leave London, cross the pond, and get home. You're probably asking, "Then what changed?" The answer, "My entire life!"

I returned to my hotel after the awards ceremony, planning on going to my room, reading, and falling into a much-needed deep slumber. It was early evening, and, as usual, I expected to find few of my colleagues holed up in the hotel bar, having more than a few pints. Preferring not to get caught up in the, "Just one drink," pressure, I discovered an alternate route past the bar; however, from my vantage point I saw none of my crew in the bar, so I was as safe. Of course, that didn't prohibit me from accidently running into one of them in the elevators or hotel floor hallways, but what other choice did I have? I had to get to my room. My journey in the elevator, down the hall to my room was uneventful and free from un-wanted interactions with co-workers, which I greeted with a deep sigh of relief.

Once in the safety of my room, I shed my award ceremony attire and robotically powered through my pre-slumber routine before jumping into bed, only to be distracted by a curious thought crossing my mind: "If no one is in the bar, and none of my coworkers appeared to be in the hotel, who would know if I went out by myself for the night to the West End gay bars?" Honestly, the two other gay guys from the company, who I could play my usual "straight not gay, but love the gay guys" routine with, knowing they'd say nothing, would be the only ones who could catch me. My thoughts excitedly danced to the beat of "This is your chance." As usual, I once again began to disengage, starting my descent into an *out of body experience*. My straight, married-man cover, the guy who only has sex with straight married men, justified my curiosity, if it was possible to, find one of my kind in the London scene. Lost in a heightened state of excitement, I quickly dressed in casual, metrosexual attire, bolted out of the hotel headed towards the West Kensington Tube station, quicker than you could ask, "One lump or two?" I headed into the heart of London, racking my memory, trying to remember the names of the gay bars I'd overheard my co-workers discuss in passing. Feeling a little bit like the blind leading the blind, I disembarked at the Piccadilly Circus Tube station. Still fearing being caught on my solo adventure to gay London, I almost turned back, a feeling that quickly dissipated once I became one with the sea of hustle and bustle of West End tourists and night life. The likelihood of being discovered by a co-worker on "Ricky's First Out Solo Gay Adventure," was about as probable as running headlong into the Queen Mum, who too was out for a quickie run to the corner pub. I honestly wonder sometimes what would have happened that night if the Queen had taken a night off to roust about Piccadilly. Might I have run into her and become one of her best beaus? Sorry, just a thought I felt the need to share!

I walked aimlessly for about 20 minutes before I finally summoned up the courage to ask a Bobby if he knew where I could get a drink that was poofter-friendly. Smugly he said, "Around the corner, down the hill, under the arches is Heaven." I obviously looked dumbfounded and confused, which caused the Bobby to repeat the directions, while muttering under his breathe, "Stupid American poofter." I'd heard of Heaven, one of the hottest London nightspots at the time. Although, I didn't realize it catered to a gay crowd. Ironically, the bar's name, *Heaven*, represented the night I was about to embark upon and the polar opposite of the journey I would start when I returned home, neither of which in that moment, as I walked towards the bar, could I ever have anticipated in my wildest, living-two-lives dreams.

Entering the bar, I immediately lost any semblance of confidence. "What the hell was I doing here? Everyone's staring at me. They all know I'm married, have kids, and shouldn't be here." In reality, those thoughts were a complete figment of my imagination. In reality, no one noticed or paid me any real attention. It was a rather quiet Tuesday evening; except for the techno beat ricocheting off the walls from speakers the size of London tube train car. Pulling up a bar stool, I ordered a pint from a shirtless, furry chested, "just my type," bartender, gazed around the bar, intently trying not to make eye contact with anyone, lest they come ask me, "Looking to shag a bit, Mr. Married Guy with kids?" How crazy was I being? I'd come to this bar, to experience gay London, hopefully meet a great married straight Brit, and possibly do what I'd always dreamed of doing – play man-on-man, hide the wienie with a British guy! No sooner had those thoughts crossed my mind than feelings of guilt, shame, and you dirty, lying, cheating, asshole took over. How strange and weird. I hadn't done anything with anyone and I was already berating myself like a loving Jewish mother. To ease my "You're a shit" thoughts, I focused instead on the gifts I had bought for my wife and little girls, trying to ward off the resounding chant of "You Suck, and I don't mean cock!" My woe is me tirade was rudely interrupted by a deep, gentle British voice that asked, "Can I get you another pint?" Ready with a canned response of, "No thanks, and cheers," I glanced up from my empty mug, only to find the bartender was nowhere near insight. Turning my gaze in the direction of the husky British voice, my eyes, landed on a slender chiseled face, sparkling eyes that twinkled with just a hint of mischief, and a genuine, slightly crooked smile. True to the English stereotype, this handsome face was attached to a lanky, swimmers-build body that exuded sexy sensuality and made me swoon like a little school "girl-boy."

Obviously and immediately awe-struck by this handsome hottie, and without a second thought for my lovely wife and beautiful daughters, I replied, "Sure I'd love another pint." This was no fairytale, and I was not being a hopeless romantic. Up until that point in my life, I had never experienced feelings anything like this for another human, let alone a man, whom I'd only spoken 5 words to. I dearly loved my wife beyond any stretch of the imagination; cherished the miracle of my daughters, loving them more than any words can describe. Nonetheless, in this moment, I was being catapulted out of my normal life into unbelievable state of ecstasy, no alcohol or drugs of any type required.

In the depths of a retired London tube station turned chic nightclub, I was connecting and getting to know a man – a gay man. Simultaneously, I was coming into my own, and saying hello to myself for the first time at a deeper level than I'd ever thought possible. We danced, chatted, held each other, kissed, and laughed. Euphoric, mind-blowing, soul-shattering feelings were assaulting my spirit, heart, and logical mind. I was experiencing the thrill of being "with" a guy without "being with" a guy. But as all good fairytales do, mine was coming to an end. I didn't realize in the next few moments that I was going to take a path I was used to taking; however, it would end up in a completely different universe than I'd ever been to before. Ironically, his hotel was just one tube station from my hotel. You see, he was British, but now lived in San Francisco, and he too was here on business. As I took in that tidbit of taunting information, he leaned forward and asked if I would like to continue what we've started back at his room. For one fleeting moment, I felt the recurring feelings of filth and disgust rise within me, only to quickly disappear as he grabbed my hand, leading me out of Heaven towards another Heaven that awaited us in his room.

During the short taxi ride to his hotel, I realized this experience was drastically different than my previous hook-ups. My emotions were stirred up in an illogical manner that I'd never encountered before. Nervous, unsure, and excited, I followed him to his room where he ordered an exquisite late night snack of fruit, cheese, and champagne. Waiting for our room service order to be delivered, he invited me to "Make yourself comfortable, and relax." Unsure of exactly what he meant, I chose to follow his cue, disrobed, donning a plush/comfy hotel robe. Lost in thought, I was quickly brought back to reality when the doorbell rang, indicating our room service had arrived. My first thought was, "OMG I'm sitting with a handsome Brit, in his hotel room, both of us commando in our robes, about to confront the room service butler. Get me outta here before I get caught!" I was freaking out. He wasn't. Without any hurry hide the gay, not gay, married American, the Brit, bounded to the door and invited the room service chap in before I could hide or cover myself fully. I'd never before been with another man in a hotel room, confronted by someone from the outside world. "How do I do this?" I did it by freezing, sitting there as if nothing were out of the ordinary for two men to be lounging in robes on one king-sized bed, smiling with an "Oh shit" grin on my face!

In an instant, the butler visit was over, and a lovely array of food and libations to enjoy was laid out. The two of us looked into each other's eyes. Once my nerves calmed and the champagne hit, I settled into a lovely evening of sharing ourselves with one another, telling our stories, basking in the late night glow of sweet nourishment and human contact – no sex required. Yes, I said, no sex required. We snuggled, started to get to know each other on a deeply intellectual level, and became sexually aroused by the experience of each other, without our cocks, nipples, or asses being the center of attention. We were two sexual human beings, who experienced the touch of one another, man-to-man. One of us gay, one of us straight; a conflicted thought I'd never experience again. In the quiet still of the early morning hours, I finally began to release my conflicted curiosity. Instead, as the morning light glistened through a slither of a crack between the curtains, I too slipped through a splinter of light into a new awareness of myself. Consciously aware that I had not slept, I turned my gaze upon a beautiful man that had awakened me from my lost self. A man, who in the months ahead would challenge me to be deeply authentic with him, my family, and myself as I stepped through closet doors, allowing my old self to die so that a new self could be birthed. A man who would help me dream of a someday that was yet to come, even though it wouldn't include him. A man who finally drew me, unbeknownst to him, into a safe place of courageous confidence to irreversibly continue my curious journey into self, while releasing the conflict that had shackled me for 38 years of my life. A man who was the catalyst, wise teacher, late night shoulder to cry on, heart-breaker, and kick in the pants I needed to say, "It's time to live my truth!"

Without curiosity, conflict, and risk, it's virtually impossible to create the courageous confidence to step into being authentically you. Diva, Leather Daddy, Lipstick Lesbian, Twink, Bear, and Dyke On A Bike: cut loose and live your destined truth!

This chapter is dedicated to G. M., the lovely handsome Brit who rocked my world, helping me see I no longer was meant to hide in the closet, and who also taught me I needed to be mature as a gay man before I was ready to be in a relationship with a gay man! You'll always hold a special place in my heart!

CHAPTER 4

Which came first? The Gay Chicken or the Gay Egg

I confess, I'm rather conflicted about the *coming out* process with regards to which comes first. In my mind, it's similar to the chicken before the egg debate. You're either going to reset your beliefs so you can have the courageous confidence to come out, or you're going to create the courageous confidence to reset your mindset. Logic leads me to lean towards resetting your thoughts regarding everything you perceive about being gay. On the other hand, I'd argue, (no scratch that) soulfully debate you need to have courageous confidence to reset every screwed up, fearful, crazy thought you're battling within. Either way, you're going forward, following your gut instinct, taking the powerful steps, shifting your mindset, and creating your own courageous confidence to "come out of the closet" to be your authentic self.

For starters, I trust you are fully capable and beyond any shadow of a doubt of finding our own path towards courage and confidence, to be who you are, regardless of what anyone else believes you should be. There's a multitude of paths that each of us can trot down to springboard into our authentic selves. It would be narrow-minded to think we should all Xerox our journey at Kinko's, so that others could follow our lead. Our *coming out* journey is a mirror image of the "cupcake shops" that have popped up in our world in the past few years. Each shop makes cupcakes with frosting. The ginormous differences from shop to shop are the variety of unique flavors each shop brings to tantalize our pallets. Likewise, if you and I as well as everyone else comes out in the same way, then what would be the big deal? Of course, here's my perspective. I believe we all come out at exactly the same time...when we're ready. On the other hand, we also learn by example...the good, bad, and ugly. Let's give the good a fighting chance. While that is a beautiful sentiment, I won't be the first to tell you, "Not every *coming out* experience is all roses, pride flags waving, and confetti celebrations." I'm not going to blow smoke where the sun don't shine, or set false expectations, just to give you some warm fuzzies. However, I do believe in sharing what I've learned as The Coming Out Coach, and from my own life experiences that I hope will shed a little light onto what seems to be the darkest moment of your life – having the courage and confidence to come out of the closet.

If you look closely at the scary, raw experiences I shared, each one of those vulnerable moments took unrestrained courage and confidence to catapult me into my truth!

» It took courage for me to have extramarital sexual encounters with men I didn't know, and the confidence to live a double life without being caught. Don't get me wrong; by no means, am I condoning my actions, nor nominating myself for an award. How I lived was cowardly, yet spawned so much by societies guiding hand. Yet, it takes courage to take risks, and confidence to hide your truth until it finally becomes too much to bear. With that juncture, it takes courage and confidence to have faith that you won't throw your entire life in the toilet by finally being honest, even if it means fully disclosing what an ass you've been for 38 years! Standing in the face of 18+ years of fundamental Christian upbringing, I found the courage to step forward, like many of you will do, to ask my maker one powerful question, "If I am made in your likeness, then why is who I am as a homosexual, considered a sin?" That question, more than any other, plagued me for years. I begged the dogma-based beliefs about Lucifer creating this sin to "Stay out of my thoughts and my conversations with God!" I wanted God, the God I believed was wise, accepting, and the all mighty, to answer me without the cross wired human interpretations of the bible. It took bucket loads of courage, and deep, deep, intuitive listening to dissect the voices of misguided beliefs, so I could clearly hear the authentic voice of my maker telling me, "You are my child, beautiful and perfect in every way." The moment I cleared the earwax from my ears, hearing those words clearly and precisely for the first time, I confidently stepped forward face-to-face with those who found me unworthy of God's approval, including some of my own family. I finally embraced the power to say, "I guess, we'll agree to disagree." And so it is.

» Without blatant disregard for my upbringing and life up until the point of "pretending to be something I wasn't," I courageously stood in the messy disregard for my own values, confidently admitting, "I've been a dishonest, disrespectful, and out of integrity son of a bitch. No excuses, any longer and no more begging for forgiveness. I needed to move forward to be authentically me. In those moments, when you stand at the crossroads of courage and confidence, pretending to be the person you're not, you can either turn left on courage, or right on confidence, or powerfully merge onto the on ramp of courageous confidence. Once you drive onto the fast lane of courageous confidence, nothing is impossible. Both lanes get you there. However, courage and confidence together are the super highway towards peace, contentment, and authentic living.

» Enlightened acceptance of self also requires equal doses of courage and confidence in the beaker of authentic living to create a magical elixir of truth, honesty, and integrity. Had I not been courageous enough to question my beliefs about being a gay father, and closely examined other factors contributing to the demise of my marriage, I'm convinced that I wouldn't be sharing my perspective about powerfully and authentically gaining the courage and confidence to say, "Frankly My Dear, I'm Gay!" Desire for acceptance and love is a strong potion that keeps far too many ill-fated relationships intertwined for all the wrong reasons. Add a couple of drops of curious questioning as to what makes a father a good father, and as you can see, first impressions don't necessarily prove to be true. Along with a big bold state of "Damn it! I gotta be me," comes the unbridled confidence to no longer settle for mediocrity, instead blossoming into a powerful magnificence of our destiny! Not one to strike out on my own, or engage in conversations without a proper invitation, I realize now, that courage, fate, and what was intended, led me to the London gay scene. Simultaneously, confidence empowered me to strike up a conversation with a handsome Brit, allowing myself to be in the moment and not go for the tried and true hook-up.

At this point, you probably sense the overriding theme. Courage and confidence are soul mates in the journey of *coming out of the closet,* and for that matter a powerful formula for *coming out* to be authentic in any aspect of life. Up until now, this concept may have been elusive, causing you to believe you were incapable of embarking on this journey. While courage and confidence are both powerful motivators, for you or I to solely rely on one or the other to catapult us towards living an authentic life, may not be enough!

For example, you may have the courage it takes to say, "I'm gay!" Now, ask yourself, "What does it take to walk the walk, and talk the talk of being confident in your own gay skin?" By mixing a strange cocktail of confidence and courage, you become an authentic powerhouse of YOU! I imagine some of you are asking, "What's the difference, and how do I get comfortable being courageously confident?" I'm glad you asked. Here's 5 Steps Lemon-Odd Pop and I came up with for being Courageously Confident in yourself!

�֎

Creating Courageous Confidence Tip #1
Get Real About Why Being Courageously Confident
Will Make Your Life Fantastic!

If you can't answer the question of "Why?" because you need, want, desire to be courageously confident, it's highly unlikely you will be courageously confident anytime soon. Now it's excavation time. Look under the covers, dig for buried treasure, and expose your hidden gremlins that keep shouting, "YOU CAN'T DO THIS BECAUSE YOU DON'T HAVE WHAT IT TAKES TO BE YOU!" Yeah right!

This is what I refer to as the **DIG Phase** for **creating courageous confidence** for *coming out* of the closet, being authentic, and stepping your truth with clarity. **DIG** stands for…

D - **Discover**

I - **Investigate**

G - **Get n' Action**

Discover

In this phase, you'll ask yourself one question over and over again, "How do I gain confidence to be me?" One of the simplest ways to find this answer is to write down 10 sentences (with 12 words or less) that explain why confidence is important for you, in your life, and how having more confidence will impact your life.

You may be asking why I recommend using 12 words or less! It's designed to help you tightly focus, right out the gate, so that you don't get sidetracked in this journey of self-discovery. No dilly-dallying through the tulips. Focus, focus, focus. Another great way to do this, if you are a visual person, is to clip pictures from a magazine or take pictures with a camera that represent what confidence means to you. It doesn't matter how you accomplish this exercise. The goal is to help you gain clarity about "Why?" confidence in your sexuality is so important to you, and "What?" having more confidence will do for you in your life!

Investigate

Once you've completed your exploration it's time to pull back the sheets and snuggle up to becoming even more courageously confident. Take an inner scan, weed out anything that you've written down just to fill the page, or set aside the pictures that were snapped or cut out just to finish the discovery task. If you're scratching your head, wondering, "How do I investigate my ability to be courageously confident?" The answer: "Questions...empowering, open-ended questions." For example:

» What does being courageous mean to you?

» Why did you choose that picture to represent your confidence?

» How does what I wrote reflect the confidence I truly want to embody?

» How does this photo accurately portray what I deeply desire?

The investigation phase is about discovering what changes to be courageously confident. It will also supports the next phase...**Get n' Action.**

Get n' Action

Now it's time to step into action, get off your duff, and start being real about existing as your AUTHENTIC and GENUINE, COURAGEOUS CONFIDENT YOU. This phase shifts you into the *WHAT'S NEXT?* mode of thought! Take a close look at your list of statements or pictures; pick 3 and ONLY 3 that represent your personal courageous confidence. By narrowing your focus, you gain clarity. Take the time to dig deep into yourself and select the 3 statements or pictures that best represent why you desire to be courageously confident, and what being courageously confident will do for you in your life. This clear focus will begin to manifest your courage and confidence into reality. In other words:

You become authenticly, genuinely, courgeously confident by knowing without a doubt, why you desire to be courageously confident!

However, here's a little cautionary note:

Make sure your authentic and genuine "why" for being courageous, and confident includes the *"i" word*.

It has to be for you, not for someone else, and it has to be so damn personal that you feel it from your heart center outward. From the tips of your toes to the peak of your head. **BE READY TO OWN "WHY" AND "WHAT" COURAGE AND CONFIDENCE WILL DO FOR YOUR LIFE!**

✄

Creating Courageous Confidence Tip #2

It's More Important To Be *Confidently Who You Are* Versus *Pretending To Be Someone You're Not!*

COURAGEOUSLY embracing WHO you are is like flipping on a light switch. It doesn't take an immense effort to flip on a light switch, right? Similarly, when you muster up the inner courage to embrace WHO you really are and take a stand to quit pretending to be someone you're not, it becomes much easier to be in your power. Confidence is built into your DNA and accessible to all. What shifts our confidence is when we're told, and buy into that we can't be something. We suddenly swallow the first pill of "not enough." An addiction that plagues many of us, for a lifetime.

Take a moment; call forth the confidence to be your truest self. Find some aspect of yourself that at one point in time you weren't crazy about. That part of you, you'd never embrace. Then, miraculously, you embraced it because it was so deeply a part of your true WHO. It didn't take much courage to finally accept it. You knew it was a part of you: no questions, doubts, or regrets. From that point forward, what was once regrettable will became acceptable and second nature to you. Here's a simple example; embracing the fact that your either right or left-handed. It's simply an aspect of who you are, no questions asked, once you realize it's just a part of you!

The key point about being confidently who you are, no more pretending, is to exercise your courage and confidence muscle over and over again! The more the "no more pretending" muscle gets flexed and used, the easier it becomes to embrace all aspects of you; therefore, the sooner you'll be pumping up the courageous confidence biceps, triceps, and abs of steel! However, here's a personal trainer for your life tidbit that's a real game changer.

Pretending to be someone you're not takes more energy than being authentically who you are!

To break the "pretend to be habit," we're going to do a little exercise called the ***REWIND***. When you have a thought that leads you towards the closet of **PRETENDING TO BE SOMEONE YOU'RE NOT**, realize you're immediately assaulting your own **SELF-CONFIDENCE.** Why? When you're pretending, you're not being the real you. When you're not being the real you, your internally telling yourself "I'm not good enough." The more caught up you get in your own trash talk and striving to be something you're not, the easier it becomes to trip, make a mistake, and fail. **NO WONDER YOUR CONFIDENCE GETS SHAKEN LIKE A MARTINI!**

Instead, take a deep breath and ***REWIND.*** Rewind your thoughts. Return to the very first time that thought first put down roots in your life, your beliefs, and your consciousness. Doesn't matter if it was two weeks, 10, 20, 30 years ago. What matters is that you ***REWIND*** to the place, time, and situation in your life that caused your first bud of confidence to be squashed.

Once you've gone "back to the future," so to speak, ask yourself, **"Is this thought, feeling, emotion, or behavior inspiring me to be courageously confident, or is it knocking the living crap out of me and forcing me into a choke hold where I can't be authentic?"** (That was Lemon-Odd Pop talking, not me. See how rough that gurl can get!)

If your answer is **"No,"** HALLELUJAH, you've just uncovered the damn source of the little disease we, Lemon-Odd Pop and I call, PRETENDINITUS. PRETENDINITIUS makes you lose all sense of reason and ability to believe you can be authentically who you are in any given situation. Now that you've been diagnosed, you have the opportunity to hold your magic wand of empowerment over yourself, casting a healing spell that kicks you in the ass to be courageously confident, even if it scares the crap out of you from time to time. It's your choice, your opportunity, your decision, and your chance to become your own "gay" fairy godfather/mother.

On the other hand, the one without the wand, if you answered, **"Yes,"** then you've already, discovered the power of not pretending, and can add this tool to your confidence arsenal. For example, if you've discovered casual dating – dating multiple people simultaneously – doesn't work for you, then each time you attempt to casual date, you're actually pushing up against a core value that you hold dear. It could be honesty, integrity, intimacy; any number of things. Yet, trying to casually date because your best friends do it with finesse and ease, doesn't mean it's going to work for you. Instead of pushing yourself up against that insanity wall, turn it into a beautiful confidence builder. *"I'm not a casual dater because I'm more content, happy, and capable of being more authentic in relationships when I'm not distracted by dating multiple people at once. I feel more invested and able to make logical decisions about the person I'm dating and our potential future."*

Doesn't it sound like the person above has a lot of confidence to be him/herself, because they are content, happy, invested, and authentic? Plus, it doesn't hurt that they want to be faithful, and highly attuned to not making rash decisions. I wonder if they're not dating anyone right now? Sounds like a catch to me!

Creating Courageous Confidence Tip #3

How You Use Your Courage and Confidence Impacts Your Courage and Confidence.

I live in a suburban area of Los Angeles, situated 45 minutes from the beach, mountains, desert, the culture of Los Angeles...a perfect place to "raise a family" and still have room to spread your wings.

Like many suburban areas, ours is an eclectic mix of interesting, culturally diverse, neighborhoods, and people. Not far from our home is the gym I go to, LA Fitness, which offers 3 facilities within a 4-mile radius of our home. For a time, each of these gyms was experiencing a crime spree of cars being broken into while members were in the gyms breaking a sweat. However, before I connect the dots with this story, I want to remind you:

How you use your courage and confidence directly impacts your courage and confidence.

Likewise,

How you take care of your wallet directly impacts your wallet.

Now back to our regularly scheduled story.

If I were to leave my wallet on the dashboard of my car, cash exposed, or not, for all to see, while I worked out at the gym, there's a high probability my car would get broken into and my wallet stolen. Why? Because of the unique crime spree that was occurring in gym parking lots across our area, not just at LA Fitness gyms! Ok, ok, so what's my point?

If I leave my wallet, out in the open and visible for all to see, even in a locked car, knowing good and well there's been a pattern of break-ins and thefts, then my car will be broken into and my wallet is more than likely stolen. And who's to blame? Nobody, but me.

Similarly, if you **HIDE AND TUCK AWAY YOUR COURAGE AND CONFIDENCE,** then it's going to remain hidden – not doing a damn bit of good to make you more courageous or confident. No one to blame, but yourself.

On the other hand, when you **BRING YOUR COURAGEOUS CONFIDENCE** out to play**,** then it's exposed for you and everyone else to see. The more you expose and flex your courage and confidence muscles, the sooner you'll begin to experience what **COURAGE** and **CONFIDENCE** look, feel, taste, smell, and sound like. What? How do you taste confidence? How do you smell courage?

Seriously, you think I've lost it, but I haven't. By embracing all of your senses, you build courage and confidence. They aren't called senses because they don't tell you anything; they tell you everything! Our senses help us sense and learn.

» You hear courage and confidence in the voice of an opera diva.

» You feel couragne and confidence when you lose those last five pounds you thought you'd never drop.

» You taste courage and confidence in the culinary delight of a chef who stretches his or her talent to tantalize your palette.

» You see courage and confidence in the determined eyes of an Olympian.

» You smell courage and confidence the moment you inhale an exotic blended fragrance that someone had the ingenuity to create.

Using all of your senses to create courage and confidence, you deeply anchor your capabilities of what you can create once you're filled with courage and confidence!

Think of it as a mirror image of the phrase, "What goes around comes around," once again affirming, "How you use your courage and confidence powerfully impact your courage and confidence."

❈

Creating Courageous Confidence Tip #4
Recognize Your Own Uniqueness Without Comparing Yourself To Others Takes Courage and Confidence.

One of the surest ways to cower in the corner and retreat into, "I'm not good enough syndrome," is to *constantly compare yourself to others.*

You're uniquely you, and for the love of Cosmos, don't you forget it. How you approach life, summon up courage, and create confidence emanates from your own personal power. And, here's a little secret! There's no definitive handbook for courage, no pretty little handbook for creating courage, confidence, or for saying "Frankly My Dear, I'm Gay!" No doubt, there are books, guides, workshops, tele-classes, blogs, and YouTube videos for improving both of these traits. Even this wonderful book you're reading, right now. However, and please highlight this line, there's only one way you'll muster up the courage, stand in your confidence, and step powerful into your sexuality – YOUR WAY!

Let's be realistic and admit it, we're human. In our own way, we each have a tendency to compare ourselves to others. If you don't, then bless you my child, you're a saint, and I have a drag queen to introduce you to who doesn't wear make-up...that's how likely it is that you don't compare yourself to others! Unfortunately, the spider web of **compare, compare, compare,** disables us from seeing our own damn brilliance. Rather than hovering in the shadows of someone else's radiance, **TAME YOUR DAMN BEAST OF "NOT AS GOOD AS THEM," NOW! RIGHT NOW!** It's your beast, and you can tame it, with a little help from Lemon-Odd Pop and me. Here's our three, bestest, and most fabulous tips to whip the comparing yourself to others beast into shape.

» **Recognize and high five other's brilliance.** If you're the least bit prone to being the jealous type, the minute you shun away from someone else's talent, wisdom, or insights, you've just done the old "Mirror, mirror, on the wall, who's the most self-confident of them all?" Like an ugly little pimple festering just below the surface of your skin, your jealousy pops up unable to be hidden by any makeup and shouts "I'm incapable of seeing my own talents and worthiness, so I'm sure the hell not going to compliment you on your talents."

» **Respecting confidence leads to respected confidence.** It's pretty hard to be respected for being confident and arrogant – unless you're Miss Piggy from the Muppets fame! Gotta love her! Nonetheless, and no disrespect for Miss Piggy, when you respect someone's confidence, you're subtly inviting him or her to return the favor and respect your confidence. Simon Sinek, the author of "Start With Why," wrote the following quote about confidence and respect: **"Self-confidence is the ability to exercise restraint in the face of disrespect and still show respect in response."**

» **Courage and confidence is your lifeboat.** The only thing that will, can, and does cause you to sink is when you punch holes in your courage and confidence with crazy making thoughts of **COMPARING YOURSELF TO OTHERS.**

Observing, admiring, and looking up to someone else is a fantastic way to say, "Your courage and confidence ROCKS." The moment you switch gears, make statements, or take actions that demean our own talents, gifts and abilities in the face of others talents, gifts and abilities, we give our self-worth the finger and tell our **courage and confidence** to take a hike.

Creating Courageous Confidence Tip #5

The Universal Handbook of *"How To Be Courageous and Confident,"* Is Not Universal, It's Individual.

It took me awhile to grasp the concept that saying to someone, "I understand how you feel" is complete and utter bullshit. No one, not you or I, can honestly understand how anyone else feels because we're not having their thoughts, experiencing their feelings, nor standing in their shoes. Nor can anyone else be ***courageous*** and ***confident*** for someone else. Why? Because:

The universal handbook of ***"How To Be Courageous and Confident"*** *doesn't exist. The only thing that does exist is how you choose* ***"To Create Courage and Confidence"*** *for yourself.*

Obviously, others play a role and contribute to our levels of courage and confidence. Often, consciously and unconsciously, others overstep their bounds, directly impacting our inner courage and self-confidence. Bless them, forgive them, and raise a Melonball Martini to them for doing what they thought was in our best interest. Then, move forward, using your own brand of courage and confidence. In the manner of our own free will. Instead of relying on others to pump us up and make us feel desired, loved, and worthy, it's time for a new prescription to manage your own self-induced anxiety, and step into your damn power with upmost courage and unbridled confidence.

Buying into a false sense of, "I need you in order to feel (fill in the blank)" means there's a higher likelihood that your need for external approval will never dissipate without working on that belief. Another bogus common belief that blows your confidence is, "I need you to understand me, so that I can feel understood and accepted." These types of beliefs prevent you from being authentically who you are, thwarting any attempt to step fully into your brilliance.

In this wicked, twisted state of needing others to understand us, or show us how to be courageous and confident, we often lose sight of one truth. It's all within our own power to be courageous and confident and rid ourselves of the "Not good enough," monsters.

Losing site and getting off track is part of our journey. It's the way we get refocused and reset our internal courage and confidence GPS! The first step is admitting and accepting that you have the capacity to be courageous and confident. The second step, without becoming co-dependent on others, is to explore and discover the magical truth that works for you. My suspicion is that you'll be surprised by what you'll discover.

To create courage and confidence your way, I suggest giving the following tips a try. If they feel right to you, adopt them. If they don't, cast them aside and commit to creating courage and confidence your way.

1. Live on the edge knowing at any second you could fall, and also trusting that when you fall is when the magic happens.

2. Breathe through the discomfort, trust deeply, breathe again, ask for help, breathe again, release any co-dependent thoughts, and own your brilliant truth.

3. Acknowledge that flipping out about what you think other people **"have,"** only causes you to lose precious time, waste energy, and lose sight of your own damn genius!

Give yourself permission to write your own handbook for creating courage and confidence your way. The sooner you permit yourself to write it, the sooner you'll catapult yourself into an empowered state of courage and confidence exclusively designed by you, for you! Giving yourself the, "permission granted" seal of approval, you'll free yourself from the constraining belief that, **"Confidence comes from mirroring what others do!"** If it were that damn easy, then there would be one fantastical model, and only one fantastical model for being courageous and confident.

The diversity of courage and confidence each of us contribute to the world, is what enables us to share our unique talents and gifts with the world. The moment we embrace that there is no universal handbook for creating courage and confidence is the magical moment we let go, fall into being our own individual, finding success, being at peace, and having the courage and confidence to say, "Frankly My Dear, I'm (Fill In The Blank)."

✄

Courageous Confidence Check-In

Answer these questions and complete these exercises before moving forward My Dear!

1. How do you define confidence? How do you define courage?

2. Who do you find exudes the type of confidence and courage you would like to have? Why?

3. Describe a time when you had complete confidence. What was it that made you feel that way?

4. Describe a time when you had an abundance of courage. What was it that made you feel that way?

5. What steps are you taking to stop pretending to be something you're not?

6. How are you feeding your confidence and your courage moment-to-moment, day-to-day?

7. What makes you unique that would cause someone else to compare themselves to you?

8. If you never gained confidence or courage to be who you are, how might your life be?

9. Who would you ask for support from in creating courageous confidence?

10. What five action steps can you take in the next week to become more courageous and confident in yourself?

Now you're ready to move onto the world of
Relishing Your Truth Before, During, and After You say
"Frankly My Dear, I'm Gay!"

CHAPTER 5

By Gosh, By Golly, By Damn - Truth Is Freedom

Honestly, truth and power wielding scare the crap out of most of us. Yet, we want to live our truth so badly that we can't wait to unwrap and relish in its warmth: kind of like unwrapping a warm little pig in a blanket so we can enjoy the weenie without the dough. Just steps beyond, courage and confidence is the delicious opportunity to relish in our truth, provided we give ourselves permission to go there. The real trick for reaching this inner state of utopia is to take a bubble bath, grab the loofa, scrub and wash away the annoying dirt, grime, guilt, shame, and self-loathing of *coming out*.

Before moving on, here's one caveat. I don't believe… WAIT! Actually I KNOW that not everyone's *coming out* experience is identical. Of course, I'd be a fool to ignore the similarities. Silly. Stupid. Foolish. That'd be like ignoring Lemon-Odd Pop when she whispers, "Honey, you'z about to make a train wreck of ya life!" Millions of unsung heroes/heroines have trodden before us, paving the way and making our *coming out* journey easier. To avoid their wisdom and insights would be akin to first time parents avoiding the brilliance imparted at La Maze Childbirth classes. Having been through two childbirths, not me personally giving birth (remember, I spawned two biological daughters before I ~~chose~~ accepted my gay truth), I highly recommend chipped ice and breathing exercises – for both having kids and *coming out* of the closet. Especially, when you're first learning to embrace, "Damn sugah, I'm gay!" Utilize the knowledge and insights that others provide about coming into your gayness, and then adapt it to your own situation. Just like the perfect chocolate chip cookie recipe. As long as the main components are there, you can always add a little extra sugar for your own personal taste. And, as for chipped ice and breathing exercises? Chipped ice is great to chew on rather than gnashing your teeth. However, consult your Dentist about chewing ice. I'm not responsible for chipped teeth. Chipped ice is also great for cooling down those people who're shouting hellfire and brimstone scriptures at you for "choosing" to be gay. Ok, dumping ice on them doesn't stop them; however, it sure shuts them up, even if only long enough for them to pull the ice out of their ass. Too bad it wouldn't help them pull their heads out of their asses. "Hush Lemon-Odd Pop! We're supposed to be helping people be accepting and understanding of others not riling them up!" And as for the deep breathing, we suggest borrowing from eastern wisdom and the practice of yoga to help you STAY CALM. Deep breathing slows the heart rate, brings peace to your thoughts, and helps you get back to, "I'm gay, I'm me, and I'm just fine!"

Truthfully speaking, I didn't get to this Zen place the moment I came out. Oh no! I bolted down the slippery, scary, "Screw you," path, much like so many before me.

✄

Slammed Out, Slammed Dunk, So I Don't Give A Slam!

You'd have to be hiding under the armpit of a Tibetan monk, wearing "speed of sound barrier proof" earplugs, and disconnected from everything Apple™, to have not heard the horror stories about people being thrown out of their homes, shunned from their churches, and banished from their friend circles for being gay! Even the Russians have made a spectacle of "Gay no ok!" Sadly, it's as common as the Kardashians being headline news! "Hush Lemon-Odd Pop, I know you love 'em and you're just bringing up the Kardashians to annoy me!" It's a sad commentary on society when Mr. Happy playing with another man's Mr. Happy, or two women being "Beaver to Beaver," is more disturbing than the number of homeless people on the street. Whatever happened to accepting each other as vessels of humanity, embracing the diverse, brightly colored, fabric of cultures, thoughts, and unique gifts each of us brings to the world. Oh wait, I forgot that thinking is fine as long as your diversity matches mine, your bright cultural colors don't clash with my bright cultural colors, and that you think and believe exactly like I do. This, "Don't be, can't be, you're not like me, so that's wrong" spiral began the moment I came out. In the name of "life is a bowl of cherries," I hope this doesn't happen to you, but the odds are damn high that you'll end up in the *coming out pits* to some degree!

I wasn't the least bit surprised that my wife asked me to leave our cookie-cutter, suburban, Orange County California home, right after I dropped the "Frankly My Dear, I'm Gay Bomb!" After all, what kind of a slimy, ass wipe, gets married, knowing damn good and well that he's kidding himself about his feelings for men. Alright, I admit, at that time I thought that getting married would cure this gay passing phase. In reality, I didn't have the balls, nor maturity to live my truth at the age of 22. Instead, I played the expectation game like a master! Right out the gate, I produced a Zen wedding that would shut a Bridezilla up! Beautifully crafted props. Tantalizing catering provided by "Moi," - all done to impress, get stroked (I'm a Leo, we need lots of stroking), and hide my truth. Taking in the, "Oh look at what a creative catch he is. He's got quite the knack for event planning," I should have stood up then and let my innocent bride know "I'm a fake and gay. The tell-tale signs are all around you!" I didn't! I couldn't because I was deeply conflicted and scared that I would be banished from the planet.

My first slammed out moment came, not surprisingly from my heartbroken, and betrayed wife. My first thought was it was the gay thing, which did ignite the initial fire, scorching our not so fairytale life forever. In spite of that issue, and due to my own lack of relationship maturity, I missed the real zinger of pain – the fact that I'd cheated on her with the handsome Brit in London, pissed her off to no end. Not unlike the Bill Clinton/Monica Lewinsky fiasco, it didn't matter that I didn't have sex with the Brit. She couldn't believe in her wildest dreams that I'd had the audacity to go to this man's hotel room and spend the night. For her that was more of a bitch slap in the face than me being gay. Having confessed, and vividly painted for her some of my truth, gave her all the ammunition she needed to tell me to hit the road Rick! Her initial emotional reaction was quickly replaced with a buffet table laden with a full spectrum of emotions and outbursts to last a lifetime, some of which still lingers and raises it's ugly head depending on both of our moods.

To avoid as many emotional landmines as possible, I immediately set my sights on Los Angeles, where my younger brother could provide a safe haven for the short-term. Even though the commute would be a bitch, Los Angeles was close enough proximity to keep my job while providing some semblance of fatherhood to my now confused a distraught 4 ½ year, and 9 month old daughters. Go ahead, say it! "What a lousy excuse of a man you were for coming clean, just months after the birth of your second daughter." Yeah, I know, I've heard that, and many other condescending remarks, under one's breathe, from a wide variety of friends, family, co-workers, in-laws, even perfectly good strangers. Yet, I persevered because my truth had set me free even though it also kicked me in the ass as well as broke up a family, as we knew it.

Something you may not know, unless you've been through a monumental crisis in your life – self-created or otherwise – is that perseverance, patience, and a positive attitude aren't just Tony Robbins hoo ha for living a successful life (Tony, you know I love you and will walk on coals with you, one day). Those three P words began their work and became my saving grace in my life. I just didn't how much until I looked backwards through my 20/20 hindsight Raybans of my life. My life became as volatile as a bitch fight between Crystal and Alexis, on an episode of Dynasty. I got thrown out of my brother's loft, lived in a friend's spare bedroom, and moved back into my own house, sleeping in a separate bedroom, of course. We fired the Nanny, plodded through marriage counseling, and I attempted to take up meditation and yoga. Each experience left deep, beautiful scars of what it takes to start to live authentically, while simultaneously helping me gain clarity, neither of which happened overnight, nor without pain and struggle.

The funny thing about clarity and authenticity is that there are more shades of clarity and authenticity then there are shades of grey in the 50 Shades Of Grey Trilogy! Each moment I spent surviving on Top Ramen and Vodka Tonics (even though Lemon-Odd Pop would have preferred I drink Lemon Drop Martini's in her honor), kept my imagination open to the possibilities that I'd one day have a lusted after, svelte body, other men would salivate over. Plus, the alcohol helped numb me from the effects of "asshole" stamped on my forehead, and in every other crevice of my grey matter. Even through the initial rejection by my parents, the false embraces of quasi "gay accepting" friends, and the "throw me under the bus" comment by a bitchy queen in a gay bar who called me a "BREEDER" – an offense that deeply wounded me for no logical reason – I slowly and purposefully saw the light of my truest self for the first time in my life. Finally, I started to accept this truth, and vowed to never to shy away from it again. Notice I said STARTED. My journey of acceptance came in intermittent spurts of luminous thoughts, only to be over shadowed by "I'm out to lunch trying to find myself!"

Would You Like a Side Of Muddled Thinking To Go Along With Your Thirteen Years Of Infidelity?

Now, don't get me wrong, amongst the ever-changing landscape of "Who's my ally today?" there were luscious islands of tranquility. Mostly from my gay and lesbian friends at the office who said, "Gurl, we were just waiting for ya put on your heels and kick that closet door down!" Actually the lesbians didn't say that! They just asked that I keep that thing between my legs away from them. All kidding aside, in less than a month, I found myself tripping, falling, being irrational, and acting as if I was the only man who'd ever been married and came out of the closet! After all, I'd never met another like me, so I had to be the only one in the world who finally took that treacherous step. Then, one day I woke up and realized, "Holy crap! I need to take a number!" There were other men and women, just like me who'd been married and tripped the light switch fantastic to shine brightly as their honest gay self. Actually, fantastic may not be quite the right adjective to describe most people's *coming out* experience. In fact, most individuals I've met, who've walked this "pretend to be hetero" to "I'm an honest to goodness gay," haven't necessarily had the positive *coming out* journey I was beginning to experience.

I was shocked by the horrifying stories I was hearing from others, which only drove me further into fear that I'd truly fucked up, and needed to strap on some ballet slippers to even more gracefully tip toe on egg shells with my soon to be ex-wife. Ironically, my fears didn't prevent me from acting like a spoiled two-year old, stomping my feet and saying, "I'm spending Thanksgiving with my boyfriend!" Exactly 6 weeks after meeting Mr. Hot Hunky Brit in London, I boarded a plane just 3 gates down from my wife and two children. They headed to my parents in the Napa Valley and I headed to San Francisco, to have my first gay holiday weekend with the man I was sure I would be my forever man. Go ahead, say it again, "What an asshole!" I resemble that remark, and that experience still causes a wishbone to get stuck in my throat at Thanksgiving. That was one of the most cowardice moments of my *coming out* journey. But, persevere I did, through that experience and many similar to it in the months and years to come. You see, one of the things no one teaches any of us about *coming out* of the closet is that there's a high possibility that you're going to make an ass out of yourself along the way. That's ok! It's part of the growth and learning process, provided you learn and grow from the experiences. Here's another insider's tip from the *"been there done that crowd."* You're going to feel the desire to go candy shopping and taste lots of candy!

❈

Lessons From A Kid In The Candy Store! Otherwise Known As The Sweet Tooth Of, "It's Just Sex!"

I'm not going to imply, nor assume (because that makes an ass out of you and me) this lovely little trip to the candy store of M4M, W4W, "looking for sex and hook-ups," is going to be your cup of tea. It may not be the path that guides you to find your gay self. We all find ourselves in different ways to finding our gay self after bursting through the closet door. I'm just sayin'. Unfortunately, there's a tendency to act like Veruca Salt from Willy Wonka and the Chocolate Factory. "Gimme, gimme, gimme! Mine, Mine, Mine! Finally, I want it NOW," because we've been deprived, self-induced or societally discouraged, from living our authentic truth as gays and lesbians. Then we go and sample everything as if it's our last date, sexual experience, or relationship before we pass into the after-life. Slow down brothers and sistahs! There's plenty of time to catch up and get into the groove of dating and mating in the gay world.

But alas, not unlike a child who's told, "No, you can't have that," we don't want to hear, "Take your time!" For those of us who've lived in a "deprived situation," being in a heterosexual marriage and hiding behind the mask our sexual truth, it's like reigning in a horse at the starting gate! Butterflies in the stomach. Stirrings of self-doubt. Deep-seeded yearnings held back and suddenly released into one fail swoop into the fascinating and scary world of "I'm out." However, what does "out" look, feel, and mean to you? Give yourself the space and make no assumptions that beyond the closet door will go the same for you as it did for Tom, Dick,

Harry, Sally, Sue, or Jane! Save yourself some trouble and frustration, early on, and own your "outness" in your own way. Whether you've waited 14, 35, or 60 years to come out, you don't want to spoil it with falling rank and file into "I'm gay and this is how you're supposed to do gay!"

I'll get off my soapbox now, and come back down to the reality of what can and does happen during the "Kid in the candy store phase of *coming out!*"

» **Gotta get hitched syndrome**. There's security in knowing you have someone. It's comforting, makes you feel loved, and helps you avoid the stillness of being alone with yourself. Ironically, that's exactly what you need to do most; get comfortable within your sexual self, so that you can be more comfortable with others in who they are within their sexuality; maybe even that person you want to be "hitched" to could use a little sexuality understanding from you. And just remember, getting comfy in our non-hetero normative sexuality can take a lifetime.

» **Let's screw like rabbits**. I'm no prude, and obviously I enjoyed more than my fair share of sex along my journey towards the real me. Please know, there's no judgment or offense intended here. If anything, I'd encourage those of you who are timid wallflowers to go peel yourself off the wall and take a few rides around the sexual tilt-a-whirl with one caveat. Stay conscious and fully aware of what you're doing and how you're exploring. Too often, too many gay individuals suddenly find themselves literally acting like a *kid in a candy store!* Some call it being rebellious, others call it losing your heads and fucking like rabbits. I prefer to call it "conscious sexing!" No drugs, alcohol, "I'm not worthy" bullshit either to drive you into any arms that will have you. Instead, consciously tangle up those sheets because you're confident in your sexual self, and ready to explore what you desire, seeing how it fits for you in your own sexual journey – shame and guilt-free.

» **Date, date, date**. Intense as screwing like rabbits, and as clingy as the "gotta get hitched syndrome" person might be, there is another animal called "the serial casual dater." Again, no harm, no foul, no judgment... just observing and sharing. Personally, casual dating never worked for me, until it did. When I finally realized I could date, 2 – 3 different guys at a time, I saw a dramatic shift in my self-confidence, and my ability to be candidly coy. However, the real serial daters, are overtly coy, have a separate Google calendar just for their dates and often may find themselves using Cliff Notes to keep their stories straight. Hey, whatever works for you is still my motto. Here's just one additional, little suggestion. Ask yourself, "Is this working for me and how well?" If you don't know your dating head from your ass, or you lose sight of whether you're a top, bottom, or versatile, then it's time to evaluate the rules of your casual dating engagement!

» **It's just sex**. More than a few, out, newbie gays have slipped into this mode of "it's just sex." And slipped, and slipped, and slipped. I'm a firm believer, some people are meant to be coupled, others single and playing the field, and still others are meant to be just plain single. I'm also not convinced, that racking up sexual conquests for a lifetime builds confidence, self-love, or self-worth. Just my opinion, so don't shoot the messenger... Lemon-Odd Pop needs a body to reside within. Sex is a beautiful and sensual experience that allows one's self to be in the moment, let go, and be vulnerable... until you aren't. You'll know you've gone astray from the essence of your sexual self and the pleasure it brings, when in the split second of an orgasm you hear a sultry little voice say, "Next!" Another possibility is that you'll disconnect from the vulnerability of sex and become a, "Let's just fuck" robot – no feelings or intimacy. Either way, check-in with yourself and decide if sex is real or is becoming a routine, numbing outlet to avoid something bigger!

Do yourself a favor. Regardless of which road you take to being the *"kid in the candy store,"* go for it and try some samples! Explore what looks good without shame or guilt. Overindulge every once in a while if it feels right for you; in addition, define clearly without apology what it is you desire sexually, now that you're out on your own in the "Free to be me world of sexuality as you define it!" Even with all the freedom, be cautious that you don't get trapped stepping from one jail cell to another! It happens more often than you might think. So let's address that conundrum, shall we?

❦

Break Out Of The Jail Cell And Dismantle The Lock

Acceptance, belonging, and love. Admit it, they're all human desires and probably what you want as well. If this wasn't true, then I'm afraid Maslow's Hierarchy of Needs would be a pile of crap. Unless you're fully incapable of experiencing feelings and emotions, our nature is to be warmly connected and feeling the heartfelt embrace of intimacy–even if that intimacy is on a social, friendship, or "my peeps" level. These types of feelings validate our existence, and ability to be social in a social world. Stripping us of these intimate feelings of acceptance, belonging, and love tend to drive most people to hole up like a hermit, or to overcompensate by being ridiculously social because they can't stand to be alone with themselves. If you're not careful, you'll end up stepping out of one closet and right into another, or stepping from one jail cell to a different, yet similar, jail cell. You may find yourself unconsciously trapped, trying to be accepted in all the wrong ways, not recognizing how deep you're about to get stuck.

For me and probably for a few of you, going off to Kindergarten or that first summer camp away from home was exciting until it was terrifying. My first summer camp, in the California Sierra's sounded so exciting - swimming, hiking, and singing songs around the campfire - until

I realized I was going to have to undress in front of complete strangers, sleep without the comforting sounds of home, and go to sleep without saying, "Goodnight Mom and Dad!" Call me a wuss and I'll unleash Lemon-Odd Pop on ya! At 7 years old, summer camp was worse than the first day of Mrs. Sawzack's Kindergarten class. At least in Kindergarten, I didn't have to change my clothes and put on my pajamas in front of the entire class. High in the California mountains, I uncovered how to cope, and cope I did, for two days until I flipped out, metaphorically speaking, and went home. All this and I didn't even know what a coping mechanism was at that stage of life!

Hard as it may seem to believe, coping is one of the most beautiful jewels of human triumph. Don't laugh. I believe it's a triumph to cope, not a weakness, until it becomes a crutch. Then it becomes a ~~weakness~~ comfortable weakness and a way to be in the world to just get by. It's kind of like hiding our sexuality from those lurking behind their judgmental high horses. Instead of jockeying into our own Triple Crown Victory – worthy, confident, and loved – we dismount into a jail cell of believing we have to step in line, coping to please others, even in our own gay community. There's a serene and humbling space to be of service and please others. It's known as compassion and caring! Yet, at our core, if we are incapable of being compassionate and caring towards ourselves, how the damn hell are we ever going to be authentically compassionate or caring for someone else?

Without self-care and compassion the spiraling cycle begins. Before you realize it, you're "doing" because others have told you you have to, you should want to, and just "do it" because I said you're supposed to. Click, unlock, and enter into the jail cell of pleasing others once again. I know! You're about to bitch slap me in that cartoon bubble over your head, with a flippant comment like, "Not all things I do are done to please others, you idiot!" Duh! I'm referring to those annoying little voices convincing you to, "Do it just this once to keep peace." Before you know it, your tiny, one time peace maker grows up to be a self-loathing, confidence lacking, not good enough adult. You take comfort in jail cell dwelling, finding it to be more comfortable than living as your true self. Now, you find that living for what others want is simply "what you do." Feeling trapped, hiding who we desperately want to be, and suddenly finding ourselves becomes a numbing way of life.

Once you've stepped bravely through the closet door, options to be yourself, or hide yourself are as abundant as there are prisms of colors in a rainbow. Whether its experiencing the rejection from loved ones, or discovering hidden support from people we least expected, there's no end to the roller coaster of emotions that lurk in the shadows on the other side of the closet door. Each teasing, taunting, and trying desperately to coerce you into losing yourself once again in a newly-designed closet or jail cells.

Driven by internal cries of, "Please, just anyone accept me," and a deep, innate desire to be surrounded by peeps with like-minded beliefs and sexual orientations, it's not uncommon to dive head first into the gay community in a myriad of ways – none of which is wrong unless its completely against your own core values. You want to be an advocate, go be an advocate. You want to be a drag performer, go be a drag performer. You want to be a Dyke on Bike, then rev up and go be a Dyke on a Bike! The only whisper of caution is to make sure you're not making moves out of a drastic, desperate, need to be accepted, or trying to fit in! You're who you are from deep within, emanating from your core inner spirit. I'm not blowing smoke and suggesting you can't change, adapt to new experiences, or embrace new peeps. Those who fail and jump back into the closet in some manner are those who are more prone to dive into some aspect of the gay culture out of a NEED to be loved, accepted, and part of the IN crowd. What if you love, accept, and be your own IN CROWD for starters?

Honestly, regardless of the age that someone *comes out of the closet,* there's a high probability you'll try to fit in, to fit in. The sub-cultures and sexual tastes within the LGBTQ community provides a delectable buffet table to sample — twinks, bears, otters, daddies, leather, muscle, lipstick lesbians, fems, butch fems, etc. Often, but not always, once you've come to terms with yourself, it's time to come to terms with the community and how you fit in the community. Why? Because one gay size does not fit all. For some of you, this will be a tricky tap dance and tight rope to walk, especially if you begin to believe that where you fit into the community defines who you are as a gay man or a lesbian woman. The best encouragement I can provide is to simply treat this exploration of "Where do I fit in?" as if you're back in high school trying to find the groups you most click with, instead of succumbing to peer pressure and molding yourself into something a group expects you to be in order to be liked!

The need to be accepted, often leads down the roads of addiction, mental abuse, sexual promiscuity, physical abuse, and co-dependency in the gay community. Let's change the dialogue, kick "need" out of the way, and call it a DESIRE. Reach deep within yourself, and ask, "How does my being embraced by this person or group align with my core values?" You're more likely to make well thought out decisions that serve your journey and contribute more significantly to your overall happiness. Plus, if you have an inner Diva like Lemon-Odd Pop, she'll keep you focused and on course.

Fortunately, I learned my fitting-in lesson early on, in my own unique way. I realized it was in my best interest to surround myself with gay friends who got me as a man—a man who'd been married, and came out of the closet late in life. I didn't I focus on only being friends with other recovering hetero-married guys like me. Truthfully, for a brief period of time, I thought I should stick with my own kind — previously hetero-married types — mostly because I got in my head about the "breeder" remark from the catty, bitchy queen in the bar. In fact, after that encounter with her, I thought I was done with gay men and being gay. I was convinced I'd never fit into this community, all due to that one snotty comment from someone who obviously:

a) needs to do some deep inner work on himself,

b) quit projecting his self-loathing outward, and

c) only define being gay "his way" for himself, not everyone else.

A few nights later, while watching my two beautiful little daughters playing in their bubble bath, I realized how cool I was as a gay man to be a BREEDER! In that quiet, loving, moment of Fatherhood, I realized I, like others who were biological gay parents, occupied a unique space in the gay community. Instead of retreating and hiding my past, it was time for me to wear my badge of pride as a father, a man capable of sustaining a 13+ year relationship, and knowing what it means for me to be gay my way. Now, I'd be lying if I said I didn't try to fit into all types of gay groups, just to feel accepted. It was part of my exploration, often leading to frustration when I felt I didn't fit in with the muscle-daddies, the butch scruff crowd, or when I got placed into the cave as a Bear – which really rankled the fur on my chest and back! Slowly, the light bulb started to glow, lighting the way for me to see that I'm just me, fine just the way I am, my way in the gay community – no new closets or jail cells to lock myself in to be accepted or to make others feel comfortable...especially a non-breeder, bitchy queen! Poor thing, I wonder if he ever found himself a 100% gay man who never touched a woman?

Ripped Shirts and Beach Runs

I'm not going to blow smoke up your cute little butt (and yes everyone's butt is cute to someone, so get over it), by telling you that moving out of the house, living at times in less than ideal circumstances, and finally adapting to life in a one bedroom studio apartment with two little girls was easy. It wasn't, and it was. Sorry, if that confuses you. The "wasn't" part included – juggling the temporary beds that needed to be made and stowed away each day, cooking on a two burner stove top, and juggling a demanding work schedule that at times conflicted with school and daycare schedules. My life was exhausting, overwhelming, and stressful; the typical life of a parent, minus one parent! Of course, my soon to be ex-wife was having the same experience as I, so no need to grand stand and say woe is me. The "was" part – positive side of things – included living in Laguna Beach just steps from the beach, surrounded by a warm brotherhood of gay men who embraced my daughters and me; in addition, now I continued to experience independence in a manner I'd never felt before.

I'd always been somewhat athletic – aerobics, jazzercise, dance – you know, the stuff people see as stereotypical gay stuff. However, now there was more, so much more! Running, cycling, mountain biking, spin class, weight training (ugh, still can't stand it) and the occasional hike! I was being an active, healthy man (except for my smoking). Even on daddy-duty days I was active, active, active and busy, busy, busy. The more I had on my plate, the more driven I became, and that's exactly what I did. Drove myself dangerously close to alcoholism, a nervous breakdown, and rapidly, excessive weight loss.

I was unconsciously unaware of the path I was sprinting down. Then, one night I drunkenly stumbled home after the Mardi Gras celebration at *Woody's* (Laguna's finest gay watering hole), and fell into my next-door neighbor's bed with him in it, out of pure desperation for a warm body. Don't get me wrong, he wasn't a bad looking guy, and the sex wasn't the worst I'd experienced. In fact, there wasn't anything wrong with the encounter whatsoever because I grew from it, and came out of a self-induced coma. After waking up next to him and realizing what being three sheets to the wind had led me to do, I had a little come to Jesus talk with myself and decided:

» I never wanted to feel completely out of control ever again

» My daughters deserved much more than an alcoholic, sex addict father

» My core values were being cast aside because I was trying to fit into a certain way of being gay, and I didn't like the feeling of that jail cell

I spent that day alone, deep in conscious thought and meditation, begging God for guidance and insight. As I stepped into this deep state of introspection, I found myself descending the stairs to the local beach, just across Pacific Coast Highway from my serene little South Laguna Beach bungalow studio apartment. Instantly connecting with the warmth of the sand between my toes, I felt each grain sending me messages of hope, faith, love, and empowerment to step into a new way of being in my gay journey. My initial quick check-in at the beach led to an extended stay, lasting most of the day. Guzzling in the sun, crashing waves, and serene peace surrounding me, I found myself drunk with new intentions; conscious and unconscious.

Up until that point, the dynamics with my ex-wife ranged from cool and collected to deranged and hateful, on both sides of the fence. Absorbed in the drunkenness of my new thoughts, I recalled how beautiful she was when I first met her in my closet-sized office on the campus of small Christian university in west Texas. That day I met a soul mate, fun mate, and temporary life mate that I couldn't do without, until I did. Of course, I was unconscious to the temporary life mate aspect of our union because I was blinded the lights and thrill of my one-man show, making its debut! "Pretend – a riveting real life drama of a confused homosexual man who pretends to be heterosexual out of fear and respect to make everyone else feel happy and comfortable!" In the warmth emanating from the beach, I looked through the haze of my irrational thinking and saw her for what she had always been to me - my destiny; and you don't *bitch slap destiny because she'll bitch slap you back ten times harder!* I realized it was time to start mending fences, slat by slat, nail by nail; with her and others in my life who'd been deeply shoved into the closet by my *coming out* of the closet. As if sent by some divine presence, a sea gull landed not 5 feet from me, staring me straight in the eyes. Without breaking eye contact with this bird of the sea sky, I gained clarity about fence mending. I could mend fences with others, only as much as they were willing to allow me to mend the fence. Beyond that, my responsibility ended.

I immediately started sobbing. Heart wrenching sobs that scared my seagull friend away and caused the mid-west tourists with their 2.5 kids (the wife was pregnant, so yes there was a .5) to hastily grab their "happy beach day" paraphernalia and quickly retreat up the 120 steps to their rental car, precariously parked on the shoulder of Pacific Coast Highway. I still question if it was my wailing, or the fact that their ghostly white skin was suddenly blazing lobster red that sent them scrambling. I still feel pangs of a Jewish mother's guilt, that I may have ruined their vacation, or proved what they'd heard, "All LA people are nut jobs!" At times, I swear I hear them still recounting their story at Sunday Church Potlucks. "Then, a really tall, stocky, guy who looked like he played defensive tight end for good old University of Michigan, sat down just a few sand plots from us at the beach and started wailing like a heifer giving birth! We couldn't decide if he was crying or calling the whales in for a Shamu show!" They were wrong on both counts; I'm not a tight end nor do I allow anyone in mine except on rare occasions, and Shamu does not reside in the wild off the coast of South Laguna's gay beach. I wondered if they even noticed that most the people on the beach were all groups of men?

I sat there sobbing for quite some time. Feeling like Goliath had lifted a tremendous weight off my shoulders, I knew I was capable of anything, provided I gave myself permission to believe I could do anything. After watching the sun slip into a slivered shimmer on the horizon, I finally headed back to the safe haven of my quaint, rustic studio apartment, to have a date with myself. Giddy as a schoolgirl on her first date, I was excited to be alone, something I'd been frightened of up until that day. Carefully playing "dodge cars" with the crazies zipping along Pacific Coast Highway, I bolted to the land side of the highway, made a quick pit stop for two grilled fish tacos, with extra guacamole, and chipotle salsa from Coyote Café (the very restaurant I'd go on my first date with the man who'd become my future husband), and excitedly went around the corner to my little slice of heaven. I spent the rest of the evening listening to Natalie Merchant, savoring my "muy bueno" tacos, and drinking a half-gallon of chilled ice water with lemons.

Drunk now on simplicity and peace, I fell asleep in my sling chair, rescued out of the *"as is"* room at IKEA. Touched by a soft finger stroke of moonlight, I awoke a few hours later, just long enough to stumble and fall face down on my bed, wrapping myself in the gentle embrace of cotton and goose down. To this day, I've yet to experience such a deep slumber – no sleeping pills, anxiety meds, alcohol, or post orgasmic euphoria to rock me to sleep.

I awoke to a typical June gloom morning. Gray fog lingered over the coast, later to be replaced with brilliant blue skies and golden sunshine – the epitome of California beach living. Ironically, my first thought concerned my encounter with the sweet mid-western family. I feared they'd awoken, blaming my sobbing at the beach the day before, as the reason they now faced a gray vacation day. It wasn't as if my wailing was some ancient call to the sky God's to bring in the cloud cover. I quickly let go of my rising insanity that I had ruined their vacation, hoping instead they were inland at Disneyland for the day, where gray skies or blue, it's still the happiest place on earth. Without conscious thought, I called my assistant to let her know I was sick and wouldn't be at work that day. Drunk from yesterday's high dive into myself, and still lingering in the state of satiated slumber, I knew today was no day for me to be at work. Or, maybe I was still lingering in the state of satiated slumber? I didn't know, nor did I care. I simply knew work was out of the question.

Out of rote repeat mode, I pulled my favorite Addias running shorts over my bare ass and privates, foregoing the jock strap, threw a threadbare t-shirt over my chest; the chest I still dreamed would one day possess pecs to cause jaws to drop. Grabbing a pair of ankle biter socks, I slipped into my well-worn Nike running shoes to get in a quick beach run, starting at Main Beach Laguna, before the parking meters kicked into "rip off the tourist's mode," of $.50 per quarter hour.

A typical run on the beach for me was 1 – 2 miles. Nothing overtly challenging, yet nothing to sneeze at either. These invigorating beach runs always filled me with a fresh zest for life, plus truckloads of eye candy to chow down on in my mind. Each step I ran, proved beyond a shadow of doubt that I was a man, a gay man, with boatloads of sex drive alive and well in my loins. Oddly though, something about this day seemed different. Not sure whether it was the freedom of going commando, or the exhilaration of waking from a deep utopic sleep. This day, I was experiencing FREEDOM unlike I'd ever felt before. In my past, FREEDOM always came with conditions. I could only experience FREEDOM if I did X, then Y, then Z. And let's not forget I also had to do Z.1, Z.2, etc. Not that day. Z was Z.

Crossing the asphalt death trap of Pacific Coast Highway, this time within the safe confines of a crosswalk, my nostrils were met with the playful tickle of saltwater air. An army of chilled goose bumps marched across my bare skin, and a new air of confidence caused my entire body to rise erect, and tall like a stallion standing on his hind legs. I was walking powerfully, genuinely smiling, and feeling extremely happy. Pride exuded from the depths of my soul outward. My core values of honesty, integrity, respect, self-love, love for others, had jolted me out of the pattern of being someone's one night-stand brought on by a drunken stupor. Laughing to myself, I cautioned the Leo within to avoid being cocky, and to gently hold space for these new truths to put down roots, sprout, and grow. No need to rush things or to assume I'd arrived. I simply need to just be. Be in this moment.

I began to run, at my normal stride, getting warmed up, before settling into a 9-minute mile pace. Dead ahead, 50 feet and closing fast was the mirror image of the self I desired to be, headed right towards me. A handsome guy, stocky build, not to overweight, sexy in his own way, slightly balding, nice strong legs, and a furry chest; the closest thing to the self I fantasized I saw in the mirror each morning. The only difference between him and I was his furry chest was fully exposed for all to admire – a daring adventure I'd rarely taken in public other than within the confines of a private swim party, or a quick shower at the gym. Even during those situations, it was a hurried rush to remove my shirt, jump in pool or scramble to the show, so that no one would see my love handles!

Closer now, only 10 feet separating us, I noticed him listening to his Disc-man (yes, it was the pre-iPod decade), singing full out to his heart content, not giving a damn who saw, or heard him. I quickly descended into to judging and questioning why I couldn't be like him. Free to sing off tune and out loud in public, run with my shirt off, and let them see me sweat! Almost stumbling while deep in thought, I suddenly envisioned Hulk Hogan ripping his shirt off after striding into the center ring at a WWE event. Don't ask me where that thought came from because (sorry Hulk) that man does nothing for me, and no, I am not a fan of professional wrestling. However, I now know where that thought arose from...divine intervention.

Driving through the sand, breaking a sweat, heart pounding out of my chest; this run was no longer about physical exertion, it was about breaking free. Pecs or no pecs. Wait. Let's rephrase. Out of shape pecs be damned! Grabbing my t-shirt right below my Adam's apple with both hands, in one riveting tear I split my shirt in half, tearing it off my shoulders - FREEDOM! Grinning like a Cheshire cat from ear-to-ear, I'd finally given myself full-permission to run in public on the beach, everything hanging out for all to see – muffin top, jiggling man boobs, sweating like a pig – and no one was pointing or laughing at me. Even if they had been, I didn't give a damn! I had arrived! I was finally able to see myself as a beautiful man in my own right, suddenly feeling possessed to say, "Yea, I'd FUCK me," and for the first time in my life, the little voice inside me was shouting, "Frankly everyone, I'm gay...free...and me!"

Stereotypical Lessons Learned

Eye opening as a FREEDOM run on the beach can be, I was far from FREE. In fact, the very next day the freedom bitch slapped me in the face. I ended up not being able to take my morning run due to an emergency meeting at work. The next two days were consumed with daddy duty, followed by a time-consuming trek up the 405 Freeway in Friday nightmare traffic to see Kyle, the guy I was dating. Lack of exercise, disappearing freedom, parental responsibilities, and a hellish traffic does not make for a "happy, horny, great to see you," evening with my guy!

Consumed in my own crap, I entered his Pacific Palisades condo with stunning ocean views, with an I don't give a damn that I'm here "Hey," which sent our evening into a tailspin neither of us had anticipated, or ordered. Screw the 1996 Clos De La Roche Pinot Noir, the lovely New York Strips and organic roasted baby zucchini, carrots, and Brussels sprouts. BTW, the Brussels sprouts on the evening menu only exacerbated the situation. I simply wanted to whine and pout my way to bed, with hopes that an ocean breeze filled slumber would re-awaken my normal hunger for snuggling and "let's get nasty" sexy man, that I was used to having with him.

Wasting no time, Kyle went straight for my weakness, a gentle, sensuous, naked full body massage, spattered with inquisitive, yet not pushy questions about my week, and of course, wine...loads and loads of fabulous wine. Pushing all the right buttons, he succeeded in loosening me up, and getting me talking. Talk, talk, talking like a gossiping little queen holding court in the schoolyard. My sweet, sexy, Russian beatnik Kyle had never seen me so free, open, and vulnerable. No, I'm not talking about the sex that followed the massage, so get your minds out of my private little porno.

My verbal diarrhea of the mouth spewed forth, bringing the Encyclo-pedia Britannica version of my week to life, including the "what were you thinking" drunken tryst with my next-door neighbor. Luckily for me, my handsome Russian didn't give a crap about the pounding I'd given my neighbor. Why should he? We were casually dating, no exclusivity agree-ment in place, nor would there ever be in the future.

Mid-conversation about my diddling the neighbor, he asked, "Which one?" Don't raise your eyebrows, assuming I was being a big "Ho!" My little slice of South Laguna Beach living had dropped me smack dab in a real life version of Melrose place...the oh so gay version! There was the trim, sexy, young, surfer boy Tom in the upstairs unit; Michael, the handsome sliver daddy in the studio apartment adjacent to me; Chad, our landlord, a nerdy, furry otter, who tanned way too much, and lived in the lower unit below Tom and across the Asian garden from me; and then of course Allen, my southern bubba gump tryst from Alabama who looked like he just got off the Greyhound bus, one too many stops past "Last stop for bible belters before entering the sinful world of west-coast living." Like me, Allen had been married with kids. The difference was, he was as clueless about living in California and being gay as Michelle Bachman is about the real "ins and outs of gay sex!" He was a country bumpkin, daily drunken mess. Something I should have steered clear of, but didn't.

Kyle's first response, once I confessed it was Allen that I'd hooked up with, was, "Oh, the other Bear!" New to the gay culture and lingo, I wondered, *WTF does a bear have to do with being gay?* Oh ye of little "gay lingo" understanding (which will be explained in a moment). Obviously, Kyle had boxed me into some label of gay male sub-culture. I'd had just enough wine to have my bitchy "Fuck You" button pushed. Unfortunately, that button caused me to raise my middle finger, so close to his face that he went cross-eyed. The next words out of my mouth were, "Gurl, don't you ever call me a bear, daddy, or any other damn gay label, other than a gay man ever again! I'm Rick, a gay man, and that's it!" Needless to say, that was the last time I saw Kyle.

Yep, another chapter of my own personal handbook on how to be "gay my way," had just be written. Feeling bitch-slapped and jilted. Correction. Having bitch-slapped and jilted Kyle, I immediately left, reversed my route down the parking lot that we in Southern Californian's call the 405 Freeway, to my little slice of serenity in Laguna Beach. Simultaneously, I was eating up my monthly allotment of AT&T minutes, whining to my closet gay friend about the tragic breakup that had driven me to tears.

Lovingly as a gay best-friend could be, and as if he had channeled Lemon-Odd Pop, he told me to get over my shit, accept certain things about being in the gay community, and too meet him at the bar in 30 minutes, so he could do his best to get me laid. Now that's true friendship. And he accomplished what he set out to do!

At this stage of my *coming out*, I'd been called a *breeder* and a *bear*. Embracing the breeder was a piece of cake. Swallowing that I was a bear was by no means having my cake and eating it to, even though most bears love to eat! But why? Why was I in denial like Lemon-Odd Pop, when she just cannot believe that she's not Babs Streisand reincarnated? Did I assume that "bear" meant I was fat, hairy, and a slob? Was that my interpretation? I admit, I was overweight, but not nearly what I'd been prior to *coming out*, carrying an extra hundred pounds on my frame. As for the "Hairy Bear" metaphor, that didn't bother me. I love me some hair on me and my man! Hairy backs, not so much! Thank God for waxing! Right, Lemon-Odd Pop? So, why was it then that my button pushed about this bear comparison? Like a Grizzly Bear raring up on its hind legs, my inner spirit stood up and growled, "Your button's getting pushed like an annoying, incessant doorbell ringing because you're not home, and comfortable in yourself!" I was out to lunch (sorry to disappoint my fellow bears, it wasn't a buffet lunch) incapable of seeing the depths of my own judgments towards my gay community. This revelation, combined with a healthy dose of reality that I had adopted my Dad's overbearing, domineering, "My way, or the highway" programming, caused me to clearly observe my own inner homophobia.

I was judgmental of effeminate men, unable to accept that my gay brothers who were into the leather scene could be spiritual, and abhorred anyone who was into BDSM. In addition, I had not an ounce of room for butch lesbians, especially when I would see one coupled with a hot lipstick lesbian. And as much as I love, Lemon-Odd Pop, I was perplexed as to why any man in his right mind would be in a relationship with a Drag Queen, other than for the campy fun! Of course, the pages of my judgment journal brimmed with thoughts of how ridiculously indulgent the Sisters Of Perpetual Indulgence were; I found Transgenders to be really screwed up people who scared me to death; and saw people in open relationship as fucked up, serial hook-up artists! Can you say "Bitter party of one, please look in the mirror?" I was a judgmental, bitchy queen.

OMG! My freedom run had done me not once ounce of good. Or had it? While I may have become free on some levels due that breakout, ripped t-shirt run on the beach, I was truly not free on so many other levels. I was trapped in the jail cell of critically judging others. I'd blinded myself with my own egotistical bullshit, unable to see people for the beauty of who they are, just as they are. I was a contradictory asshole, incapable of teaching my daughters how to be accepting others because I wasn't walking the walk, and talking the talk. I'd become a hypocritical, gay, asshole; a reflection in the mirror of all the people who were being hypocritical and unaccepting of me.

I'd literally become one of the people I despised most – the holier than thou critic with no regard for the beauty of human diversity. I was hurting my gay community and myself simultaneously, unable to recognize this hurt until it slapped me in the face. We're all human, but by no means am I some righteous being who's been miraculously cured from judging others. I'm not sure any of us are capable of experiencing that type of complete freedom on a regular basis. However, I believe we can strive to be as non-judgmental as humanly possible.

In those dark moments of having faced my own judgmental homophobia that I was lobbing on my own gay community, I realized I had a tremendous amount of inner healing yet to experience. Blind and unconscious to what was yet to come, I continued on a path that led me to be consistently in and out of relationships, having my heart stolen and broken, questioning my sexuality, trying to find labels and comrades to help me find my footing in the gay world, and finally, surrendering to the realization that *coming out* is a life long journey that is never finished until I step out of this human experience at the end of life!

Blinded By The Light Of The Stolen Hearts Club

The fact that I'm a Life Coach doesn't make me invincible. I'm well aware of my own vulnerability and wear that badge proudly. One of my favorite sayings is, "I can be hurt only if I let you," much easier said than done. Like most of you have or will, getting hurt and owning it comes along with the wonderful ritual of gay dating, or dating period. But it's not just a gay plague. We're not going to let the heteros- get off that easy. Don't get me wrong; I dated way more than three guys on my way to homo-matrimony. Of course, I'm excluding…

"One date, you're doners;"

"Just coffee" didn't make the cut;

"Three strikes you're out,"

and of course the "You call that sex?"

Those little diversions don't count in my gay dating book, and my gay dating book only! Although some of those were truly little, tiny diversions, but I'm not one to kiss and tell!

I encourage you to navigate your gay dating journey just as you are, in your way, and don't let anyone throw you off track. Be persistent, open, vulnerable, and wear a lot of armor with sparkles or leather – whatever floats your boat. I'm not bitter, just better having had Garrett, Kyle, Thomas, and Harrington in my life. Yes, the names have been changed to protect the innocent and not so innocent. A couple of them I'd like to call some names that would make me sound like a foul-mouthed Navy man who's gone without sex on a 6-month tour of duty. Woof...Navy men! (Fanning myself) Before jumping into the deeper truths that each of these beautiful men brought into my life, and stole from my life, I need to share one of my core personal beliefs.

"Everything that happens in our lives has a purpose!"

I'm not the *"Everything for a reason"* guy. Reason, just my perspective, implies something was wrong and needed fixing. Purpose, on the other hand, is a nudge from the universe to grow. These handsome, sexy, challenging, loving, and frustrating guys were brought to me, and I to them – I think – to deliver a much-needed-wake-up call so I could GROW AS I WAS INTENDED TO GROW!

Let's get down to the juicy lessons learned each of these guys taught me that enabled me to get over myself (not all the way), step authentically into me (still stepping), and to stroll further down the path towards my intended purpose on this earth (still getting there).

My first man was Garret. Handsome, sexy, British, whose dynamite blew the closet door off its hinges and set me free to live my gay truth at the ripe old age of 38. He was my own personal Eckhart Tolle, Deepak Chopra, Oprah Winfrey, and Tony Robbins all rolled into one. Yes he was a deep, intuitive, "never stop questioning," sort of guy. He inspired me to look deeper, be aware, and start questioning why I felt I could never be happy without a man in my life. Two of us feeding off of each other's deep introspection (good thing), separated by 400 miles (not so good), and my "newbie out and not ready to be in a relationship status" (definitely not good), didn't make for a rich, healthy, trusting relationship. Layer on the mix of my impending divorce, trying to find myself as a gay man, juggling parenthood; no wonder, I got caught up in the fairytale fantasy of dating a British Prince Charming. It masked my pain, which caused me to look the other way on so many things I should have been looking right at, which inevitably led to the accident waiting to happen.

I was swept away with his accent, sexy svelte swimmers body, oh so beautiful manhood, and his hip, jet setting lifestyle in the fashion industry. Of course, none of that held a candle to his spiritual, calming presence; an essence I'd learn to embrace and practice many years later in my own life. The fact that I didn't know how to be with myself – a reminder he cast on deaf ears, more than I want to admit - constantly threw a wrench in our already unstable long distance relationship. Thank God, he finally let me go to learn that lesson and many others so I could blossom into a much more mature gay man.

There's magical beauty in being with self right after *coming out* of the closet and ending a long-term relationship. Being by yourself is different than being *lonely* or *alone*. In moments of being by yourself, you've got nowhere to hide but within your own thoughts, feelings, and emotions – what a frickin' trip! It's the playground where you uncover YOU and get to know all the different playmates within YOURSELF that make you unique, lovable and that also cause you to act like a buffoon. Thanks to the lovely Brit Garret, I began, and still work towards, mastering the art of being with me. Loving the solitude of my essence, my unique perspectives, and my scary vulnerability. I learned the hard way, through my first gay break up, the lesson of how to be with one's self was Garret's purpose in my life. Once I realized this, I was able to release Garret to the VIP table in the Lost Loves Club of my life.

Kyle: my Russian/ Spanish amore. Obviously, I have a thing for foreigners. Don't get too excited, Kyle always gave off a mysterious, mystique, never knowing exactly what he was thinking, except for in one area of our relationship: sex. Ok and marijuana... that makes two. Kyle's purpose was to teach me the raw beauty of cutting loose, in the sexual arena of life. Sounds like a fortune cookie fortune that you finish with the words 'in bed!' "To be happy one must cut loose...in bed!"

If someone had told me then, "When you start making changes in one area of life, all the other areas of your life will magically begin to shift and transform as well," I would have told them to go smoke a bong with Kyle. Of course now, I throw that same phrase on clients as frequently as Kyle lit up a joint! Kyle pushed my "Just let it go button," as much as he pushed his...you get my drift? Because of Kyle, I quickly began to let go of other things in my life. As you already know, him calling me a BEAR led me to be more welcoming and accepting of the diverse sub-cultures in the LGBT community. It was also while dating him that the rip my shirt off FREEDOM beach run occurred. Most importantly, my sexy, pot smoking, Russian/Spanish, push the erotic boundaries Kyle, taught me I couldn't be in a relationship with someone who ran in the LA entertainment circles. No judgment, no harm, no foul towards him. I'm not a prude, nor am I immune from a past sprinkled with recreational pot use. At that time and being a newly out gay man, I realized that I had to be a clear-headed father, facing a multitude of challenging decisions about my future; therefore, I couldn't be wrapped up in fast times of LA life, no matter how thrilling running with the "A" listers sounded, nor how awakened my sexual appetite had become to go where Ricky had never gone before! Kyle's purpose was to always be a reminder of one of my truths. I am a sexual being, will always be a sexual being, which is nothing to be ashamed of, nor afraid of exploring. With that understanding, Kyle took his own table reserved at the Lost Loves Club in my life.

Thomas, dear sweet Thomas, was my first, "Let's date another guy who was married and had kids!" Sounds perfect, right? Well...there was a purpose for this relationship too! He helped me see that "Sexy only goes skin deep!" Nice guy. Nice otter type build (Look it up in the gay bear dictionary. I don't have time to explain!) Furry chest. Easy to look at, until I realized, his looks were the only thing that he had to offer. I'm all for looking good, just not looking at myself 24/7, saying "Looking good!" I'm pretty sure Shania Twain ran into him and he became the inspiration for her song, "That Don't Impress Me Much"...

I never knew a guy who carried a mirror in his pocket

And a comb up his sleeve-just in case

And all that extra hold gel in your hair oughtta lock it

'Cause Heaven forbid it should fall outta place

It was the performer in him that couldn't let go of seeing himself as anything other than handsome and needing constant grooming. Plus, he seemed perfectly content to settle, without an overt fight with his Mormon ex-wife, to have little to no interaction with his kids, other than a couple of times a year. I finally admitted to myself that we were on completely different value plains, after he insisted I keep a detailed journal of every conversation I had with my ex-wife in case I should need it some day in court. I had a hard time swallowing that pill, only because I was still not comfortable being that brash with my ex, even in the worst of times, but yet I followed his suggestion for about one page of notes in a journal. It didn't work and caused huge havoc with the mother of my children. Yet, I held tight to my fantasy that, Thomas and I both having kids would somehow cause his ex-wife to soften up, see that his kids would be well-taken care of with another parental figure in the picture, and that we'd all live happily ever after. That unrealistic someday never came. However, purpose driven messages often hit you when you least expect it. The sledge hammer over the head message I received about my relationship with Thomas was, "Rick, you're disconnected from your core values, treating others in ways that is uncharacteristic of yourself. It's time to reexamine your relationship with Thomas, look at what he's influencing you to do, and figure out why you're in a relationship with him. It's for your own good and for the good of everyone around you." Thankfully, Lemon-Odd Pop ensured I heard that message loud and clear, that Thomas really didn't want to be a family guy. With that kick in the ass, I realized the relationship with "Mr. Don't touch the hair," wonderfully endowed Thomas, was meant to be at the back booth in the Lost Loves Club of my life! Ironically almost 15 years later, I ran into him online and he didn't even remember that we dated…go figure!

Having just completed my eye-opening experience, dating a former "heterosexual," recovering Mormon, man with kids, named Thomas, you'd have thought I'd have learned my lesson. Or at least gotten a clue that dating another *like type* guy wasn't my destiny. But, alas, along came Harrington. Prim, proper, and exquisitely cloaked in tradition – from his tastes in décor to the labels he wore. Blinded by my own insecurity and NEED for companionship, I didn't see him for him – the "not my type at all guy." Not his fault, it was mine. I've never been a Chintz, Louis

Vuitton, Tiffany, Swarovski Crystal, type of guy. I'm more of a Modern Minimalist, Lucky Brand, Teno jewelry kind of guy. True, opposites do attract. Also, true, polar opposites don't last and never should, especially when both people are *coming out*, going through separations with spouses, navigating divorce, and child custody battles, simultaneously. Yet again, there is purpose in every experience we're thrown into the arena to experience.

The relationship with Harrington, possibly for the first time in my life, helped me clearly understand the fruits of holding the line on what you DESIRE and not allowing yourself, or those fruits of thought, to fall far from the DESIRE tree. There's no need to stand stoically in the corner with a corncob up your ass, not being flexible. That kind of behavior is painful and everyone around you sees your discomfort in being of rigid mind, thought, and spirit. Same holds true when you're not being authentic to yourself and trying to fit your round peg values into someone else's square hole values. Yes, I'm talking about trying to put a square peg in a round hole. Any other picture you just conjured up from that metaphor I just used is on you and your imagination, not me!

Harrington's purpose was to provide me with delicious insight of being proud of my own tastes, desires, and intentions for living. He also, taught me that friends come first. I'd never really been with anyone, to date, where our mutual friendship got in the way of our intimate relationship. Regrettably, and thankfully, Garrett and Harrington both stayed true to their friendships by helping me start a new journey of growing up and allowing the person I'm in a relationship with to be independent and dependent. It's a tough lesson to learn, yet well worth learning. I filed that *life lesson* into the rapid access memory banks of my mind. Shortly after our disconnect over friendships and styling homes, Harrington dropped me and I dropped the velvet rope to the Lost Loves Club of my life; therefore, granting Harrington a lifetime, good riddance, bronze club membership with no benefits of any kind.

As each of these relationships faded into the archives of my life, I realized I had one final bullet of healthy gay adult maturity to bite off – "How to, and why would I, maintain a relationship with an ex? A gay ex?" After all, I'd managed to do it with my ex-wife in a very unique way. Ok, the ex-wife collaboration is a gimme because I gave a damn about being an active player in my daughters' lives and trying to somehow make it work with her. Staying connected to my ex-wife was also a conscious choice to ensure I learned to grow through the tangled, twisted, and challenging world of divorce with an air of decorum as much as possible. The investment was worth it as she was the mother of my children. But the ex-guys in my life, now that was a little bit different mix of drama and story.

Like many of you will, I at first hung onto these "wrong guy, wrong time" relationships, forcing and trying to make them into friendships. I had false expectations of possibly reigniting the flame of intimacy that'd been lost. I've come to realize that relationships are relationships and can, if mutually agreed upon, continue as friendships provided the maturity level exists on both sides of the fence and the expectations are clearly defined. It's also imperative that freedom, respect, and individuality co-reside to make the friendships, family relationships, and intimate relationships thrive on paths that go their own separate ways.

✤

Peddling Me, Myself, and I To Deeper
Levels Of Authentic Freedom

Shortly after *coming out*, and right in the midst of the divorce, not an ounce of tranquility in sight, I discovered two life-altering discoveries. Well, more than two! However, these two gems in the rough changed me physically, mentally, and emotionally. They also contributed to my snippy little feelings in my head that finally said, "I'd Fuck Me." After years of being the little fat boy, overweight adult, and buying into inner rationalizations of "I'm just a tall, stocky guy" I finally broke free of my obesity excuses. I saw the light because of Crunch Fitness and a bicycle.

The last few years of my marriage I'd begun to find my joy factor in being physically fit. I'd become a runner and even had the privilege of running a 5K run with Cheryl Tiegs, only to find running wasn't my passion. I tried Jazzercise (surprise, surprise), and loved it (surprise, surprise), but because seriously, what kind of a "straight man" does Jazzercise? Try as I might, I couldn't find my physical fitness stride.

Six months after *coming out* of the closet, moving out of my home, and finally stepping into my life as a gay man, I decided to try a gym. Crunch Fitness no less; you know the ones that at that time, were cool, hip, gym experiences that inspired you to get your booty in shape, for a paltry $650 a year membership. I didn't think twice about the money, or the fact that I hadn't had a gym membership since the Black Adonis shower days of Oklahoma City. I was caught up in the quest of a ripped body and a better frame of mind. I'd convinced myself that both were needed to live my liberated gay life, and by God I was going to do it.

Needless to say, I wasn't immediately enthralled with weight lifting; however, I was immediately drawn to this thing called "Spinning!" Plus Dave, the 6'4, Gerard Butler look-alike instructor, knew how to motivate a room to sweat and also causing a lump in my jock strap. Somehow this Spinning craze was able to kick your ass, making fat fall, pump you up, all while riding a stationary bike to the beat of Madonna, Pet Shop Boys, and Stone Temple Pilots. I was enthralled, addicted, and loving it so much that before I knew it, I had become a Certified Spin Instructor, purely by accident. Out of necessity and urging from my fellow spin classmates, I lead a 5:30 a.m. class one morning because an instructor had "no showed." Before I knew what was happening, I found myself being a much sought after spin instructor, teaching 8 - 10 classes a week. Thank God for the little blessings that precede the big, "Oh shit's!" Within weeks of launching my Spin instructing gig, I suddenly found myself fully available to teach as many classes as Crunch had on the schedule. I got laid off from my position as Director of Marketing at the software company that I'd given my lifeblood to for 6 years. At first, I felt devastated that I'd been laid off. That lasted about a week, before I decided to relish my Golden Parachute, and began enjoying my Laguna Beach life. I was a single gay man, teaching spin classes, which quickly led me to the thrill of road cycling. Not the being a single gay man part…the spin classes part. C'mon folks stay with me here. I know, crazy as it may sound, I took my singing spin instructor talents to the streets and started riding my Trek Mountain bike up and down Pacific Coast Highway (PCH), every chance I had. Of course, it was a challenge to balance the fun, fun, fun of cycling with the "Oh crap, I need a job to sustain my lifestyle and to cover the mountains of alimony and child support I took on the moment I said, "Frankly My Dear, I'm Gay!"

Ironically, even though I was not a trained cyclist, nor was I riding a traditional road bike, I began to cycle daily between 30 – 50 miles a day. In the blink of the eye, and a shimmy out of my Lycra, I'd dropped 100 pounds. I'd become a cycling junky and was addicted to the thrill of dodging cars on PCH. My dramatic weight loss, also led many to question whether I was in a healthy state of being. I never quite understood why my parents were wigged out so much about my health status, until years later when I saw photos of my skeletal self, a drastic comparison to the stocky man I'd been for years. I continued to ride, ride, and ride because it brought me peace and contentment, much like the day I ripped my shirt off, and ran bare chested on the beach.

Driven by a desire to ride like the wind, I signed up for the MS Ride from Newport Beach to San Diego. Surrounded by cycling friends from spin class, my married life, and even a few from my gay life, I was beyond excited about the prospects of a two-day ride that would challenge my stamina and new found love for cycling. The bonus of this adventure ended up being a man. A man I'd met when I was least looking for one. This man showed up just days after the tragedy of 9/11. How we found each other, and why we found each other weren't part of either of our individual life intentions at that time. Our meeting was simply part of the master plan that was yet too revealed for both of us. This handsome, svelte, Hispanic, salt and pepper haired, man with a beautiful smile, came into my life just a few weeks prior to the MS Ride, providing me with the added inspiration to get to the halfway point of the two day ride. This man, now my Supreme Court of the United States, Gay Marriage Ruling approved husband, met me at the halfway point hotel to spend the night. It was our first intimate night together! Little did he know, nor did I, that he'd be helping me recover from a nasty first day cycling spill, where I bit the asphalt.

At the end of the first day of the ride, while basking in the exhilaration of completing the first 50-miles of the ride, and while nursing my black and blue ravaged body from a stupid crash, I felt the deepest level alignment with myself that I'd ever experienced in my life. Admittedly, I was in excruciating pain, but also in the most genuine essence of pure joy. I'd accomplished something that a few years earlier would have made me the laughing stock of my imagination. And, even in the pain of my injuries, I experienced a night of pure ecstasy with a man I realized I was beginning to fall in love with. A feeling that led me to unexpectedly wrap my arms in the warm embrace of lovingly accepting myself in the new form of my authentic self. Even though, I awoke the next morning ravaged with soreness, and dreading the departure of my newly found love (he was off to spend the day with his BFF straight girlfriend), I straddled my bike, stood at the front of the starting line, and dug deep into the vault of my inner strength. I took off and rode on a wave of pure adrenaline, knowing I was a man in love, and in full acceptance of myself. It was a feeling that only catapulted off the charts knowing that in just 25 miles I would cross the finish line at San Diego Bay.

Lost in the beat of Cher's "Believe" album playing in my ears, I drove myself forward. Side-by-side thousands of fellow cyclists, all within arm's reach for the first mile, I peddled with the wind beneath my wings and the shimmering Pacific Ocean as my inspiration. Stimulated by a new found zest for being in life, I knew then, more than at any other juncture thus far in my life, that living my truth would never feel as sweet as it did in that moment. The sweet nectar of authentically accepting myself as a father, ex-husband, son, brother, uncle, marketing professional, cyclist, spin instructor, human being, and a gay man with a beautiful alter ego diva named Lemon-Odd Pop, was far more important than ever, ever again, pretending to be something or someone I wasn't.

No longer settling for mediocrity or contorting to live under the thumbs of other people's standards, I was not only driven by the thrill of completing a 100-mile cycling event under my own strength and power, I also realized I'd rounded a corner and had started to ascend into the reality of becoming me, in my truth, my way, which was truly in the best interest of me and those closest to me in this journey!

Out Without A Doubt!

It's Not About You or Everyone Else...It's About We.

The first memory I recall of realizing, *coming out* isn't solely about me, came during my cycling trek down PCH from Newport Beach to San Diego. Maybe it was the overdose of salty sea air, or the nasty tumble I took during day one of the ride that made me realize, "I can be out of the closet, but now, everyone else in my world has been let out, too." It's a hard pill to swallow, and the lesson(s) learned from this epiphany, take on many unique forms for everyone in the *coming out* journey.

Despite the fact that you've been waiting your whole life to authentically be yourself, others - your family, friends, and acquaintances - haven't had the luxury of processing this reality for years. They're now having to wrap their heads and tongues around, "This is my (fill in the blank) and he/she's gay." As difficult as it was for you to say, "I'm gay," those in your inner circle are having just as hard of a time coming to terms with the "new you," even though the "new you" is exactly who you've always been.

One of the overwhelming thoughts I kept struggling with was, "Why aren't you happy for me now that you know I'm gay and being truthful and honest with you?" Nice thought, and quite honestly it comes from a genuine center of truth. However, I now clearly see that was a selfish, one-sided perspective. Of course, I was thrilled, excited, and ready to be me, even though it broke apart a 13-year marriage, and forever changed the landscape of what family would mean to my two lovely little girls. I also can't set aside the reality of how *coming out* impacted my parents, and my brother's view of the Rick they knew. Therein lies the slippery slope of assuming we fully know someone else.

Regardless of sexual orientation - gay, straight and everything in between – when we start to ASSUME (making an ASS out of YOU and Me) anything about anyone else, we march blindly into the danger zone. The assumptive nature of assuming, leads to false expectations based on our own beliefs of what will happen, rather than looking at situations from "How can this be a win/win for everyone concerned?" Now, don't make an ASSUMPTION that I'm insinuating that you need to, or should, live your life for everyone else. Instead, I'm suggesting that you live your life for you, and consider how you can make it a "win/win" scenario for everyone in your life. Easier said than done, until you've flexed that "win/win" muscle.

I wasn't all that far from a "win/win" mentality the day I came out, or so I thought. Oh no! I was far from evolved. It took years of tripping, falling, being an asshole, and even to this day, getting a swift kick in the ass to help me grasp that I would be a *better me* by being a *better me* for others. Whatever you make room for in your life is exactly what you attract into your life.

» Want more understanding? Be more understanding.

» Desire more acceptance? Be more accepting.

» Wish people were more open-minded? Be more open-minded yourself.

Regardless of what it is you desire for yourself during this phase of *coming out,* you'll be more likely and capable of achieving your desires if you turn your thoughts inward towards a "win/win" proposition rather than a "my way or the highway" stubborn stance!

In the excitement and newness of being authentic, it's easily and unconsciously tempting to have it all about you. How do I know this happens? Because I lived it myself. I lost myself, my dignity, my integrity because it was too much about "Look at me, I'm gay and you should be celebrating with me!" I had a huge circle of supporters who were celebrating with me, but I had an equal number of naysayers who weren't in my court. If you believe you won't experience negativity during your journey, then bless you my child, and I'll await your phone call or email when you need the support, once that blindsided, bitchy, negativity slaps you in the face!

Through the boxing rings of negativity, I got caught up in the "Fuck You" mentality many more times than I'm proud to admit. It happens! Once I realized the "Fuck You" mentality was emanating from my own inability to allow others to authentically be themselves, my energy shifted to a deeper space of compassion, respect, and valuing the diversity of others opinions. By no means did this mean I agreed with them or was willing to change who I was to make them feel more comfortable. The chapter of "Fuck you, if you don't love me for being gay," was quickly being shut down by a new perspective. I began choosing to bend, without breaking. A lesson that taught me the purest essence of acceptance of others for who they are, with the hopes that my modeling that behavior would encourage them to more readily accept me for who I was!

CHAPTER 6

Embracing Our Truth...One Hug At A Time!

Truth can be scarier than fiction, and it can send us down a funky little rabbit hole of insanity if we allow our fiction to become our TRUTH. Taking the road less traveled to fully embrace ourselves as we are, in our truth, only requires one darn thing...that we accept ourselves - just as we are, in this moment, and every moment that we take a breath. There's no point trying to accept ourselves in the yet to come, until we arrive in that future moment, living it in high definition reality. As for our past, we've been what we were in our past and there's nothing but a lot of wasted worry, shame, and guilt that can come from wallowing in what was. Thank goodness we can grow from the past, choose to be different in the future; in addition, realizing we can't change the past, nor predict the future. We can kick our self in the booty and launch us forward into a bright new future where we accept with open arms and vulnerable grace, the powerful possibilities.

If you take the brave step to embrace this philosophy, choose to wake up and be yourself, and only yourself in each and every moment, then surprise, surprise, things will naturally shift for you as they were always intended to from the start. Not because you've said it's "now or never."

Your shift will happen because it's in your best interest. This may be a new concept, and a new way of being in your life, but so was the first time you paid over $3.00 for a gallon of gas. Now that type of money spent at the pump is a norm. Doesn't mean, pump, pump, cha ching, cha ching, will always be the new normal; it's just what is for now. The truth is, this can become your new normal as soon as you allow it to be your new normal, regardless of the chaos you may be facing right now, as you get into the groove of embracing yourself, in your new life.

✤

Taking Nothing For Granted and Everything For You!

I'm going to hand you an honest to goodness truth that I hope starts making things easier for you. Because you've staked your claim in your sexuality, everything is going to be a new experience. You've never been down this path, with yourself or your inner circle, and they've never been down this road before with you or themselves either. Let's get real. They may have had other people they've known, or heard of, who've come out of the closet – a distant uncle, a cousin, a sister in-law, a friend from college – yet, they weren't expecting to have this experience with you. It's a big difference! Regardless of the relationships you have, no one in your inner circle has experienced a *coming out* journey with you, and you haven't experienced this journey with them or yourself, so be patient: no matter how hard or challenging it may be to keep your sanity at times.

The moment you step into a tunnel vision space of being incapable of seeing the journey from the other person's perspective, you've purchased a one-way ticket on the train of misunderstanding and hellish communications: not always, but usually. Quite honestly, this isn't a unique anomaly found *only* in the *coming out* experience. It's an everyday, in every way, lesson to be learned about being in any human relationship. I know you've heard the phrase, "Until you've stood in someone else's stilettos..." Ok, maybe that's not exactly the way you've heard it, but you get the drift! Trust Lemon-Odd Pop and me on this one! You gotta give people space to grow into the *coming out* experience with you. It's one of the keys to *coming out* success. Of course, sometimes that key is unable to unlock the door to understanding and acceptance. When that occurs you've got to let people fumble around in the dark to find the right key, before they'll unlock their heart to loving the new you, which is the old you with a fabulous new twist of authenticity! It takes time, patience, and allowing others to process how "Frankly My Dear, I'm Gay" affects them, and their relationship with you. Grant them a beautiful loft space within their thoughts to breathe in the new you. By the way, the same goes for you – breathe in, give yourself lots of space, and lots of processing time to think!

�֎

Unwrap The Gift With Joy and
Be Damn Grateful That Ya Got a Gift!

Excitement, freedom, honesty, authenticity, and a big boost of sexual energy, pretty much sums up how most people feel once they own up to their truth – sexually speaking or otherwise. Often, once the, "WHEW, glad that's over," feeling hits, it's like the Heavens open, doves fly, confetti drops and then suddenly an ASS shows up because you ASSumed it's over, and all is well in the "I'm gay" world. Oh my dears. If only that were blissfully true. Granted, the acceptance of us queers in the world is shifting, more rapidly than at any other time in history. Yet, like the fight our brothers and sisters of color endured for freedom not so long ago, "It ain't freedom 'til its freedom for all!" And, that's where many of us end up making ASSumptive ASSholes of ourselves, right after we've come out of the closet.

Not everyone is going to be happy that you're gay! If you just gasped at that thought, then honey, we seriously need to chat! As much as you're excited and wishful about your newfound truth and being accepted, it ain't gonna happen with everyone overnight. Wake up, smell the coffee (Starbucks or otherwise), and remember how deeply you've wrestled with your desire to be authentically you! In fact, when you begin to unpack the Samsonite of your sexual identity, and start sharing with your peeps the excess baggage you've been totting around your entire life, realize, over the weight limit, extra bags don't fly free on planes or in life. There's a cost for ASSuming your inner circle should and will hop on the next flight with you to Gay Celebration Island. Candidly speaking, making those ASSumptions will hurt you and them equally. If you dig in your Manolo Blahnik heels without giving space for others to come to terms of endearment with your news, then you might as well have said, "Screw you and get over it!" There's plenty of time, and more than ample opportunity to tell a few people to "Get over it." Just be cautious doing it with some of your inner circle right after you come out. You might end up regretting being so quick to say "Screw You," in the moment. Plus, now that you've revealed your truth, there's a closet full of stuff that people are going to throw at you that will make you want to shout, "Get the fuck over it!" Breathe, breathe, oh and breathe!

Let's do a quick little check-in. "Are you getting this concept of not being an ASS and ASSuming anything?" If not, here's a great way to wake up and understand it. Try to think back to when you were in the womb. Oops. Not that far back. Think back to when you first realized, "OMG, OMG!" (Again, if you need this translated...gay card revoke alert!) Now, back to our lesson. How long did it take you to "Get over it," accept yourself for who you were, in your sexuality? 5, 10, 30 years? More? Whatever amount of time you gave yourself, you <u>might</u> consider giving the same to those in your inner circle who are struggling with your GRAND REVELATION! Don't misunderstand me; I'm not diminishing you or your trek towards authenticity by one iota! Quite to the contrary, my dear! Get over yourself and realize, I'm actually celebrating you by handing you a beautifully wrapped, hand written invitation to allow others to be authentic in their acceptance of you. Once again, it's like forcing a square peg in a round hole.

If you force others to accept you, are they truly and really authentically accepting you? Lordy, lordy, lordy, NO!

One of the most powerful ways to be in the "give me breathing room space" with someone is for you to be the gift of giving, so they can receive and vice versa. Each opportunity you have to authentically let someone step into your new world with you in his or her way is a frickin' brilliant gift. This type of gift doesn't require a gift receipt for returns nor does it run the possibility of becoming a white elephant at the next holiday party. Conversely, when someone asks you to give them space to process the new gay you, you should be jumping through hoops of joy. They've just extended the olive branch of consideration and an attempt to understand your new reality, which is their gift to you. Put ya damn ego aside, take it for what it is, and let it be! Nothing more, nothing less, until it truthfully becomes an issue that they won't accept - then we'll take a new course of action.

✳

Sweet and Salty Childlike Innocence.

One of the things we adults let go of without a second thought is our ability to be childlike and have fun. On the other hand, you know the hand that causes problems, we often act like spoiled, little bratty, kids. Guess what? Nothing changes, for most of us, when we come charging out of the closet on our very own pride parade float! Whether we're driven by the excitement of a whole new, fabulously gay world, or we're finally rubbing the pain away from wearing the shackles of pretending to be someone we're not, we can suddenly become little, excited, immature kids after kicking the closet door open, almost breaking it off its hinges.

For some of you, you'll once again become the shy, nerdy, "Don't call on me, don't call on me," introvert including: being afraid of your own shadow and scared to death to step into the reality of your sexuality. Others of you will dive fearlessly, head long off the 50M high dive into the synchronized water ballet of the gay world. Falling right into place without creating a ripple in the pool of life. No matter which way you travel, even if you escape down your own unique route, all that matters is doing what works for you, with a caveat. Make your *coming out* journey work for you without you being rolled over by the bulldozers of outside influence that may derail you. Take heed, dear friends! (Geez...I'm starting to sound like Lemon-Odd Pop's preacher daddy!) As soon as you step out of alignment with your core values and beliefs, some of which are just now being formed with your newly found freedom, the more quickly you may lose sight of yourself. For example...

There's a kid in the candy store mentality around sex and *coming out*, that a grand majority of us face. First, as shared in Chapter 5, is the "Gimme, gimme, gimme," stomping your feet, arms crossed, spoiled little child mentality. Nothing wrong with that behavior. Ok, maybe it's not pretty behavior. However, as long as you're highly aware that what you desire is attention and acceptance, to be fully out and proud, experiencing your newfound sexuality. There's no need to beat yourself up because you're out tasting the candy, provided you're consciously aware of your actions, embracing fully the myriad of possible outcomes from those explorations – feeling like a tramp; finding you enjoy certain sexual practices; admitting you don't want to be committed; accepting that you do want to be monogamous.

Most of us encounter similar feelings that remind us of our younger self standing outside a candy store, staring in the window at all the delicious delights, only to discover we don't have enough money to buy our sweet tooth's desire. The same holds true when we find ourselves staring at the gay culture wondering if we have the looks, the bodies, the (FILL IN THE BLANK) to be accepted in the community. More prevalent than we'd like to admit, many brothers and sisters in our community who come out believe they still have to pretend to be someone they're not versus living their authentic life and being in their truth. It's as if the yummy chocolate bar of authenticity is still just out of reach because they're not quite the right flavor of gay to be accepted in the community unless you act and behave a certain way. Oh so not true, unless you eat that poisoned candy of liar, liar, pants on fire. You can be who you are and you will find others in the community who will embrace you.

An additional candy store breakthrough of *coming out* is discovering that your sexual energy is a unique blend of a sweet and salty. Sometimes, the curiously sweet side of exploring your sexuality is like indulging in a luscious Godiva chocolate; a pure joy to savor and relish without remorse. Other times you may find your experiences a little under salted or over salted – each taking you into a different taste dimension of discovering who you are in your own gay skin.

Clearly understanding how you're playing in the candy store of coming and being out, enables you to grow, shift, change, and be more authentically you. The real you! Regardless of what others think or say about you, there is immense personal power in staking your claim, your way, to be in the candy jar of your gay life. Taking a stand empowers you to be more truthful with yourself and others. Simultaneously, you're adding bit by little bits of sweetness to the mix by being fully aligned in your own core values, and by sharing dollops of your authentic self with the world.

Now, to be clear, some of ya will come out and jump immediately into the pulse of the gay community! Bravo and go shake your little bubble booties away in the gay disco. Others of you will discover it's more your style to be a "normal gay," which actually doesn't exist. There is no normal "gay club!" There's only the "gay your way club." Regardless of the way you step into the community, don't force yourself to be anything other than who you want to be as a gay person in the LGBT community, and in the world at large! Often it's the *forcing and molding yourself to mentality*, which causes you to get lost deep in the abyss of our own stuff - emotionally and mentally. Whether you're *coming out* of the closet, going through a nasty divorce, or facing a job loss; the common human yearning is for love, understanding, and acceptance... unless you don't give a damn. Even if you're not yearning for your own "You love me, you really love me," Sally Fields moment, then you might simply desire a "love me for the quiet wallflower that I am" small group hug. The key is to be who you are, until that no longer works for you. If, and when that happens, it's a "Hello! Wake up and smell the cappuccino" sign that your values are missing the foam on the top. The true you, in the cup of your life is crying out for some attention from the head barista – YOU! Answer the cry, take the time to have a little coffee chat with yourself, so you can bring back the balance of the rich full flavor of living a life that's fully aligned with who you are and who you desire to be. Once there, your cup of living a fulfilled life will runneth over!

Unlock The Final Frontier, So To Speak!

Coming out is like the smoker who's finally committed to quitting-smoking, or the overweight person who's setting the éclair aside so they can lose weight. Stepping into your sexuality is making a commitment to unlock the magic and throw away the padlock and key on the closet door that was you. At least a piece of false you! Think of it as Beauty tossing away the Beast who's been hiding the real prince/princess. It's an astounding self-expressed moment when you realize; nothing has kept you handcuffed (at least not handcuffed in a fun way) more than your own beliefs, expectations, misunderstandings, and those funky, crazy making little diva gremlin voices telling you that you're not enough. Bottom line truth time! Nothing, and I do mean nothing, changes if you high step out of being the person don't want to be, only to step right back into another closet of people pleasing a different crowd who want you to "Be this way, so I can feel comfortable with you!"

Don't get me wrong, there are plenty of roads, back alleys, and paths that will lead you towards more acceptance in this world. In fact, there are more routes towards acceptance than Lemon-Odd Pop's shoe collection, which is huge! However, the teapot of life all boils down to, "Why are we so hell bent on reaching for acceptance from others?" Yes, I realize that seems like a deep question, and I'm not expecting you're going to pick up the phone and speed dial me with your answer. Of course, if you have me on speed dial, then I must either love you to bits or you're stalking me. However, I have a question I'd like you to ponder. I love the word ponder because it's so deep! Any who, here's the question to ponder: Why? Why do you crave, desire, want, and need acceptance from the gay community, or from anyone for that matter?

» Does it stem from a deep space of past rejection?

» Are you hoping that in some way you will find a new identity in the community that brings happiness?

» Do you need a new "family?"

» Are you craving love that is currently "non-existent" in your life?

» Do you fear deeper rejection by not fitting into some pre-defined sub-culture of the gay community?

No matter what's driving you towards the warm embrace of acceptance in your sexual identity...BE CLEAR. Get very clear with yourself, your intentions, and how you DESIRE – not NEED or WANT – to be in your new world, and new you. Reminder, make sure you take the closet door padlock and key and throw them away. Do it. Do it right now. Admit once and for all that you never want to feel the hell of being locked in another jail cell brought on by false beliefs, assumptions, or interpretations that cause you to fail and jail yourself, again! While you're at it, go ahead and tell the your supreme gremlins to shut their traps too, or face the wrath of Lemon-Odd Pop. You don't want that... trust me!

Cut Loose, Run Free, and Be The Raw, Naked You!

Remember the story of me ripping off my shirt and running free on the beach? (Something I wouldn't do now because I can't find my 6-pack abs...LOL) I'm challenging you, not threatening, challenging you in a loving manner to cut loose, run free, and be raw and naked in your own skin – however that looks for you, and only you as your gay self. There's just one itty-bitty caveat to this challenge. I want you to be ready, willing, and able to cut loose, run free, and just be your raw, naked, gay YOU!

Breaking out of the starting gate living your raw naked truth isn't always going to be a smooth up at the bat. It takes practice. In fact, sometimes it might be as embarrassing as a pre-mature ejaculation, or having to fake an orgasm. It can feel really good in the moment until you have performance anxiety. In those cases, you may be left wondering, "Is this raw naked truth really me, or am I not really gay?" Whoa, whoa, whoa! Authentically living freely in your sexual orientation isn't a one-time event that's done and over when you say, "Frankly My Dear, I'm Gay!" Being gay is a lifetime journey that starts with a powerful opening note "I'm Gay," that crescendos and ebbs in the rock concert of your life.

The musical score of authentic "gaydom," includes notes of financial, intimate, spiritual, personal, career, and of course sexual interplay. There's not a single gay note of gay life that is exempt from the essence of your gay being. When fully appreciated for its contribution to the gay score of your life, each note brings a unique harmony to the overall experience of you being authentically yourself. Remove a note or become pitchy in one part of the score, and the entire gay harmony spirals out of key. Not a chair turn for you in this metaphorical version of the "The Voice" which is now your life. Your goal is to realize the WHOLE of you is greater than the GAY of you. If the GAY of you dominates the score of your life, you might find yourself disappointed, crying the blues, and never singing your own version of *Hakuna Matata* from the "Lion King."

Let's be honest, striking the cords of freedom, and cutting loose may be a scary new, live stage experience that will cause you to freeze up. No worries, it happens to the best of us, even Lemon-Odd Pop! Take a deep breath, suck it up, and realize you haven't exercised your freedom muscles yet. Activating those muscles will make it easier and easier to take step after step towards your authentic destiny. One of the easiest ways to cut loose, run free, and be naked in your truth is to do so with gratitude.

Gratitude is easy to come by, provided you allow it to come forward without an iconic event to remind you to have gratitude. During your *coming out* journey, give gratitude for waking up, being able to cut loose with a big belly laugh, having a hot shower to wash yourself in, or give gratitude for the simple feeling of a cool breeze on your skin. Each powerful step towards gratitude guides you one step closer to cutting loose, running free, and just being your raw naked truth. Why? Do you really need to ask? It's plain and simple. You'll experience an awakened state of gratitude for wrapping yourself up in your sexuality, so that you can cut loose tethers of false beliefs, run free from other's expectations, and be you, as you are, with no second guessing.

✄

Surprise, You're a Little Jaded Bitch!

Take no offense honey, none is intended, but don't be surprised if you step out of the closet and suddenly find yourself being a caddy bitch towards the gay community. You're not doing it intentionally and the reaction is quite human and normal. Any time an earth shattering, monumental shift kicks us in the ass, most of us quickly run into the arms of like-minded cohorts who've endured similar pain. Admit it. You need and desire to have a sense of acceptance, unity, and family. *Coming out* of the closet is no different. We run into the arms of our like-minded peeps only to realize some of them in the gay community need to be still and chill. No need to be shocked, surprised, and at times even judgmental towards your own gay community. HELLO! We're humans who get annoyed, critical, and BITCHY about the people in our lives. That's ok! Being gay or straight doesn't change this reality. No one on the planet is immune from judgment – giving or receiving.

The diversity of sub-cultures within the gay community may throw you off, and have you begging for a gay pocket-guide to help you find your way. Pocket guide, schmocket guide! Just be ya damn self. For example, just because I'm a 6'4", 280 pound, hairy-chested, six-pack deficient, goatee wearing, bald-headed guy doesn't mean I'm a BEAR. Others might see me that way. However, I don't buy it. That doesn't mean you have to buy into whatever box someone tries to put you in either. I am me. A tall, stocky, hairy handsome, daddy who knows how to rock a goatee and a baldhead. Likewise, if you can strut a nicely tailored pantsuit, straight off the couture line at Nordy's, with a Tiffany's sliver leaf cuff from the Paloma Picasso collection, that doesn't mean you're lipstick lesbian. It simply means you can rock it as a woman who happens to be lesbian. Labels are just labels to help us sort and sift as humans. That is, unless you think that bear, dyke on bike, twink, butch lezbo, are labels that help you rock your world in your own unique gay way.

The moment these boxed in boundaries make you feel trapped and jaded, brothers and sistahs it's time to take that crazy making thought and ask yourself, "What's really getting under my skin?" We all do it; let a snotty comment, or a less than subtle insinuation about our character from time-to-time, get under our skin. IT'S HUMAN NATURE. Instead, let's think big picture. Don't be afraid to be naked with your raw truth. To expose your real feelings of vulnerability. To get real with the honest to goodness truth of why what others think keeps preventing you from being authentically who you are – yourself, your way, in your world.

Enjoy The Ride, Relish The Heart Swoons, and Don't Let Heartbreaks Break Ya.

I'm not assuming I know you or exactly how you feel. However, it's not uncommon for newbie gays to feel immune from becoming members of the hearts clubs – stolen and broken. You can't avoid it, so, buy the

2-for-1 special and get ready to face the music. No matter what you think gay means, the tango of "love me tender," and "dropped me bitch," doesn't discriminate based on your sexual orientation. I swear this is the truth, and if I'm lying, then may the divas of "living truth" cast me out of the chorus, never to perform live on the stages of Provincetown during Carnival Week! (If you don't know what this is, look it up and you'll have your tickets booked to be there before you know it!)

The damn straight (shudder) truth is, whether you're 14, 44, or 74, any intimate relationship – homo, hetero, bi, or any other flavor of sexuality – doesn't mean you have a heartache free hall pass for life. No, I've not lost it. I know you're smart, and most of you are scratching your head saying, "And this is news?" Ahem. I didn't say that. In your best interest, I want to ensure that as you venture out of the closet you're fully prepared for any false fairytale pretense you may create about gay life. Hetero or homo, we've all been bombarded, from a very young age that "Love is happily ever after" (thanks Disney). Glad that's working for Mickey and Minnie. But alas, even a grand majority of heterosexuals haven't found the "red brick road" to wedded bliss. For crying out loud, there are more divorces these days than hairs on Donald Trump's head to pull up and comb over.

Each of us, creates our own versions of "to infinity and beyond," lofty expectations, dreams of having a perfect relationship; friends with benefits or otherwise; monogamous or open; long-term or casually dating. Despite the Technicolor, 4-D picture we create of waltzing onto the dance floor of blissful love, like a betting fool, we go for the 100-to-1 odds that we've got the winning love horse for life! Of course, to win:

a) There's got to be a winning horse

b) The horse needs to be in the race with us

c) And, winning for the long stretch around the track has to be on each horse's agenda.

My dear friends, just because you're the latest to venture out of the closet, doesn't crown you flavor of the month, even though in some circles you may feel that way. If so, enjoy the moment. In reality, you may very well be the newest distraction on the scene, until another new distraction comes along, which is what's likely to happen. Being the "new meat" distraction, and hot kid on the block is a great ego boost, provided you see it for what it is, and have fun with being the Belle Of The Ball until the clock strikes midnight. Unfortunately and fortunately, this pivotal crossing is where many well-intentioned "newbies" coming through the closet doors get off track. Unfortunately because seeking others approval and vying for acceptance takes us outside of ourselves to feel complete. Fortunately, this "flavor of the week" lesson is given to us, to teach us the priceless lesson of being ourselves. When we are our true selves, cupid's arrow will hit the bull's-eye on the freeway of dating and mating in the gay community. The fun, joy, and adventure of disappointments in "relationship rugby" are no different, except for a few interesting twists than how we learned to do relationships in the "heterosexual" world. A lot of frogs will be kissed, until one day your prince, or princess, finds you and you'll be with them, just the way you've always dreamed...unless you end up being someone who believes you're destined to be alone...but that's a different book.

A-U-T-H-E-N-T-I-C! How Do You Spell It?

No matter where you're going, how you get there, or what you want, if you're not authentic, then nothing else matters. You'll be terminally stuck in the clutches of PRETENDINITIUS – pretending to be something or someone you're not. Best wishes for experiencing FREEDOM. It's likely to never come knocking. Just sayin'!

Know FREEDOM...Know PEACE...Know HAPPINESS!

The only thing to make this statement a Nobel Peace Prize winning quote would be to add...

Be CONFIDENT...Be AUTHENTIC...Be YOU!

If you're sitting there, yelling at me underneath your breath, saying, "Gurl that's just a bunch of lip service, mumbo jumbo," then tell me something. When was the last time you were really being you and happy? Correct me if I'm wrong, in order to be truly you and happy requires CONFIDENCE, FREEDOM, AUTHENTICITY, and PEACE. Just sayin!

I know this idea is not the gospel truth for everyone. Nor am I asking you to come to the mountain of Rick and Lemon-Odd Pop to adopt our outlook on life. I'm simply offering these little appetizers of empowerment, so you can step into a deep, warm, Jacuzzi tub of authentic freedom. Now, some of you may be saying, "What the heck does that mean?" It's story time, so gather round, lighten up, and open ya mind.

As a child, Tommy loved to play with Lego's. He lived and breathed to create everything his crazy cool imagination could conjure up. One day, while on an expedition to his favorite toy store, he once again found himself in the Lego section, surprise, surprise. While standing there lost in thought, the store manager came up to Tommy and offered him a special treat for being such a good customer. "Tommy, I'm willing to give you all the Lego's you desire, so you can build anything you like. How does that sound?" Of course, to an 8-year old boy, the thought of having all of anything was almost too good to be true. "That sounds totally cool," Tommy replied. Smiling, the manager continued. "There's just one catch. If I give you all the Lego's you want, you have to stay here in the store, and only play with them here in the store." Suddenly, the excitement left Tommy's eyes. Gone was the vision of his room filled with every Lego imaginable. His Lego wet dream had just been cast aside like a used condom. What's the moral of this story? Dreams vanish when they become boxed in by boundaries set by others!

Authentic freedom has no boundaries!

Along the lifelong journey of *coming out*, you'll find yourself limited by your own thoughts, and the expectations of others, but it doesn't have to be that way! When these limitations arise, ask yourself, "Is this how authentic freedom is supposed to be and feel?" If your answer is no, then redirect your focus, change your thoughts, experience new feelings, and create new actions that launch you into the space to be authentically free as you are intended to be – today, tomorrow, and every day of your life. You're only limited by your own inability to change focus and direction.

❇

The "Out" Factor.

There are many shades of gay when it comes to being "out." Here's a little secret, no one knows better how to be 'out' in your life than you. Not your best fabulous friend, your aunt who's marching in the pride parade in your honor, even before you do, or the hot Adonis you just met who thinks you're adorable. Each of us has our own unique way of being out, and it doesn't necessarily mean waving a rainbow flag, wearing a pride ring, or showing up at the 'in' gay bar or chic brunch spot. There's no need to be *out* except the way being *out* fits for you.

It may seem overtly obvious that you'll be confronted when, where, and how out you are in your life. Be prepared that some people will get annoyed, and try to influence how out you choose to be in your life. Others will celebrate you as the person who takes a stand in life to declare, "This is me, hear me roar." All that should, and does matter is your comfort, in your own skin, in your environment. Your "out factor," doesn't make you "less than;" unless you are being measured by someone else's measuring stick. Buying into this self-depreciating standard, you're once again signaling your willingness to live by someone else's expectations.

Consider this example: Samantha is a swinger, yet she doesn't talk about it at work. Does that make her less of a swinger? Of course, not! Extreme as that example is, what Samantha and her hubby do on their own time is their business. Same holds true for you and how you want to be in your life. Provided how "out" you are doesn't put you in harm's way, then be out your way... After all that's what living your authentic truth is all about... RIGHT? And, as for those in our community who think you're not "out" enough... since when did it become YOUR responsibility to make them more comfortable in their gay life by you being more out. If you being "out" has an effect on their life, they need to have a chat with me and Lemon-Odd Pop. We'll give them the inside scoop for finding peace in their own gay skin!

✖

Relishing Truth Check-In

Answer these questions and complete these exercises before moving forward My Dear!

1. What does living your truth mean to you?
2. How do you define authenticity?
3. Who would you say personifies authentic living to you?
4. What scares you about being authentic?
5. What areas of life do you wish you were more authentic? Financially, spiritually, intimately, socially, career, family, personal growth, sexually, and etc.
6. How does living your truth impact your ability to be loved?
7. Who could reject you for being truthful and authentic and why would they?
8. How could you be truthful and authentic in your response to the person(s) you listed in question #7 to let them know you've been hurt, without being hateful or accusatory?
9. Who do you need to ask forgiveness from to be truthful and authentic?
10. What do you need to do to give yourself permission to be truthful and authentic?

11. On a scale of 1 – 10, how truthful are you in your overall life right now?

12. *How important* is it for you to change the rating of question #11?

13. What could you do to change your rating of question #11?

14. On a scale of 1 – 10, how authentic are you in your overall life right now?

15. *How important* is it for you to change the rating of question #14?

16. What could you do to change your rating of question #14?

17. Using two words, and two words only, describe how being more truthful would make you feel.

18. Using two words, and two words only, describe how being more authentic would make you feel.

19. Based on your insights of self, your desire, and beliefs about TRUTH, write a short mantra that will support you in being more truthful with yourself, others, and in life.

20. Based on your insights of self, your desire, and beliefs about AUTHENTICITY, write a short mantra that will support you in being more truthful with yourself, others, and in life.

Now you're ready to move onto the world of Relishing Your Truth Before, During, and After You say, "Frankly My Dear, I'm Gay!"

CHAPTER 7

Fear of Freedom

What I'm about to share may seem quirky, crazy, and even harder for you to buy into, even more than Cher's going on her Farewell, Farewell, Farewell Tour. While *coming out* is liberating, there's going to be moments where you'll find it a little bit difficult to feel free on the other side of the closet doors! "What? You don't say!" I did say. Did I just go off my sanity pills? Um, maybe a little bit, because Lemon–Odd Pop has been hoarding them. Cutting loose negative beliefs about being gay and building confidence to come out leads to truth and releases us from the constraints of living a lie, which is also constricting and freeing. I see you scratching your head and saying, "I don't get it!" I didn't either until it went from being muddled as Lemon-Odd Pop's facial mud, to being crystal clear!

Freedom to be you, no matter how it's ingrained in your heart's desire, may feel awkward and unnerving once you're actually holding it in your precious authentic hands. It's O.K.! Don't fret. It's a new experience and will feel awkward until you get comfortable being "free to be you!" It's like breaking the smoking habit or learning a new dance step. Both take concentration, commitment, and determination. Before you know it, one will have you breathing more freely, and the other will have you breathing harder by shaking your booty like there's no tomorrow. Same thing happens when you finally take the brave step out of the closet. You'll breathe a whole lot easier into the lungs of your authentic self, dance through life with a new powerful strut in your step; all the while, taking shaky steps in your new stilettos of freedom.

More than likely, when you least expect it, you'll catch yourself saying, "Wait, can I do this?" Or even better, "Is it ok for me to feel this free?" Yes and Yes! You've simply never been given, or given you permission to experience this level of freedom. In those moments of doubt and questioning, allow yourself to relish in a state of fearless, untethered freedom, and enjoy it. You should bask in the glow, open your mind so that you can grow and learn as you burst through the dazzling doorways of *Free To Be Me*. Once I learned that freedom to be me was a tremendous gift I gave myself, I found I became more and more grounded in the luscious liberty of fearless freedom.

❈

Um, "How Do You Do This Man-On-Man/Woman-On-Woman Thing?

For starters, learning how to date, mate, be intimate, have gratifying sex, and be in an emotionally available relationship with someone of the same sex, won't be found in the latest issues of G.Q., Cosmopolitan, Single-Man Hunting, or the Gay Wed Book! (Trust me, I wish). You might be tempted to rush to a *coupled couples* bedside, asking for their advice. Not a bad idea, just be prepared that some couples might ask you to join them in bed. However, that topic will be covered in depth in my next book– "How to be your own gay man, stay sane, and keep your sanity in a 3-way monogamish relationship!" The best place to uncover how "YOU' will conduct yourself in a same-sex relationship thingy is to take a deep look within yourself, your reality, and get in touch with your M4M, W4W dating and mating desires – needs and wants don't count.

DESIRE is all that counts. Once again, my disclaimer states clearly, this is my philosophy: take it or leave it. If you leave it, know that Lemon-Odd Pop will come find you and mess you up, leaving you looking like Sarah Palin pretending she didn't spend a torrid night with Joe six-pack, playing with his plumbers crack! (Author sits with devilish grin across his 5 o'clock shadow face, musing over that last sentence he wrote!)

To look fearless freedom in the face, and step in for the bumpy ride of man-on-man living, I had, yes had, to let go of my NEEDINESS. I didn't need a man, even when I brainwashed myself into believing I did…which most gay men tend to do. Same thing applies to you my dear sweet Lesbian sisters. Well of course you don't need a man, and you don't NEED a woman even though you think you do! None of us NEEDS someone else to complete us. Even the $6.50 Hallmark cards that clearly state, "You complete me," are frankly my dears full of bullshit! And, no I'm not being "Bitter, party of one!" We each complete ourselves when we believe we can be complete within ourself.

To be complete, you only have to see yourself as your best gay self, just the way you are, each and every moment of your life. Once you've gotten at least a B+ in being yourself, then you'll be able to move onto the real fun, challenge, joy, and pain in the ass of being in a relationship with someone else of the same sex. My true colors finally started shining brilliantly once I wrapped my discombobulated grey matter around this ironic concept of being my best self in my own way, which had nothing to do with being gay. The secret wasn't going to be found in online dating, speed dating, or matchmaking. The secret was me allowing me to freely be me in the man-meet-man, date man, mate man world. All I had to do was release my grasp on overcompensating to please, settle into the steady breath of being in the moment, and trust that my DESIRES were being met exactly as intended – in my best interest.

The deeper I stepped into my meeting guys, dating guys, mating guys, map of reality (NLP term, look it up), the closer I came to defining what

I desired in a M4M relationship. I discovered this part of the journey to be a little more challenging than expected, mostly due to my own lack of dating experience – hetero- or homo-. Honestly, I jumped on less than 10 Filly's (not literally, nor do I mean to sound demeaning to women) during my spins around the heterosexual carousel. Ten times around, hetero or homo dating carousel, does not make one an expert at dating or mating. Thus, I found myself in a conundrum with no clear-cut direction, for dating men and finding Mr. Right.

I'd never felt more free to go hunt hunks, ride cowboys, and rankle the sheets with whatever Mr. Right Now I desired; however I desired, yet...I felt incapable and ill equipped to be a dating dynamo. Alas, true freedom once again seemed elusive. What the hell? I'd worked so damn hard to get here; waited an eternity to be me, and salivating beyond my wildest dreams to be with a man, and not just for the sex. Nevertheless, freedom hung down around my ankles; a shiny new set of shackles that prevented me from stepping fearlessly forward to live my authentic life because I'd never been this deep, in the M4M world before without sneaking around behind my wife's back (a huge shaming thing I had to also get over to move forward). For instance:

- » How do I date a man without him running for the hills?
- » Do I touch him in public or not?
- » Is talking about the ex-wife appropriate and when?
- » What about the kids? When, where, and how do I bring them up in a conversation?
- » When do I discuss sex and sexual preferences?
- » How do I share my life goals without sounding like I'm ready to set up house?
- » Who pays for the date, and is it even considered a date?
- » What qualifies as a "let's do this again" nod of approval with a guy?
- » Where do I go to meet guys like me?

» Why should I date more than one guy at a time?

» How do you introduce him to the family and meet his?

The more I stumbled through these crazy making yet mostly logical thoughts, the more I realized I wasn't free. I was consumed and trapped by my own inability to do "gay life." This was the freedom I'd been yearning for all these years. Call me "naïve party of one," in the millennium of years I'd fantasized, and mentally masturbated (in more ways than one) about my life with my Mr. Right, I hadn't prepared myself for the realities that were now kicking sand in my romantic face with less FREEDOM than I'd had as a pretend heterosexual!

For a time, I let the "less than" thoughts consume me, stunting my growth as an authentic gay man. Even though I was 38, I was far from being an adult gay man. I struggled trying to find my footing in this FREE new world on the other side of the closet door. Aching, yearning, and try as I might, I was failing, if only in my own mind. Subconsciously, and consciously, all I kept hearing was, "You're free to be free, so go be free damn it!" Finally, one typical night at my favorite gay watering hole in Laguna Beach, Woody's (how apropos), someone finally had the balls to shake me loose from my bullshit beliefs with one comment. "You're an adult man, in an adult man's body, living your gay teen life as if it's your first orgasm! Grow up and go with it!" Time stood still in the moments following this "oh so circuit boy, yet wise old queen's words!" I immediately was transported back to high school, the vision of my gargantuan adult body playing the lead role while trapped in the mind fuck of an awkward gay teen. I started laughing hysterically; so hard in fact, that I had to leave the bar before I got thrown out for being TOO GAY and disturbing the fabulous pounding beat of remix #5025 of Cher's Believe. I mean, come on…as if it's possible to a) disturb CHER, and b) to be too gay in a gay bar. In the midst of that frenzied laughter, I realized I was just starting my ascent towards being an adolescent gay man. Yes, I was truly free to ride into my gay life, training wheels included, being the little gay boy I was, trapped in an adult man's body, just as I was intended to be…with loads of "bitch slaps" upside the head, and wonderful gay life lessons to be learned in my newly found FREEDOM – gay and otherwise!

※

Kids And Loving A Man… Are They Mutually Exclusive or Exclusively Mutual?

As you now know, I didn't take the traditional route to my GAYDOM (gay kingdom) and as such, I brought "baggage" with me. Not the kind of shoulder bags that cause irritation as you streak through the airport. Nor the kind of irritation that an imitation Louis Vuitton roller bag has with wheels that go every direction but the way you want them to. I'm talking about the baggage that comes from being a late bloomer, going through a divorce, and trying to find myself after 38 years of living a lie. Of course, I didn't see it as excess baggage whatsoever, even though many gay guys were turned off by the fact that I'd dipped my dicky wicky in the vagina. Coming to my senses, I realized their perception of me and my so-called "baggage" was their shit not mine.

> » "Oh, you have kids. Well I'm not going to be a mommy!"
>
> » "Gay and divorced? How'd you screw up your life that much?"
>
> » "Ex-wife? I don't want my ass infected with vaginal juice!"
>
> » "I think it's great you've been married. **TRANSLATION:** 'You're way too complicated for me!'"
>
> » "You just came out and have two kids. How Sweet! Good luck with that. Now if you'll excuse me, there's my friend Todd. Gotta run!"
>
> » "I like Daddies, but ones that aren't really daddies!"

Once I'd been through a few excursions into the superficial state of the gay man, and the even more superficial state of what they think they are looking for in a gay man which really isn't what they are looking for at all, I began to feel trampled like damaged goods fallen off the shelves at *Kohl's* *after a $10 Kohl's Cash With Every $50 Purchased* sale. What's the big deal with being sidetracked in the closet of heterosexuality for 38 years of my life? Intimately attuned to my own state of mental wellbeing, I attempted to tune out the negative, catty chat these "men" lobbed at me. Even Lemon-Odd Pop tried to drag me out of the dumps to no avail. Drowning my sorrows due to the lack of a man in my life, I retreated into alcohol and emotional eating, as a means to cope with an illogical question of "Why I'd ever come out of the closet?" It didn't take long before I began to keep certain information hidden from potential suitors in order be *out* in the male-to-male dating world, and to feel acceptesired (accepted and desired). This false sense of security led to a false sense of "dating" and falling for all the wrong guys. My wake-up call finally came when I woke up next to a guy that I had no freaking clue how he had landed in my bed. Round 2 of my days of being something I wasn't, for myself or anyone else, for all the wrong reasons, were coming to a screeching halt!

Thank God for those moments of dysfunctional functioning which opened my eyes to the light and triggered my desire to start acting like man...a man with integrity and undying loyalty to the people who mattered most in my life... my daughters and my ex-wife. My about face came, not out of guilt, but out of respect and honor for three women who'd be an integral part of my life until the day I die. Well, maybe not every day. My ex-wife and I still get ready and rumble from time-to-time. Yet, there wasn't a studly Adonis out there who'd cause me to lose my head and lose my girls — even if we weren't a family living under one roof behind a white picket fence any longer. I started getting my priorities straight! Now, to some, this "gotta take care of the shattered family" mentality, might seem the obvious way to be from the get go after *coming out*. Others of you, might be compelled to think, "It's my turn, to live my life, so please get out of my way and let me enjoy what's left on the gay side of things!" Regardless of the path you choose, you have a journey you're on called life. How you choose to live that life is your decision. No harm, no foul. The crossover to conflict happens when you choose to tell me how I should live my life, and I tell you how to live yours; including how to live your gay life.

The decision to live my gay life, my way, catapulted me forward, moving me into my essence as an adult gay man who started dating like the adult gay man I desired to be. My criteria? Honesty about being a dad, having been married, and not sacrificing either of those relationships in order to land the man. Ok, the more than occasional sacrifice if you were to ask my ex, but that's how ex's see things so be prepared for it. Now don't get me wrong, I simultaneously found the balance to enjoy being gay, without guilt or shame. I created a harmonious and healthy space for being gay, a father, and an ex-husband 24/7. Was it a challenge? Sure. Was it worth it? Without a doubt! The instant I started being real in my new direction, I also began to balance room for my dating and family life. I began to relax and enjoyed being in my life. Ironically, along that path and like an epic Disney movie, my guy, the guy that really got me, showed up in my life and accepting me and my past without a catty remark, the moment I invited balance and living my gay life my way into the picture.

I wasn't sure at first, if I was dreaming, and my defenses were up, standing taller than my morning woody. I was cautiously trying to accept that this guy:

a) really liked me,

b) didn't seem to have an issue with me having kids, and

c) was willing to explore the possibility of a future with a former heterosexual.

All of this left me skeptical with a capital "S." I was too gun shy to buy into the belief that a gay man, had the capacity to take me, my kids, as well as the lifelong relationship I'd maintain with my ex-wife. Fortunately for me, my guy showed up when I was least looking for a relationship, and when I was best ready to walk my walk, and talk my talk about being authentic. Authentically me – a dad, an ex-husband, and an available gay man for the right guy... no apologies, no shame!

✖

Meeting The Family Or Not

Gay, straight, married, single, or divorced; at some point we have the beautiful pleasure, or pain, of meeting the in-laws...or not. Given the dynamics associated with *coming out*, there's an inherent divorce from the self that occurs and a re-acquaintance process with the new self that follows. Likewise, for most of us who move through the *coming out* process, into dating, and a potential long-term relationship, it's inevitable that meeting the in-laws is just around the corner, unless said in-laws don't even accept their own gay child, in which case, really sucks. When this happens it gives you all the more reason to keep the in-laws at a comfortable arm's length. Meeting the potential in-laws is an elementary thought process, and overtly obvious move to most people who fully invest in the dating and mating process, and isn't one to be easily be brushed under the rug, left to be forgotten. The moment you forget the in-law meet is inevitable. That's the exact moment it will suddenly show up, like it or not. It's that unsuspecting instant cloaked in day in day out normalcy, when your boyfriend/girlfriend says, "I'd like you to meet my family!"

Faster than Dorothy clicked her heels to return to Kansas, panic, underarm sweat, and crazy thoughts of "What do I wear to meet my potential in-laws?" consume your every waking moment! Skitzy fritzy, senseless thoughts take center stage in your relationship. Whether it's been 2 months or a year that you've been together, the ante just got raised and you're about to show your cards to the family!

From the moment you desire a deeper, more intimate relationship with someone, you set the wheels of "Meet the in-laws" in motion. The interesting twist, for those of us of the gay persuasion is the "acceptance factor" from the in-laws takes on a whole new flavor due to our sexual orientation. Yes, heterosexual relationships also face the in-laws acceptance, yet they don't have to deal with the sexual orientation piece of the pie because it's not even up for discussion. It's assumed, without being spoken, that meeting the family comes with the territory of being a heterosexual. Heterosexuals accept heterosexuals (not meant to be a blanket statement, just more a truth than fiction statement), no questions asked about sexuality and what happens in the bedroom. Of course, they have their dirty little bedroom secrets too that aren't put up on the table for discussion either. Once again proving the point, "Whose damn business is it what happens behind closed bedroom doors?"

On the other gilded hand, we homosexuals, going home to meet Mommy and Daddy dearest could open up Pandora's Box and a plethora of delicate questions. Oddly enough, most of the questions they'd like to ask never get asked because they lead to unchartered territory for everyone involved in the "I'll take awkward questions for $500 Alex" genre. Stepping into a new space of gay and "meeting the family," leads to discomfort, until it becomes comfortable. However, until you've done something for the first time, then you don't have the experience of experiencing it to know what it feels like. Honestly, for crying out loud, jump in, call upon past experiences of meeting new people that were a cakewalk for you, and go "make it work!" Bake them a cake covered in delicious rainbow butter cream frosting and decorated with the words "I'd love to be a part of your family!"

Faced with meeting in-laws (a trip for both of us), plus the added twist of me coming to his family gatherings with children, caused both my partner (now husband) and I to face uncertainty, stress, and curious questioning as to what might happen to our relationship as we took a deeper dive into couple hood. This is not a unique journey. The popularity of divorce leads many to come to the table as "previously married with children." The uniqueness is the sexual orientation lemon zest on the cake. Venturing into the realm of meet the family, and then family meeting the family, I was transported back to the memories of little Rickey standing on the threshold of the Kindergarten door, scared, tightly grasping Mom's hand afraid to go in the classroom. The only difference in this case was Mom's hand of security was missing each time I met new members of his family; a feeling I'm quite sure he felt as well. It took patience, intention, and desire to land in our relationship at this deeper level, but we did it. Patience to allow the relationship to grow beyond casual dating. Intention to be in relationship, not only with my guy, but his family and vice versus for him! Desire to create a life that honored both of us as individuals, as a couple, and as a modern family before it ever became a hit T.V. show.

✂

Money TALKS

Sex and money is the most deadly combination to kill any relationship, outside of the realm of infidelity. Yet, society makes an assumption that "the gays are all about sex," especially gay men. I don't disagree to a certain point, but only because I am a very sexual person and I truly appreciate sex and see it as a bond that is not the only glue, but a powerful glue in a relationship. Not because of the actual intercourse, but because of the intimacy created by the many facets of a healthy sex life. The only thing that can truly get in the way of a powerful, titillating, and passionate sex life is MONEY, and MONEY TALKS! I literally mean having MONEY TALKS! You know discussions! This being the case, then why don't we talk about MONEY? Because those talks are often scary and lead to money minefields that nobody wants to step on in a relationship. Which then begs the question, "What is one to do when faced with the money, money, money dilemma?" We talk!

Avoiding money discussions, even from the onset in a relationship can consciously and unconsciously lead to bitter discontent and avoidance of other critical, "Love ya but..." conversations. It only takes one "A-List" conversation to be avoided, and suddenly, the whole damn relationship is based on "B-list" assumptions where things are OK, even though that's complete and total bullshit. Not talking may seem a like a safe bet to keep from getting feathers ruffled, having doors slammed in faces, or being deprived of sex (yes, us gays know how to play that game too). If you believe avoiding money talks is best, then I'll let Lemon-Odd Pop take you to her little Diva sofa for a chitchat, and good luck with her!

To start, be clear, sincere, and admit that money talks make you uncomfortable! If your own relationship to money needs to be addressed, then address it. Before you can be in relationship with someone or money, you have be in relationship with yourself and your own beliefs around money and finances. This is one of the truest tests of getting to know yourself and your other half. How the two of you relate to each other through the eyes of money about your combined incomes and sharing of financial responsibilities, will be an eye-opening experience about the foundation of your entire relationship. Similar to other aspects of life, financial responsibilities and money issues do not discriminate based on sexual orientation. Talk, communicate, talk, communicate, and if all else fails, talk and communicate more, even if it means being subtle and overt all in one conversation.

Often, the things that get forgotten when we encounter the "sticky conversations" in life, is to recall how we best handled them the last time we found ourselves up against a dollar and a dime, sexual desires, or any other "I have something to talk about," uncomfortable conversation. In these situations, it might be best to dive in one step above your comfort level, never forgetting to be authentically you in a way that catapults you forward instead of shrinking into the corner. If nothing else works, look at it as if you were taking your first step as a toddler. The only difference is you're taking your first step as a gay adult, in a gay adult relationship, having a gay adult conversation, so be a gay adult about it. You've had the empowered audacity to come out, surely, you can have the powerful honesty to talk about money and finances with someone you love and want to be in relationship with...right? If not, then there's some work to be done before you're ready to be in a relationship.

My husband and I both put things forward in our own way to make our money, and sex life, come into balance. These conversations continue to this day because our relationship isn't perfect; we both change each and every day. Just like everyone else (I know, shocker). Obviously, my obligations towards my children came with built in expenses that were part of the territory! From a loving and powerful place, we talked, defined, and shared the load of expenses as it made the best sense for the two of us. What more can you ask for when you're authentically being who you are in every aspect of life, including MONEY TALKS!

❖

Open vs. Closed Relationships

I'll be the first to admit I carried a steamer trunk full of judgments and bitchy thoughts when I heard about people in the gay community having "open relationships!" What the hell? Isn't being in a relationship about being in relationship? Sure! But it all comes down to how you define a relationship for you and your couplehood...plain and simple!

The thought of an open relationship had never even crossed my mind, and yet, I still couldn't help but get caught up in the thoughts of "How do people do this type of relationship?" At times I was completely consumed with these thoughts, even to the point of anger. On one side of the coin, I couldn't grasp how fighting for equality and gay rights could ever be achieved if you played into the stereotype that all gays and lesbians want to do is have sex and multiple sex partners. To me, and from my limited view of gay life at that time, these types of relationships feed the societal view that gays were promiscuous and were bringing about the downfall of the gay community.

On the other side of my judgmental coin, I realized what an asshole I was, given the fact that basically, I had been in an open relationship my whole married life. The only difference was that my lovely wife didn't know we were in an open relationship nor did she agree to it. I was a cheating ass, and I admit it, so get over your bad self and let's continue this "open vs. closed relationship discussion!"

Far from proud of how I'd lived my married life, it was my cheating ways that began to shed light on my hypercritical view of my gay brothers and sisters who chose to be in open relationships. After all, how far does the apple fall from the tree when you compare having sex outside the bounds of marriage and having an open relationship.

This concept of an open relationship to the outside, normal, heterosexual world seems so foreign yet, it really isn't that uncommon... it's just not talked about. Mistresses, bisexual relationships, hidden infidelity, swinging, they're all different spectrums of the open relationship rainbow. While it's assumed that gays and lesbians are particularly prone to "sex at the drop of a dime," that assumption truly makes an ass out of anyone who has those judgmental thoughts.

Hard as it may be to believe, a larger majority of gays and lesbians desire and do committed relationships. The flavor of those relationships is what trips most people up. As a newcomer into the gay world, the basic relationship types (my personal definitions) are:

Casual Dating – Dating regularly, multiple people, which may or may not include sexual relations.

Committed Dating – Dating one person and being committed sexually to that one person.

Committed Monogamous Relationship – This relationship usually goes beyond the committed dating relationship. At this juncture, most individuals decide to cohabitate, but not always.

Committed Open Monogamous – This type of relationship the couple agrees to have sexual relations with others but only in the company of one another. In other words, "We play, but only together!"

Committed Open Relationship – Similar to the committed monogamous relationship, the only real difference is the degree of openness in the types of sexual activity the couple experiences. Basically, these are polyamory relationships.

One-Way Open – One partner or half of the couple desires to have sexual relations outside of the bounds of the relationship, while the other chooses to stay sexually monogamous.

Two-Way Open – Both partners choose to have sexual relations outside of the relationship with others. This type of agreement may include "playing together" or separately.

Regardless of the type of relationship, for most couples, the key is having as much open communication about their open or closed relationship as possible. When the doors of discussion get closed, or for those matters never opened, it leads to a shaky relationship built on distrust and dishonesty – not the best foundations for building a strong, loving, and mutually respectful relationship.

As our relationship grew, discussions of "open" vs. "closed" came up and we crossed those bridges as we came to them with communication – clear and unclear. Regardless of the differences and sometimes silent communications, it was clear to each of us what we both wanted and how we desired to be in our relationship, proof positive of the power of clearly communicating. In the state of clear communication, you enable yourself and one another to step into the space of fearless freedom; in addition, there's not a damn thing to fear about talking about what you desire from your relationship when you're actually talking and communicating. What a novel concept!

Often, especially when someone comes out of the closet after being in a long-term heterosexual relationship, the first place they jump to is the committed monogamous relationship train. Yippee! No harm, no foul, unless you haven't given yourself the opportunity to live outside of those types of constraints. Don't take this the wrong way, living in a committed monogamous relationship doesn't mean you're handcuffed (unless that's part of the pleasure) and that you can't enjoy the relationship to its fullest. The message and philosophy I hope you pick up is to give yourself time to breathe into why you want to be in a relationship, and what that relationship looks, feels, and acts like for you, so that you're better capable of being in the relationship with your partner.

If it feels constrictive, then it is constrictive. If it feels open, then it is open. If it feels comfortable and supportive, then it is. Plain and simple. Listen to your gut feelings and emotions, then follow them up with the logical question of, "Is this what I really desire?" What you'll find is this benefits you and your partner in far greater ways than you might have ever expected, and it alleviates a lot of unnecessary negative energy and worry along the way. Plus, in my case, it helps me keep Lemon-Odd Pop in check!

To "I Do Or Not To I Do" That Is The Question!

Gay marriage, at least in the United States and a few other countries, now makes what was once impossible, possible. At the same time, the ability to get legally married is now one of those sticky-wicky conversations that will take place somewhere along the route of casual to serious dating... but not on the first date! Well maybe on the first date, if you're that needy!

Versus dodging conversation bullets, or waiting for an award-winning moment to fall in your lap, give yourself the confidence to open up to conversations about the future, when it feels right for you. Fear of losing a relationship because you want to get a barometer reading on their views about marriage should be a clear sign that a) you're probably in the wrong relationship, or b) you're being a drama queen with no balls! You're not alone and your other half probably does feel the same trepidation about going one step deeper into the relationship. If the conversation leads to the realization you're not meant to be, you may have to date a lot of toads to find the marrying kind amongst the gay Lily pads.

As awkward as money talks, *amplifying up the relationship commitment* talks can be just as uncomfortable. Having the long-term relationship talks too soon may cause Mr./Mrs. Right to take a hike. Waiting too long to speak your truth about the long haul, could lead Ms. Right to drive her U-Haul down the street to the next available lesbian on the block. Sorry, I just couldn't resist the proverbial stereotype reference. I do love my lesbian sistahs! It may feel awkward to have this raw conversation about the future. However, if you stop and think clearly, "How different is having this conversation from opening up and having other difficult conversations you face in life and in your relationship?"

One of the major reasons couples – gay or straight – end up facing irreconcilable differences regarding moving the relationship forward is that subject didn't get breeched appropriately or at all. Often, one person has their ideas about the future, and the other person a completely different perspective. Totally understandable, not uncommon, and a perfect launch pad for saying, "It's time we talked about what we each desire for our future as a couple!"

A long-term relationship may be the ultimate goal for many of you on the other side of the closet door, yet what often gets missed is the "Why?" Being completely honest with yourself and admitting, "I want to be in a relationship because..." helps you more quickly, with clarity, arrive at the burning root of your desire. Once you land in this space, it's much easier for you to relate your honest expectations and desires to your partner about the future you envision. It also is imperative that you know specifically "What" you desire, in and from the relationship, to take the relationship to the next level.

It's very common for those of us who've just come out of the closet, to immediately run into the first open arms of acceptance, love, and intimacy we encounter. Wrapped snuggly in the comfort of these feelings were able to repair the thoughts of rejection, self-loathing, and possibly of never finding true love. No matter the path that leads you to being loved, desired, and in relationship, the greatest love you can give yourself and your partner is to first love yourself and then to be authentic regarding your desires for a long haul relationship.

⚜

Parent, Parent, Parent – A Modern Family

Ranking right up there with the money, open relationships, sex, long-term relationships, and marriage talks, comes the parenting discussion – whether to become parents, or that you are a parent and bringing kids with you into the relationship. Either way, this conversation has only two possible outcomes – good or bad! However, I don't believe a good or bad conversation exists. My perspective is that conversations are purposeful. The possibilities of having children, or that you're bringing children with you into the relationship are "eye-opening" insights as to your own nurturing instincts.

I get it! Not everyone is cut out to be a parent (Lemon-Odd Pop for example), and even those that think they are, aren't always the best parents. Swimming into these waters of dating and mating, knowing you have kids or would like to have kids would be a wise thing to bring up sooner rather than later. Of course, showing up on your boyfriends' doorstep, spawn of your loins in tow doesn't leave any room to gently drop the bomb, "Surprise! Have you met my kids?"

Full transparency about your desires to start or that you have a family may break the relationship camel's back right out the gate. In the words of my wise alter ego diva, "Better to break that hump than be a lying chump!" Thanks Lemon-Odd Pop for those… interesting… insights! Depending on the situation, sharing your predispositions to have a family of your own, "might" even be appropriate on the first date. Don't groan and throw rocks at me. I didn't mean, "Hi, I'm Rick and I want to have 3 kids. How about you?" Subtlety is a gift. Let's try this approach. "I'm very family-oriented. I love spending time with my family, especially nieces and nephews. Who knows, one day I might even make a great parent." Of course if you have kids, I believe in being forthright and honest right from the onset.

Taking a simple daring step to declare you lean towards "married/

partnered with kids," doesn't mean you're committed to it, nor that you've got the adoption or surrogacy papers in your hip pocket ready to be signed. If anything, it's a thermometer check to see

a) How you personally feel when you're being completely honest and vulnerable,

b) If the person receiving these insights is on the same playing field, and

c) How well the two of you dance the tango of open and honest discussions about big life moments – moving in together, finances, open relationships, parenting, etc.

Coming from the other end of the spectrum, as a gay biological parent, I've found truth, honesty, and full disclosure pave the way for truth, honesty, and full disclosure to be reciprocated. It's not like you can hide the kids. You could if you're ok being brought up on charges of child abuse for locking them in the basement when your girlfriend comes over. Of course, you might be estranged from your children because your ex didn't give you any other choice in the matter; sad situation in and of itself. Hiding the truth that you have biological children is grounds for being thrown the verbal dagger of "You can't be trusted!" Unveiling the truth of who you are, and the lives you've brought into this world after you've been dating for months on end, is simply not right, not fair, and doesn't paint you to be a person of integrity or honesty. Just my opinion, so take it for what it's worth.

It may feel like an annoying pebble in your shoe to admit your desire to be a parent or that you are a parent. Truth is, that's who you are, and that's what you desire, no shame, guilt, or flogging required. Even if pecs and abs of steel gets you all worked up, or a lipstick lesbian with an edge of masculine femininity rocks your boat, Mr. Hot Body or Ms. Curves of Steel don't impress you much if they run at the thought of being Mommy or Daddy Dearest. No judgment on him or her, it's merely who they are, and what they desire for their life. Even the best parents who come out of the closet feel a little hazy and disjointed when they find someone genuinely digs them, truly gets them, and really loves them, only to be told "It's me or your kids!" Personally, that wasn't even a fractional consideration. My daughters are my world, my responsibility, and the lights of my life. One guy tried that ultimatum with me and was immediately shown the door and given back his pants and underwear a week later! (Luckily for him, he didn't get a ticket driving home naked. Yes, I threw him his keys.) Not every parent with kids, who comes out of the closet, feels the innate parental calling to stay connected with their children. Others are given no choice other than to disconnect out of spite from a spouse or court order.

I lucked out. Scratch that, I was blessed to meet a guy who valued family, and made it a top priority. That's not to say at the beginning of our relationship there weren't challenges balancing him and me time vs. daddy duty. He came into my world having been out of the closet since his early twenties. He'd been in a couple of lengthy yet not long-term relationships. It wasn't that kids weren't on his bucket list, but having an instant family did come out of left field. Like any couple dancing through the "getting to know each other phase," we shifted, grooved, and made accommodations to step into each other's lives. Me with kids, him without. Numerous times, it felt like we were living polar opposite lives, which we did to some degree. Additionally, I brought my own built in expectations to the dating table assuming he would instantly dive into the co-parenting role. My bad, not his. He helped with the kids in his own way and to the best of his ability. The bottom line, in the honeymoon years of our relationship, was that the girls were my responsibility. Mine, mine, mine. I just needed to get him trained to say "Ours!" Now that he's house broken into parenthood, I just sit back drink Cosmo's, watch porn, and eat bon bons! (NOT!) Ok, maybe I watch the occasional porn but that's a whole different confession to write about in another book somewhere before the universe calls me to my next life.

One of my most challenging yet greatest growth periods in my *coming out* process and learning to adapt to a regular guy in my life was learning to "Make Space," and I'm not talking about closet space, although that was necessary too. I admit, my marriage was a somewhat co-dependent relationship. My ex-wife and I were our own best and worst company, rarely leaving each other's side. Not a healthy way to live, nor did it help me help me grow into an independent, trusting, married man. And, being a cheating loser myself, led to my own levels of misguided and projected distrust. All of this co-dependent, hiding truths behavior contributed to my childish possessive conducts that sucked the life out of the first few male-to-male relationships I had in the post *coming out* years. Lessons and relationships that had to happen in order for Ricky to get a kick in the ass and start acting like a mature gay man.

Once I started making space for others, things began to change. I created room for me to be a single-father, a gay man, dating gay men, juggling career transitions, and navigating relations with my ex-wife from a space of "let's make this work!" Not all the time, but a bigger majority of the time. Along the way, I also carved out space and time to learn the value of being healthily independent and dependent in my relationships, not only with my husband, but also with my kids, parents, friends, co-workers, and ex-wife. For me, this was an excruciating transition. Years spent depending on others to make me happy, or so I thought, had become my standard of living, my existence. Simultaneously, living to make others happy had blinded me, causing me to forsake myself. In the beautiful throws of this new real-deal relationship with myself, I began to own my responsibilities, and only my responsibilities for myself, my children, my boyfriend (now my husband), my ex-wife, my family, and my friends. It was no longer necessary for me to slice and dice myself into little slivers of inauthentic truths to please others.

Like most gay parents, I'd always wanted to be a parent. No that's not the reason I got married. I'm not that conniving and shallow. I'm also not insinuating that heterosexual parents don't have the same deep desires. The difference, especially for my gay brothers and sisters, is they have to jump through 3-ring circus hoops to adopt or surrogate a child into being. Anyone who says gays shouldn't be parents should take a closer look at the immense sacrifices of time, effort, and money gay parents make to have kids. It's no different than what heterosexual couples do who can't have kids, except the gay experience is on steroids, especially in areas where gay marriage and gays adopting children is not law of the land. The legal fees and joint adoption process alone is enough to drive anyone batty. In cases such as these, it takes work and commitment to be the parent you want to be. Likewise, I worked overtime, as did my ex-wife, to maintain the life I started with my daughters. True, I could have given up, let go, and been a walk away Dad and just paid for it with the all mighty dollar. I chose differently. My experience turned out better than I could ever have imagined for the most part, and I am truly blessed to be an active participant in my daughters' lives. Even being so fortunate, I know one thing for sure, if I'd chosen to hide my kids, not making them part of my dating conversations, or disclosing they existed too late in my dating journey, then I'd still be living in the closet, hiding a very valuable part of my truth. I chose not to hide. Did I miss out on some great dates with hot guys because of this choice? Not in my book. I took the path that was meant for me, which might not be the path meant for you. However, the path I took led me to the right guy who gets the disco beat of "We are family." (Knock on wood and I don't mean a hard penis). I made a few false starts before I learned the value of never regretting saying, "Yes, I was married and I have two beautiful daughters that rock my world. Do you have a problem with that?"

Guess you could say, that's what fearless freedom means to me. Authentically being who you are in the face of any challenge. I value myself as a gay dad, partner, ex-husband, friend, son, brother, uncle...it's all good and freeing to just be YOU!

CHAPTER 8

Boppin' To The Freedom Beats

There ya stand in your naked truth, finally being you. You've crossed over the great divide from the dark, lonely closet to "I've arrived and ready for my close-up in my own gay skin." The essence of your newfound freedom hangs in the air like morning fog, creating grey doubts about your decision to come out of the closet. On the polar opposite extreme, there's a new light brilliantly shining on the your authentic self that stirs up excitement that is beyond control. Emotions run the gamete from moments of serene peace to unbridled fear of "How do I do this thing called freedom to be me?" The answer? With patience, flexibility, vulnerability, and deep-rooted trust in yourself.

Drawn from your spiritual center that's guiding you into the milky depths of yourself where you came to terms with your sexuality, it's now time to cast your bucket into the well of "give me inner strength" once again. Go ahead! Nudge your toes right up to the stone's edge of the well, grab the handle and release the bucket of exploration into the depths of your inner self. Every powerful intention, belief, and value are floating right below the surface once again ready to support you in the next phase of being your honest truth – a bee boppin', freedom loving, out gay person who loves their freedom as much as they love a comfy pair of jeans. Now ya just gotta get used to wearing those new threads. (I'll turn ya over to Lemon-Odd Pop. She gets into new wardrobes more frequently than the rest of us change our underwear!) There's no better place to test out your new threads than in the gay "dating and mating" world.

Stepping Lightly With Caution Into The Dating Scene

My values are guiding me to be fully transparent, and fully ~~disrobed~~ disclosed. I'm not a dating coach, nor do I profess to be one in any way shape or form. I've dated, mated and been through my share of, "OMG, why can't I find a man?" moments! However, passing along insider information doesn't mean you have to end up in jail, literally or figuratively. Here's my own personal version of inside intelligence to hopefully help you land on the right track after you come out of the closet. First and foremost, get it out of ya head that there's a right track! There's no right track except the one you're on and take for you! Dammit, stop rolling your eyes. It's true. In fact, whether you're living the high life in prime time, Reality TV, on the *Bachelor* or *Bachelorette*, or trying to figure how to write the perfect profile on Match.com, OkCupid.com, or settling into the pain of carpal tunnel syndrome due to over use of Grindr, Scruff, Tinder, Her, or Growler, you'll find your own unique path to be alive and well in the gay dating scene. Sorry if I'm disappointing and not delivering you a magical dating and land a relationship formula. I hate to be a disappointment, so let me make it up to you by providing a few tricks and tools for getting in the gay dating game.

1. **Be kind.** It's the golden rule of dating (and for EVERYTHING) – gay or straight. In this lovely little iridescent bubble of dating, all anyone really desires is to be noticed, appreciated, liked, and loved. Exactly in the order. You want it, they want it. And, as Lemon-Odd Pop says, "Karma is a bitch, even if you haven't met her yet!"

2. **Be real.** Pet peeve alert. Whether you're hooking-up or attempting to match and mingle on the LTR (Long-term Relationship) online dating front, nothing says "I'm seriously insecure..." than those who taunt you with a picture that's a decade old, boast to like hobbies that you've never even attempted, and falsely claim to be looking for friends when what they really want is a hook up! Hello! You're free to be the real you instead of walking around pretending to be someone you're not. That was your past life, now step into your real self and attract some real people who will accept you just the way you are! Do it. Do it now!

3. **Be open.** Ladies and gentlemen, please note! Being open is not a reference to having your legs or ass up in the air, even though that leads to ecstatic fun. The point is to be open to experiences, no matter how out of your comfort zone you may feel. You will for damn sure kiss a lot of rainbow-striped toads before Mr. Right/Ms. Right hops into your life. If you're closed, you're closed off to the possibilities of enjoying the full buffet, dessert and all, of gay dating. Freedom to be you is all about sampling, so that you can settle on what tastes good, and makes for a sensible relationship diet for life.

4. **Be slow.** Not slow out the starting gate, or slow at getting your dates jokes, unless they're really bad. The suggestion is take each date slow. No jumping to picket fences or renting U-hauls before calculating the tip. Take the date-to-date, mate-to-mate journey at a pace that's enjoyable and at a stride that allows you evaluate progress based on where you're at in your *coming out* and same sex-dating journey, so you can clearly determine where you'd like to be. A powerful exercise you can do at the end of each date is to ask yourself, "In 5 years, would it be possible for this same date to still feel like our first?" If so, then damn gurl, go get the U-Haul and I'll even send you a Lowes Gift Card to build that picket fence. Just kidding. Slow down sugar and enjoy the ride.

5. Be accountable. This suggestion starts and ends with you. Hold yourself accountable for moving relationships forward, not the other person. Relying on the other person leads to co-dependency. Check your values frequently, and keep asking "What is it I really want, and why I desire to be in this relationship?" Don't falter, selling yourself short, because his or her kiss sent you over the moon. It could be a whole different story, once the drawers are dropped and the moon rises over the edge of the bed. During these first few days, weeks, and months of your freedom, you deserve to be deeply in touch with someone who won't steer you wrong, provided you stay awake and listen. This powerful trinity is not the father, son, and Holy Spirit. It's you, yourself, and you. Lean into them, follow their lead, because you're never going to lose them, and they know ya best.

If you choose to follow these "Steps For Success" (which by God you should cause I took the time to write them and give them to ya), you might find yourself stepping into the long-term relationship or matrimony ring sooner rather than later with a firm head on ya shoulders, and a pat on the back from the person who knows you best...you.

✂

Mucking It Up With Kids, Exes, and Whatever Else Came Along For The Ride.

Honestly, we've all got baggage! It comes with the territory, and stepping out of the closet is no different. Most of us have past boyfriends/girlfriends who served as our mask of normalcy to help us hide our truth of our sexual orientation. Others of us, bit the bullet and have ex-wives, ex-husbands, kids, parents, and in-laws who are standing there like a deer in the headlights thinking, "WTF do I do with this gay person in my midst?" Also be prepared for more than a few in the gay community to judge you, and ask, "WTF were you thinking getting married, hiding yourself, and spawning stuff from your loins?" To them I say, "If you can't handle me and my truth, then get the hell out of my kitchen because you're not on the guest list to the party of my life!"

In your freedom march, happiness should be a top priority. Those who get their feathers ruffled because they can't handle where you came from, don't deserve to step past the red velvet rope, into the shimmering light of the disco ball hanging over the dance floor where you're celebrating your new way of "Stayin' Alive!" However, certain relationships in your life can't be ignored. You have two choices for people, like parents, siblings, exes, etc.: you can either beautifully choreograph them into dance routine of your new life, or respectfully ask them to sashay off the dance floor.

Two of the most brutal places you'll be judged, is in your own "trusted" inner circles, and by your new family – the gay community. Regardless of which corners of the earth the JUDGMENT flies from, take a deep breath and repeat after me, "What someone says is all about them, what you hear is all about you!" Keep that little bit of wisdom tucked in your back pocket, clutch or wallet, ready at a moment's notice when you need to go all Deepak Chopra on someone. Being consciously aware of your own reactions provides you time to unpack the Samsonite you bring into your new tour of life, and be a little more understanding of what the "others" are going through as well.

1. **The Ex's** – Unless you've been hiding out as a hermit, or ceased to date after your first heartbreak in Kindergarten, there's a damn good chance that you've got an ex and probably a string of them. Thank God! Without those exes, you wouldn't have learned to deal with heartbreak, have experienced a relationship that wasn't good for you, or discovered the specifics of what you don't desire in a relationship. Now that you're on the open market in the gay world, use what you've learned from your exes, and unless there's any logical reason to stay connected to them, walk away, putting them on the shelf of "learned from," and move on. They don't need to be mixing

it up in your new relationship, unless you're beholding to them due to alimony, child support, custody, or joint property. In those cases, do your best work to keep things as separated from your new life as possible, only intertwining when absolutely necessary. You can "trip the light fantastic" by keeping everything in perspective and moving forward as smoothly as possible.

2. **Disclose only the necessaries**. Too often we say what we think needs to be said to all the wrong people. The God's truth is not everything needs to be disclosed, unless it's going to upset the apple cart of the new relationship by not saying something. Don't accuse me of talking out of both sides of my mouth because I really don't know how to do that. I'm a firm believer in transparency and authenticity. Why else do you think I love to see a man in sheer boxers? Wait, wrong book. In all seriousness, I've found from personal experience, and by working with wonderful clients that the more you expose, the more you're exposed. I'm not advocating lying, or telling little white lies. I'm encouraging thinking carefully about what you have to say to make your newfound relationship work. When stuff comes up that you haven't disclosed, be honest and say, "I didn't share that part of my life with you because I wasn't sure it had any monumental bearing on our relationship!" Feel free to wordsmith your own version.

3. **Share because it compels you, not because it scares you**. One of the biggest mistakes I made *coming out* of the closet (see, I admit my flaws, what few there are, LMAO) was trying to hide my ex-wife and kids, as well as my outlandish sex addiction from potential suitors, and the world. It didn't work. Probably because (**ATTENTION:** here's where you take notes), hiding any of this was so out of alignment with my values. Ugh! There's those damn values again, but trust me, you'll always get more of what you want being in alignment with your values than you will veering off course from them. Rather than hide your honest to God true stuff, share

it where it serves a purpose. Put your bitch slap hand down right now, and don't even think of suggesting I'm talking out of both sides of my mouth again. I realize I just suggested you "Disclose only the necessities!" Yet, I also know for some of you that won't work. Wait, scratch that. For most of you that won't work 100% of the time. Thus the reason we have one pretty little hand holding of "Disclose only the necessities," and the other holding "Share because it compels you, not because it scares you."

4. **Make it a non-issue.** One of the things I learned early on about being a gay dad, an ex-heterosexual, and an active member in both the gay and heterosexual community was to not make anything an issue. Even *coming out* doesn't have to be an issue, unless you choose to make it a big to do! I realize, in certain parts of our country and the world, it is a big WTF Bomb when you come out of the closet. One of the greatest lessons I learned was, the less I made a big deal of my sexuality, the less it was a big deal. Does this mean I retreated back into the closet? Hell no! I simply refused to never again be untrue to who I was, because I played that game for way too many years. There's a delicate balance where authenticity and "no big deal" play nicely in the same sandbox of life. How you navigate this tight wire, is up to you. Yet, for all the advice columns, self-help books, and gurus who claim to know best, I personally found that being me in my best self and not making things an issue seem to work just fine.

5. **Don't settle!** This may seem like an overtly "Duh" moment, but seriously, "Don't settle!" No matter how hot he or she is or what they bring to the table that you've never been able to sample before, if you settle into "Oh this is everything I've been needing and wanting in my life," then that's exactly what you're going to end up with...what you've been needing and wanting! I get slapped constantly for saying needs and wants are the bullshit that complicates life. Go ahead and slap me now. Needs only provide what you need to survive. Wants

are what you think you need to be externally and maybe internally happy. For me, "Desires," are the bee's knees that rock your life! Provided you've done the work to stretch deep into yourself, align your values with your deepest "desires," then you'll never be settling, you'll be getting exactly what you've "desired" in your life.

There's is no "mucking it up" in a new relationship with your past unless you "muck it up." When, where, why, and how you muck it up all comes down to you, or how you allow yourself to get mucked up by the person in your relationship or by your past. I'm going to challenge your beliefs and have you ask yourself, "Am I really mucking it up in this relationship with these details, or lack thereof, or is this just the way it's supposed to go?" Interesting thought, isn't it? See, there you go being all consciously aware in your new freedom, just as you should be!

The Family Ties That Bind Or Release You!

Being candidly honest, I really don't give a flip if my extended family, or even certain members of my immediate family accept me as a gay man. At least now I don't. I've never been an uber, snuggly, hug me, and love me, family guy except with my now ex-wife, daughters, and my husband. I'm still working on that. My kids and the love I have for them and vice a versa is damn important to me and I'll snuggle them until the cows come home. The same thing goes for my husband and to some degree my ex-wife (depends on the day and how we're feeling towards each other). Outside of those relationships, if my parents, my brother, and the family that extends beyond them don't fit into my world, then so be it! I've given it my best shot, with what I have to shoot with, and that's all I can do. I still love and respect all of them. However, if my sexuality is a game changer for them, then they need to huddle with their inner coaches and therapists and figure that out for themselves. It's not my responsibility to make them feel comfortable any longer on the couch of our relationship.

Right. I hear you mumbling, "What an asshole," or "Yeah, I totally agree!" I'm not asking you to love me, agree with me, or step in line to march in time to my beliefs. I'm simply sharing with you where I stand on relationships and how I've chosen to address them as they have shown up in my gay life. What's funny about these relationships is at their most simplistic essence, they have nothing to do with you or me being gay. Before the gay "issue" even came up, people either liked you or didn't. They may have seemed to be in your corner, but if you look closely at your most intimate relationships, they've always had some little inkling of not quite being in your corner. That's ok, and I'm not saying that my perspective is the God's truth. I'm just inviting you to consider this perspective. Think about it. Why should who you are attracted to be the complete game changer in a relationship?

When you decided to step out of the closet in your rainbow finery, more than likely you had concerns about what this would do to your relationships. Justifiably so! Now that you've marched boldly into yourself, there's a multitude of questions to be addressed. And, as you address each question, stay focused on two things. "What is it you really desire?" and "Why is what you desire important?" By keeping these questions at the forefront of your thoughts and decision-making, you will more than likely never trip into a dismal state of "I did it for them!" You can still respectfully "Do it for others," while staying very aligned with being true to yourself! Here are just a few ideas to help you navigate your own version of being you with those around you – family or otherwise:

1. **Be yourself.** I know it sounds trite, but it's right. Enough said!

2. **Be clear about meeting family.** Discuss as a couple why meeting each other's family is important at this stage of the relationship without losing your cool, or throwing dishes at one another. Putting your best "let's communicate" foot forward, as best as possible, place all the facts and feelings on the table well in advance of the big reveal day!

3. **Leave second-guessing behind.** You don't know until you know, how anyone will be until you meet him or her and share yourself with him or her. Let the element of surprise prevail, and then deal with what comes your way in the moment.

4. **Practice honest, loving, and living in reality.** It's a rare relationship that all the family and friends will love and appreciate your beau, gal, spouse, and vice-a-versa. Being gay doesn't change this fact. Even if your sweet love has an overtly "out and proud" family, you may find yourself suffering from verbal diarrhea of the mouth spewing, "I just don't mesh with your fam!" The real trick then becomes how the two of you will then make your relationship work, just like all the heterosexuals with in-laws, family, friends, co-workers and spouse/partners they can't stand. You'll do it with a lot of patience, understanding, and a bonus room in your heart filled with space to be individuals as well as a couple.

5. **Determine if meeting the family or embracing friends is a game changer in the relationship.** More often than I'd like to admit, many a "newbie out" individuals, prematurely jump with glee at the opportunity to be introduced to family and friends, only to find, it ain't no Cinderella story! Damn it, as much as you thought he/she was the one, family blood ties and friendship, even in the gay meets gay world can be stronger than, "God you're hot, and we're so meant to be together!" Once this revelation comes to light, you'll at least have affirmation of where you stand. Unfortunately, the fires of family and friendship ties burn so deeply, and may lead you to the junction of "Can I make it work?" and "Get me outta here before my heart breaks again!" If it's a game changer, then it's a game changer and move on.

It's always an interesting dynamic observing when familial ties and long lasting friendships waltz into any relationship – gay, straight, or otherwise! Even more profound is when the inevitable question gets asked, "Can you Tango with me, my friends, and family, or are you going to sit this one out?" You're the only one with the answer. It doesn't require family-friendly dance lessons at Arthur Murray or your own guest appearance on *Dancing With The Star's* to determine if you're up for the dance off. Your answer's already on your dance card, so just follow its lead!

�֍

Money Talks Or The Relationship Walks!

I'm not going to beat around the bush about the subject of Money Talks. As you know by now, I don't beat around the bush on much of anything. Let's get right down to it and talk about money! Gay or straight. In the closet, or out. Married or dating. If ya don't have the balls for money talks, then ya don't have the balls to be in a relationship. Ditto goes for sex talks, but we'll get to that discussion soon.

Money talks can be sticky and suck. Why? Because if you don't have "enough" then "life sucks!" Actually, I don't buy that philosophy, but we'll just go with it for now. It's ironic how money is all about worth...YOUR OWN SELF WORTH! Money is a funky medium we use to define who we are, where we fit into the pecking order of society, and how dollars and cents play into our relationships.

Rather than get all up in each other's faces, let's be proactive, and figure out how you do the money dance – no g-string required – with your guy or gal. Size queens or money queens be wary that your desires can lead you to run from what could be a relationship of a lifetime. Don't always judge the book by its wallet size. Be bold. Be honest. Be financially vulnerable...in a good way. There's no reason to screw up a perfectly good afterglow of an orgasm by saying, "Now that that's over, let's talk about our finances!" Quell your fears, and jump bravely into the money pit discussions once you realize the relationship is moving to the point of "Is this what commitment, and a LTR (Long-term Relationship) looks like?"

No need for money talks to be ugly, pointed, or embarrassing, unless that's your modus operandi for tackling sensitive couple chats. If so, then it's time for you to break the mold, humbly get vulnerable, and have some heart-to-heart cash chats.

» **State your truth**. Hiding what you make, what you owe, might come bite you on the successful relationship ass. Financial non-disclosure is infidelity, only there's no lingering scent of another on your skin. Getting into bed with a partner takes on many different flavors, one of them being, "Here's what my relationship with money looks like, now show me yours!" Candid honesty may cause him or her to run. If so, then Hallelujah, you just struck the jackpot because that asshole wasn't meant for you!

» **Talk about the future**. I get it. All couples headed towards the goal line of commitment talk about the future. Make sure you don't get lost in the happy, happy, joy, joy, white picket fences moments without asking, "How do you manage your money?" During my marriage, I came to realize how royally screwed women are with the cost of hair, nails, make-up, clothing, the works. However, I believe this is a moneymaking, culturally induced racket to keep the economy afloat. Now I'll step off my soap box and share with you that the same sort of stuff may and will show up for you in your gay relationship, if you choose to spend $50 for a haircut and your partner/spouse chooses a $10 Super Cut. If that grates you the wrong way, then you better make sure you are both in balance with these type of money differences and get to the bottom (no pun or insinuation intended) of that discussion, sooner rather than later, before financial hair pulling ensues without the use of tweezers and a proper back wax.

» **Crossing the great divide**. I'm not talking about who's the top who's the bottom. Similar, but different. I'm referring to where do "you" as a "couple" divide up the responsibilities for "your" financial welfare! This will be different and unique for everyone and it's a discussion that can go haywire. For instance, in my case, I had alimony, child support, and previous life obligations that prevented me from contributing, as I would have wished financially to mine and his future, and not being able to contribute to home in an equal way was a bitch to navigate given the fact that I felt less of a man. Yet, I'd made my bed and I was remaking a new bed, with a new life partner who lovingly understood my position of, "Here's what I got, and here's what I can do!" How did we fill the gap? Not by me topping him, so get your minds out of the sexual realm. We're talking money, not sex here. We'll get to the sex talk soon, I promise. We talked, worked it out, like most couples that decide, "Let's do reality house playing, and not play house." We were serious about playing and being in the house of relationship.

» **Money is energy.** I'm not going all woo woo or new age on you. I'm taking you into a space of where you can explore, understand your relationship with money, and learn how to lovingly talk about money and finances with your partner, spouse, significant other, and see how to keep the health of your relationship alive in a same sex relationship. Similar to sexual preferences, frequency of sex, and your energy around intimacy/sex, if you're not talking about money matters, and the negative energy it may bring up for you, then you'll soon find a whole lot of bitter feelings building up with every slide of the ATM Card your partner/spouse swipes – maybe even your own swipes. It starts with you and your energy towards money. If you've never had a good relationship with money, or always felt a lack of abundance, it will show up like a big zit in your relationship. Add to the equation your inability to chat about money matters, planning for future financial stuff and you've got a relationship spreadsheet that spells D-I-S-A-S-T-E-R! Do yourself and your partner a favor, and get to know each other's money energy as well as you knows their favorite sexual position. You won't be disappointed and you'll avoid the awkward post-coital pillow talk about "How much money do you save on a monthly basis?"

Rather than put the fear of God in you, I hope you see the beauty in "In money talks we trust!" Why waste a perfectly matched relationship because one of you invests his retirement funds in edible lube while the other invests his in plastic fabrication of the edible lube bottles. Crazy as that sounds, same page financial stability reduces the chance of something slipping out when least expected. Those slip ups can and do cause relationships to plummet based on financial hardship, rather than the inability to get hard...pun intended!

❈

Did We Say We Do, Or We Do With Benefits?

Admittedly, I'm not a lesbian. Nor, am I a bisexual, even though I may have appeared to play one based on my previous ability to have sex with a woman and spawn two beautiful daughters. And, as much as I love my transgender friends, no one's snipping what's between my legs. I'm 100% pure gay man. But, what exactly does that mean to you in your relationship, to be 100% gay or 100% lesbian? Does it mean, monogamous, or open?

I'm keeping this check-in simple, just like the Money Talks check-in. Either you desire an open or closed relationship, period! Doesn't mean there's no shades of grey on either side of the fence, it simply paints the image you're either A or B for discussion sake. Ironically, until after I "came out," the thought of "open" or "closed" relationships never crossed my mind, so to speak. I've already admitted that I was in an open relationship; my wife just didn't know she was married to a guy having open relationships. Once I stepped into the man-meet-man world, things became one dysfunctional, carnival, madhouse in my mind. I wanted the "monogamous" relationship, which seemed similar to every guy I was dating, until I realized monogamy had very blurred lines in the gay man's and my world. The explorations of these different tiers of monogamy were covered in the previous chapter, so no need to repeat. Flip back a few pages and take a refresher course.

What's now at hand to explore is how your freedom, being you outside of the closet might be impacted or expanded by an "open" vs. "closed" relationship. This was one of those awkward discussion moments with my guy where I needed Lemon-Odd Pop to hold me together. Thank ya sistah for being there for me! Not only might the discussion between you and your guy/gal be an awkward discussion, it's the one rattling around in your own head about being in an "open" vs. "closed" relationship that can take you on the world's greatest, high-speed rollercoaster. For some, this kind of conversation is no biggie. For others, just pick up the phone and call me, so I can chat you down off the ledge. From my personal perspective, there is no right or wrong in this arena, and it's personal to you and your guy/gal. Here's my input, ripped off from Tim Gunn of Project Runway fame, "Make it work!" Even with eyes wide open, and being consciously aware of how you want to be sexually and intimately in a relationship, things can get muddy quickly if you haven't done the following:

» **Define what a relationship means to you!** Take everyone else, and all their societal expectations out of the equation. Focus on what being in a relationship means to you from a sexual, intellectual, and intimate level. That's what counts and is what will make or break your relationship. Be clear, very clear, and don't deviate, unless flexing makes sense for you. However, if the deviation gets messy then think twice.

» **Admit you like sex!** I know, that may sound funny to some of you. Yet, so many people get uncomfortable just at the mention of the word, sex? Strip off the awkwardness and simply admit, "I like sex, I enjoy sex, and I love it!" Your ability to be open and honest, takes you one small step closer to being even more candid and saying, "I like sex with people other than my partner, I enjoy sex with people in addition to my partner, and I love sex with people other than my partner!" If this isn't you, then be bold and proud to state the polar opposite; "I like sex only with my partner, I enjoy sex only with my partner, and I love sex only with my partner!" Honesty with yourself leads to honesty with your partner, which leads to an honest relationship from the start.

» **Never say never.** Coy as that may sound, there's always an anything's possible silver lining in just about every situation. Doesn't necessarily mean you'll act on it; yet, leaving the door open for experimentation doesn't make Jane a slut or John an app vamp! It's kind of like saying, "I'll never eat Brussels Sprouts!" Until you've tried them BBQ'd with Garlic, you never know. Never say never might also apply for opening up your relationship. My theory is that we're all sexual beings; without numbing alcohol, or intoxicating drugs, it wouldn't take much for anyone of us to have a sexual liaison outside of how we view our sexual self in our *best behavior, logical mind*. Stop rolling your eyes, and for a moment consider this fantasy. You're in a room. Blindfolded (ok, so we're going a little *50 Shades of Grey* right now). Your only senses being aroused are your hearing and touch. Breaking the silence is the padding of bare feet coming closer to you. Suddenly, a light touch hits your erotic ignition switch, whatever that is for you. You can't see the person, nor touch them back, all you know is that, they've hit your happy spot, and that climax is just around the corner. Notice, I didn't mention the gender of the person or that it came from your partner or spouse. As I indicated before, "Never say never!" Sexual arousal might be interrupted by the most unexpected of sexual pleasures when you least expect it, from about anywhere in your life.

» **Talk about it.** Rather than sound like a broken record, talk about your sex life, what you like, what turns you off, and whether, or not you're open to an open, slightly open, or shut tight relationship. Once again, this is the murky stuff that just doesn't get talked about until it's often too late. When infidelity rears its ugly head, or a honest conversation pops up at the dinner table, "I'm just not sexually attracted to you anymore," it's probably too late. Hell hath no furry like a sexual conversation never had! For whatever reason, "Let's talk about sex," is way too scary for many people, even if it doesn't involve, "Do you like to be blown or blow?" We skitter away from sex talks because they're the "brush them under the rug" topics of societal norm. Well by golly by gosh, shame on society! We're sexual beings, with sexual energy, and that's as much a part of who we are as apple pie, baseball, and waking up needing to take a leak in the morning! It's time to get your *let's talk* heels on and start talking about sex without feeling weird, pointing fingers, and accusing your other half of not getting who you are sexually. After all, how is he/she supposed to know our most intimate sexual secrets and desires if you don't share them? Last I knew, crystal balls weren't all that effective for creating an orgasm.

At the end of the night, afternoon, or after a morning romp in the hay, all's good, provided you have adult conversations about how you like to enjoy sex, be intimate, and the number of partners you desire, in a relationship.

✵

Going To The Chapel, or Not?

Society's barometer is shifting towards the acceptance of "those gays!" Along with this shift, new check boxes are being added to "What does Mr. or Mrs. Right really look like for me?" Checklist:

» Do I really want to get married?

» Who pops the question?

» Do I take on his/her name or keep my own?

» Who claims the dependents on taxes?

» Prenup? (Egads, sounds like a Kardashian move doesn't it?)

The option to marry or not is a very personal decision that only YOU can make. Versus, starting to sound like yet another broken record, this exploration starts with you, your guy/girl and how the heck you'd like to move the relationship along!

Let's not be stupid. There's benefits to tying the knot – emotional, spiritual, physical, and financial – no aspect of your life will be untouched by "I do!" On the other side of the rainbow, every aspect of your life might be touched negatively if you haven't fully thought through this new adventure of being in a deeper gay commitment. Let's be really clear, and not to insult your intelligence, no one says, "Just because gays and lesbians have the right to be married" (future projection across the globe), doesn't mean every gay and lesbian must ride the "Going to the chapel and going to get married gay pride float," any more than being gay means you have to participate in sex parties, or pull a U-Haul up to the front door at the end of the first date.

Commitment to be in a domestic partnership, civil union, or marriage is serious business. I may be preaching to the choir. I've been down the aisle twice, now. If you don't realize this then go back to the start of the book and begin re-reading. I know for a fact, to be in a committed relationship takes commitment, however that works for the two of you, and only the two of you. If marriage works, then get married. If a civil union works, then get civilized. If a domestic partnership fits, then get domesticated. If being in a dating relationship brings you joy, then date on in the name of dating. Freedom truly rings when we wear our unique ring of freedom in all aspects of our lives, including the biggies like, domestic partnerships, civil unions, and marriage. If you're not free to hitch up in your own way, then honey you're handcuffed, shackled, and torturing yourself for no good reason.

I'd be remiss, and not fulfilling my duties, if I didn't provide you some of my own personal insights for domesticating your partnership after saying, "Frankly My Dear, I'm Gay!" I won't bore you with more than 5 quick tips!

1. **Take it slow and stop it if it doesn't feel right!** Your inner self is one smart cookie and will tell you exactly what you need to know in any given circumstance. Listen, take it in, and save yourself regrets later. Although, there really are no regrets, only wonderful mountains of lessons to be learned along the road, even in the detours!

2. **Never act out of fear.** For crying out loud, you don't have to be alone, nor will you be, if you're not the marrying/partnering kind. This is who you are, so don't get all caught up in ya fears about getting old, and only having one chance at love, and always being alone. Honey, it's all a bunch of screwing with yourself and running up a bunch of debt on your credit card of false beliefs. You're acting out of fear, and allowing yourself to buy into it hook, line, and sinker.

3. **Be ready and willing.** Regardless of how long the two of you've been dating, be ready for slight shifts to happen, the bigger, longer, and deeper commitment becomes. In these moments, realize you're taking your relationship to a new level and don't fly blindly fueled by pipe dreams of long-term relationship bliss. The trek towards a more committed relationship, however it looks for the two of you, means being ready and willing to flex as the relationship morphs. Trenching in and living by a distorted view that by day 33 a relationship is supposed to "look like, feel like, and act like this," will only disappoint!

4. **Talk about *coming out*.** This may seem weird to talk about your individual *coming out* experiences as a launching pad for enhancing your relationship. The beauty of this sharing is you'll both gain insights by showing each other how you react under stress and adversity; plus, quite honestly, you never stop *coming out*...and I don't just mean about your sexuality. How each of you navigated your own *coming out* will have bearing on how you come out as a gay couple in gay culture, society, and to family. You'll also find the

coming out process influences how you each come out of any life challenge. The better you understand each other's process, the more likely you'll be to successfully navigate challenges as a couple.

5. **Give space, take space.** One of the keys to a successful relationship – intimate or otherwise – is to provide space for each other to breathe and to be individuals in the couple hood. It's easy to get wrapped up in everyday life, rushing to work, quick check-ins at the gym, plans with friends, and suddenly, unless we stop and "give," or "make" space for each of person to be an individual in the relationship, it never happens. If this occurs, wake up darlings, its a little pink warning flag that communication is needed. Even if it means insisting that each other goes and does something for themselves, in the long run, it could save the relationship that's already on rocky ground, or starting down a slippery slope. Take action when action seems least necessary and you'll flourish in your relationship as well as in other areas of your life.

Similar to other monumental decisions we face as humans, the decision to cohabitate shouldn't be done under the gun, in a vacuum, at the spur of the moment. Overzealous, let's play house decisions often lead to quick relationship death, especially in gay relationships where one partner just came out of the closet. Taking the "let's move beyond booty call and dating" step requires extra special care and communication: particularly in the realm of same-sex relationships. Why? Same-sex relationships weren't covered in "Dating 101," not that there really was a "Dating 101" course actually offered in high school. We all learned how to play bride and groom, but groom and groom and bride and bride, weren't in the "Let's play house..." handbooks in my kindergarten class, and I'm sure they weren't in yours either.

Mommy? Daddy? Are Ya Cut Out For Parenthood?

Many of you who embark into the realm of a committed same-sex relationship, may also find yourself experiencing another classically oriented heterosexual stirring within – the desire to be a parent! Don't get confused! I'm not suggesting that you'll have to dip your dicky or open your va jay jay to make this happen. There's lots of alternatives to party of two +1, or 2, or 3. At some point, you may sit across from someone and the question will get popped "Do you want kids?" Don't run, and for God's sake don't throw this book at them. You spent good money for this book, so don't mess up the cover with blood from someone's nose! Discussions about starting a family and raising children are going to happen, more, and more, and more, as gay rights and gay parenting become the new normal.

Be honest. At some point in your lifetime, you've probably asked yourself the question, "Do I want to be a parent?" For some of you, it was a definitive, "No, end of discussion!" For others it was an enthusiastic, "Yes," accompanied by a pearly white, once a month bleaching treatment smile! Then there are others of you who answered with, "Let me think about that," or "Let's cross that bridge when we get there." Regardless of your answer, it's a thought that will cross your mind guaranteed if you don't already have kids. For gays and lesbians, parenthood comes fully loaded with an above average set of challenges, whether the kids are your own biological children, or otherwise.

The nuances and challenges range from "How To Conceive," whose sperm and eggs to use, will it be a domestic or international adoption, acting as foster care parents, or integrating into a built in family relationship, are all common conversations that gay couples are having more frequently. Of course, there's still those states and countries blinded by their own stupidity where it's illegal for gays to be parents. A fact that has become more complicated given that in some states and countries gays and lesbians can be married, but aren't legally deemed to be suitable parents. It's an anomaly that makes me scratch my head and wonder "Why?" given the number of throwaway kids living on the street, yet us gays aren't parent material. Go figure! While the conversations are still occurring in these states and countries, it makes it exhausting and daunting to consider the possibilities of being parents when you have to fight this type of battle on top of all the other red tape as well. Of course, Lemon-Odd Pops response is, "Then, move to a different damn state that's obliging to ya!" Realistically, we, you and me (not Lemon-Odd Pop) know that's not always possible.

In all honesty, the where, when, why, and how of "kids or no kids" conversation takes place, you should be prepared and know there's a high likelihood you're going to be pulled into this conversation with someone you're dating, after you "come out of the closet." It could be a quick, slam-dunk, hands down conversation where you're both on the same page, or it could lead to a deep dive discussion where you uncover nuggets of wisdom and treasures about yourself and your love for each other. Either way, "Wisdom and knowledge is power!"

Equipped with this knowledge of "Yay" or "Nay" in regards to spawning rug rats conversation, you're now able to walk more deeply into a committed relationship, or run like hell. Either way, the preparation for these types of discussions, and holding true to your own inner values and desires, sets you perfectly in our power to be authentic and on course to be honest. There's no harm/no foul in saying, "Parenthood's not my cup of tea," or "I want to rock my socks off while rockin' my babies!" Difficulties and challenges arise when you're not clear with yourself. If you're in a state of elusive clarity, it's easy get distracted by, "He/She's hot and maybe I really don't need a kid to round out the equation." Or by default, coming to the table with kids in tow, could cause a strain before there's even a chance for the relationship to get off the ground.

Honesty in the moment with your self is key, whether it be with regard to popping out babies, or having an open relationship. The moment you sacrifice your deep seeded desires and values to be with someone, the door's been left open for the uninvited relationship disaster to make an appearance. That being said, the question then becomes, "Why do this to yourself?" – sacrifice your desires and values to be in a relationship! I'm not suggesting you can't have everything in life, without flexing and compromise. You can have what you desire provided you understand what you're being given and are willing to flex on is exactly what is intended for you, for your best life, if you accept it as part of your intended journey.

If parenthood is part of your human DNA, then it's already present and will show up in your desires for life happiness. Start by trusting that your feelings and desires to raise children is truly part of the experience you're meant to have on this planet. In my foolish mind, I believed that the best "out" gay parent experience I could have was to be with another "out" gay dad! For me, that belief turned out to not be in my best interest. Trust you're desires to be your desires, and "stand your ground" in them until it's been proven that they're actually not in your best interest. Once clarity steps in and slaps ya upside the head, which shows you what you desire is not in your best interest, let it go, refocus, and run with these new insights and internal energies.

The parental experience may be high on your bucket list. However, that experience may not be as important for the person, you've been chatting with online, via app, or even dating. If that's the case, step back, re-evaluate, and step into the uncomfortable zone of releasing this person from your future, and go get someone who is comfortable, as a parent with you, in that future.

One last tidbit on the gay parenting/potential gay parenting front: there's a wide spectrum of parents, within the world of parenthood. Figuring out how you and your other half view parenthood will help you be well on your way to dirty diapers, teen attitudes, and empty nest syndrome. So get this crap figured out, so you can be in loving pain and agony like the rest of us gay parents.

Free To Be You Check-In

Answer these questions and complete these exercises before moving forward My Dear!

1. What does freedom mean to you in the following areas of your life?
   a) Financially
   b) Intimately
   c) Socially
   d) Family relationships
   e) Work relationships
   f) Spiritually
   g) Communication with others
   h) Relationship in the LGBT community
   i) Sexuality
2. How does, or might a relationship impact your freedom?
3. What people in your life make you feel LESS free?
4. What people in your life make you feel freer?
5. If you could be more free in two areas of life, what are they and why?
6. How does freedom impact your life positively? How does freedom impact your life negatively?
7. Who has shown you how to enjoy freedom? How would you like to thank them for sharing that gift?
8. If you could overcome your fear about being in an intimate relationship, how might that make you feel more free?
9. When you don't feel free what happens? Be as specific as possible.
10. On a scale of 1 – 10, how free do you feel in your overall life right now?

11. How important is it for you to change the rating of the previous question in the next week, month, 6 months, or year?

12. What could you do to change your rating of question #11?

13. Where do you feel the most freedom in life?

14. What could you do to replicate the freedom you feel most in the previous question to other areas of your life?

15. Using two words, and two words only, describe how experiencing more freedom would make you feel.

16. What do you hear yourself say when you wish you were freer?

17. Write your thoughts about this statement: "Freedom isn't earned, it's abundantly present. We just forget to grab it and run with it!"

18. Write down 5 times in your life where you've felt less than free. Write down 5 times in your life that you've felt fully free. Now use the second list to help you in the future when you feel less than free. Use the first list to help you answer the question "Why?"

19. In 10 words or less, write how freedom will make you a better person.

Now you're ready to move onto the world of living a more powerful, passionate, purpose filled life, before, during, and after you say "Frankly My Dear, I'm Gay!"

CHAPTER 9

Pour Me A Passion Purpose Martini For Life

Words like passion, purpose, and enlightenment were never really used around our house when I was growing up. Faith, destiny, and "If you don't do this, you'll go to hell," were more commonplace. Of course, we were also selectively religious, as it fit our needs. I'm actually pleased to have had this "spiritual" experience growing up. It led me down a quirky pathway to God, while also leaving a delectable taste in my spiritual center that told me there's a hell of a lot more at play than just one spiritual way. Again, that's just my perspective and I'm not asking you to drink the Kool-Aid of my spiritual beliefs, so calm down.

I've already shared how my parents were of the hippie, free love, 60's and 70's rebel era. That makes me a flower child in my own right, I guess. I witnessed my fair share of Free Lovers, and Groovsters on our treks from our home in the Napa Valley (no wonder I'm a wino), into San Francisco, Mill Valley, and Sausalito. Just a few "groovy" and "outta sight" cool spots we frequented. I now, realize there was something about that era and those trips (no, I wasn't smoking and tokin, and neither were my parents) that already had me yearning for a higher level of enlightenment, even at a young age.

Gays, lesbians, streakers, porn, drugs, hippies, Laugh-In, Nancy Sinatra, and "no more war," were just a smidgen of the culture that fed my consciousness along with Gilligan's Island, The Monkees, and Scooby Doo! The plethora of cosmic, blue light on velvet experiences bombarded my young mind, which left me thinking in psychedelic "What if's?" and "Why's?" Even then I knew my passion and purpose were running just out of reach in front of me, leaving me perplexed with feelings that excited and scared simultaneously. Additionally, frequent solo sojourns into the woods adjacent to my grandparent's house that overlooked the Napa Valley, led me to solitude or meditate even though I had no idea what either of those words meant at that elementary stage of life. In those moments I was already questioning, "What's next? Why do I feel this way? Is this how a normal boy my age should feel?" Never sharing the feelings and experiences I encountered during the brief respites from hide-and-seek, cowboys & Indians, and war, I stayed the course by inhaling and exhaling to the beat of a "normal" boy's life. Normal being the state I felt most unfamiliar with except when I felt the excited stirring within me as I hung out with my uncle and his "friend!"

My Dad's family was a large loving family, who all pretty much resided in the and around the Napa Valley. Family gatherings were almost always in excess of 30+ people, making holidays, birthdays, and even anniversaries a nominee for prime time reality TV, way before Ryan Seacrest birthed the Kardashians. Even though my gay uncle and "his friend's" relationship was fodder for family snickering, gossip, and catty talk behind his back, they were accepted warmly at these gatherings provided they gayed it up to make the events fabulous, and gayed it down, so as not to embarrass anyone. In fact, no one batted an eye when it came time for Uncle Will and Bill to cook, or throw a party. How rude we'd be to shun their tantalizing culinary delights, or say a negative word about the fabulous decorating job they'd done of the tables? They were after all two of San Francisco's finest restaurateurs. "Thou shalt accept the gay man's fabulous talents, yet not the fact that he is gay! Thus sayeth some big guy upstairs who also said we are all created equal!" Go figure!

Flamboyant and gay with a capital "G", my uncles (yes, I called them both my uncles) were tolerated and accepted by the family as the family novelty that didn't get discussed. Funny how nothing's changed! The only difference is today, I'm the "Let's not acknowledge it, that way it won't be true that Rick's gay," and sweep it under the rug. Don't snicker. I see you nodding your head. You have one of those lumpy family rugs too where all the family crap gets brushed under don't you? Needless to say, from that shameful seed of "let's not talk about it," regarding my uncles, grew a twisted vine of confusion that began my unconscious state of "not talking about it" for 38 years. Even though this cover up was more effective than anything that L'Oreal ever created, all was not lost, and I learned immense lessons about truth telling from my family's version of "Don't Ask, Don't Tell!" By no means, did I put blame on anyone in the family for me practicing this standard of behavior. Ok, maybe I did blame them for the manual on how to brush things under the rug and how to pretend to be someone you're not. Family influence was only part in partial a contributor to the way I designed my life, but they're not completely to blame. Ok, maybe there was something with someone in the family (not with my gay uncle) that shouldn't have happened, but I'm not going to kiss and tell.

None of these factors had any deep dark influence on the essence of who I was, or the man I became because I was gay, gay, gay from the moment I was born, born, born. If you've been convinced that your "gayness" is due to some taboo explorations of the family kind, I'm going to suggest you don't buy into it, unless you feel that being gay is a learned behavior. If you do, then I would recommend seeking the help of a licensed therapist or psychologist to help you gently work through those feelings. For me, witnessing the catty whispers, hidden snickers (not the candy bar type) only strengthened my subconscious resolve to be passionately who I was in my truth, regardless of what others thought. Those precious moments in which my uncles were freely, gaily themselves, taught me that true freedom means never apologizing about who you are, for all the wrong reason!

My life as a young, curious, and confused boy in the 60's and 70's, initiated my quest to drink a life Martini with a twist of authenticity that would quench my thirst for passion and purpose. Of course, it took me 38 years, *coming out* of the closet after a 13 year marriage, two children, and a layoff from a job that fed my ego to finally wake up and say, "Drink up bitches. Screw who I thought I was. I'm going on a quest to find what I'm meant to be in this life and world!"

❋

Honestly Speaking...I Never Had!

Honesty wasn't a foreign concept to me. After all, I wasn't holed up in a jail cell, serving time in solitary confinement because I'd killed someone or embezzled money in a masterful Ponzi scheme. I left that to Madoff! Honesty was always one of my core values, except for that little lemon twist in my life's Martini about my sexuality and my cheating ways. My dishonesty, lack of integrity, and denial were so deeply rooted in my life, that I easily dismissed my actions as normal, in a mind-boggling manner, all the while allowing them to set in my consciousness like an annoying pebble in your shoe that you can't find. It didn't matter how often I took the shoe of my sexuality off and madly thrashed it about to remove the stone of truth, it always found a way to hide. Of course it would then return to annoy me when I felt most vulnerable.

Looking through the rear view mirror of my life now, I know it was impossible to be honest because I was hiding. Hiding a truth that was strangling my capacity to experience my deep seeded passions and to live a purposeful life. My core essence strived to be honest, happy, joyful, fun loving, spontaneous, and free. Deep as my desire was to have each of those things add up on the balance sheet of my "Damn Good Living" life, I always lived in the black. The numbers of my life overstated, undervalued, and out of balance. I borrowed from the bank account of my own happiness, to pay a debt I felt I owed to help others feel more comfortable with me for their sake, versus being who I was in my own eyes for my sake.

My honesty and integrity towards myself and others were tied up in an interesting Tango where the two values constantly stepped on one another's toes. The honesty of who I was and was meant to be was in direct opposition to what others expected of me. To stay in my integrity of being *in service to others,* I faked my life. This dynamic caused me to fall face first on the dance floor I called my life. Fortunately, I was the only one who was watching the reality TV showoff my life called "Dancing With A Farce!" The paid programming that I'd produced for others viewing pleasure, kept them far removed from channel of scandal. My charade was as strong as the glue that holds Lemon-Odd Pop's wigs and false boobies in place. In this checked out state of being – with the men I hooked up with and the people who were in my life – I was constantly tuned into regularly scheduled programming that was the false truth of my screwed up life. I was making it work. That was only one problem. I was being eaten alive inside by the pretending and lying, rather than tasting the sweet nectar of living a passion and purpose filled life of truth.

Throughout the years, I sought solace in my sacred Zodiac energy, Leo. Cunningly and manipulatively, I led the cast of characters that took center stage, basked in the accolades for my talents as a father, husband, and star employee. Each mask I wore meticulously helped to keep the mask of false happiness from slipping off the façade to reveal my true misery. Rip away the appreciation, or show any sign of turning on me, and lord help you. The wrath of Lemon-Odd Pop would erupt, kidnapping the kind, big-hearted, loving spirit of Teddy Bear Rick (even before I knew, or would admit I was a bear). In these truly erratic pain-filled and anguish-ridden angry moments, my honesty locked up. The inner pain left to boil over the rim, leaving me with no sense of sensibility or sanity whatsoever towards others, let alone myself.

In true Leo fashion, my headstrong ego – nominated for narcissist of the year award – marched forth. I'd become an arrogant, dominate, cynical asshole, trying to control everything and everyone, especially puppeteering my grand sham lest anyone see me sweat!

Reeking of bitter sadness and quickly losing all sense of integrity, my façade began to crumble. My truth yearned to come out as much as I needed to leave the confines of the dark closet. It was time for me to drink the elixir of passionate, purposeful living once and for all. Conflicted as a sailor with a 5-minute pass in a whorehouse, I found myself repeatedly rolling the dice between being honest, exercising integrity, and lovingly protecting my truth to avoid upsetting the apple cart of everyone else's life. Each moment spent in inner turmoil and denial only reminded me that my true passion and purpose remained locked up in a password-protected file in the data processing center of my soul.

It seemed that the others around me were living fully exposed, passionate, purpose filled lives. I believed I was completely incapable of living as they were, even though deep down I knew the password for unlocking my own passion and purpose filled life. Nudged by this deep knowing, I set off on an expedition to explore every possibility that might miraculously bring these two elusive desires permanently into my life. My adventures led me to read new age books, smoke pot, explore new religions, and even became a parent, in the hopes that "P" and "P" would join me in my secret life. Nothing, except the births of my daughters, ignited the flames for me to live with some slightly heightened level of passion and purpose. Yet, parenting two bundles of joy wasn't enough to douse the fires burning in the voids of my life. I remained a dishonest, miserable man, who had been nominated to receive a lifetime achievement award for best portrayal of a happy heterosexual.

In hindsight, I pretended to be a straight guy who had sex with other straight guys, which hampered me from discerning truth from fiction. Towards the "end" of my heterosexual journey, I became known as Mr. Miserably Moody; often finding myself distracted, screwing up at work, and becoming overtly self-destructive, but not suicidal. I was naked and taking a bath in my own self-loathing. (An extremely painful predicament given my disdain for baths.) Scrub as I might, I was still blinded from clearly seeing what I needed to commit to in order to live a life with passion and purpose. Little did I know, two words, "I'm Gay," would release the gale force winds of change in my life, forcing me to my knees in humility, but also release me into peace and tranquility. My passion and purpose were soon to be revealed, no forcing, no pushing. Simply asking my ego to retreat, if only for a bit, in order so my truth could shine. (A truth that would become the foundation of my life's work.)

For Now, Put It In The "When You Feel Like Shit, Read This File!"

Even though the dimmer switch controlling the light shining on my life had only shifted slightly brighter, I began to see clearly that *coming out* was going to be more than about *coming out*. A deeper passion was to be discovered beyond the sheets, and my life purpose would be revealed in this journey. For most of my life, I'd chosen to file away certain hopes, dreams, and aspirations in my "When you feel like shit, read this file." Do you have one of these files? If not, start one, and start one now. It's a lovely little place where dreams go to rest, but not to die. You'll find this folder to be a wonderful respite from the chaos of *coming out*.

For as long as I could remember, I'd felt I was destined to do something big. No, I'm not referring to doing a big beautiful penis, or having a luscious bubble butt rubbing across my face or furry chest. *Sigh!* Ok, where were we? My big desire was to play bigger in the world, making a monumental difference in people's lives. Yet, no matter what I attempted to do, I intentionally kept making notes and filing them in the wrong file; the "Someday, I'll Do This File!" You'll notice I have a lot of files. I'm not only a coach, author, and podcaster, but I'm also my own version of the Container Store! Hell, if I'd known that dropping crap into *someday* would possibly lead me to living in my car, afraid of losing my kids, and never finding love with a man, then I would have never invested time and energy into someday thinking. Here's the interesting juxtaposition about the crap in the "Someday, I'll …" file. Ironically, I didn't file away that someday I'll be gay, I'll have fathered two lovely daughters, and I'll have gained a lifetime of knowledge about being in a long-term relationship. Those things really weren't even on the radar. Nor did the "Someday, I'll..." file contain any junk about someday being "Me, Myself, and I!" Yes, someday those things did happen, but I wasn't setting them aside, pining over the day when I could be any of those things.

What I've learned is there's always an inherent danger in keeping the "Someday, I'll…" file alive and well. What if "someday" never comes? Of course, the same applies to filling your, "When you feel like shit, read this file," with stuff you never have time to read. Trust me! Clipped articles from magazines, inspirational cards, fabulous quotes, all poured from the confines of my first manila folder of "Read this when you feel like shit folder," birthing two, three, and four more offspring folders. Finally, I awakened to the realization that I had a proclivity for hoarding; gathering inspirational goods because it felt good to gather and on some occasions read. Well boys and girls, men and women, it doesn't mean a thing until you take the time to do more with them other than organize them into nice little folders! Quicker than Lady Gaga could ever shock the world with one of her stunts, I lit the fire under these folders of inspiration, not literally of course; however, it aroused my inner muse to step forward to lead a passionate life. A dream I'd dreamt of living for longer than I can remember.

Shortly after *coming out*, I began shuffling through each of the "When you feel like shit, read these files." It was a cathartic process that opened my eyes, healed some wounds, and scared the hebejebes out of me. I began to feel alive, experienced clarity, and even ran from vulnerability, all within the confines of my 600 square foot studio beach apartment in Laguna Beach. One dark evening, as I wallowed within myself, I grabbed one of the sacred inspiration folders, trudged down 200-hundred treacherous steps onto a cloud-covered beach with only slivers of moonlight and stars to guide me. I was fully intent on throwing the whole damn "When you feel like shit read this" folder into the water. I'd convinced myself there was no purpose for anything I'd done in my life, especially *coming out*. All that lay between the covers of the manila folder were demonic lies, tempting me to live a happy, authentic life, which I tauntingly laughed off as a complete joke. Thank God, I was shaken back to my senses by the crashing waves before I disrespected the Pacific Ocean by intentionally casting my litter into its beauty!

Standing at the water's edge, tears rolling down my flushed cheeks while screaming silently at the moon, universe, and God, and begging for a frickin' break, I stumbled through this new life with a different cloak of shame and guilt, all in the name of being true to myself. My new destiny had me deeply regretting the pain I was bringing into the heart and soul of my daughters and soon to be ex-wife. I flogged myself daily with cynical thoughts of, "You're not worthy!" To numb the agony, I began to swallow erratic advice from men I was convinced were my destined life loves. (Advice that almost cost me my relationship with my daughters.) As the tide came in, sand wedged between my toes, and cool ocean water gently lapped up my legs, my truth began to come into focus. No, there wasn't an angelic light or booming voice from heaven that awakened me. That was just Lemon-odd Pop Burping up her Martini. What descended upon my consciousness was knowing that within the confines of that manila folder were pages of wisdom to guide me towards a destiny I was yet to experience: a destiny that hid in a closet, not yet ready to be revealed. Confused and slightly intoxicated by the moonlight and ocean spray, I set free my frustrated cries of "What's my purpose?" at the ocean's edge, letting those taunting cries be carried out to sea. A subtle tickle at my core was turning me towards the answer, while a new stirring within began to ask two additional questions, "Why is this my purpose, and how can I better manifest it into life?"

Flashlight Please!

I believe passion and purpose take on a myriad of faces, some of which we can't see until we're shown. Some of which also take on the face of newfound love. Not long after my night at the ocean's edge, almost lobbing the manila folder filled with the crap of my life into the ocean, I met a guy. A guy who helped me see my passion was well on its way to coming to life, and that my purpose was just slightly out of reach. On the surface, this new hearts a flutter relationship seemed destined, to be the one. Luckily, it was destined to move me one step closer towards my authentic self, and he was "so, not the one."

I lovingly call this my flashlight relationship. It had the power to guide me out of the dark, and taught me the lesson of not sacrificing me, all of me to be with a man. For the first time in my life, I completely understood that while being alone and single seemed scary, it's also a time to learn to love you, without loving yourself being a selfish thing. I repeat, learning to love yourself doesn't mean you're BEING selfish! I know I just struck a chord, which means it's time to keep moving into the light... shall we?

Throughout my life I'd had numerous friends whose life focus was all about status – what they had, and who they knew. Yet, I'd never had an intimate relationship with someone who was wired this way...up until now! Blinded by my desire to avoid loneliness, I landed in a relationship with someone who was the polar opposite of my values, my desires, and me. We were truly, the epitome of polar opposites, or at least more opposite than alike. Before I share more, I admit, I like nice things, love rubbing shoulders with good and even sometimes famous peeps, and I relish experiencing the wonders of the world. However, the wake-up call of this relationship came when I showed up at his condo one day, and suddenly awakened to the explosion of the Chintz and French Provincial everything in his home. How had I allowed myself to be sucked into this relationship with a person who was not a Modern Minimalist in style?

In that moment, other realities began to awaken. I didn't give a damn about designer labels. I sure the heck didn't freak out about getting a fountain drink out of a machine at an AM/PM. Nor was I going to call the paramedics when my date ate a tortilla chip that fell out of the basket, onto the table, at a Mexican food restaurant. I was a simple, happy to be me kind of guy, with stylish minimalist tastes who wasn't afraid of contracting a food borne illness from dining at a buffet! I was so not supposed to be with this guy, except for the wake-up call he unknowingly gave me to be myself.

Without sounding hypocritical, I did love dressing my two little princesses and myself in hip fashions. However, to do so, I mastered the art of fashion sleight of hand with no label fashions. I had no choice. I was a divorced, gay dad, living on a shoestring budget, who had to pull a Houdini at every turn to sustain a moderate standard of living. It was all part of the universes master plan. After 39 years of pretending and making others feel comfortable with me, I was stepping into a passionate place of being me. No second guessing. I was finally drawing real lines in the sand to stand in my truth. The faux finish of feigning certain ways of living to please others were getting a new coat of life paint because they were out of alignment with my values, beliefs, and desires. I no longer was content to unconsciously exist without heading towards my intended purpose, even if it wasn't clear what that purpose was at this stage of the game. Funny how all it took was a difference of interior decorating style, a few dinners out with the germophobe, and one too many designer labels to get me pointed towards my true north.

Do That Again. It Feels Right!

Funny how we all have those "AHA moments," that we ignore. Damn it boys and girls, wake up! As Lemon-Odd Pop would say so eloquently, "Pay attention! If you don't, then ya higher self will keep poking, nudging, kicking ya in the ass until you do! And how much do you really enjoy getting ya ass kicked?" Wasn't but a ~~few minutes, few hours~~, ok, it was a few days after the break-up with Mr. Labels (nice enough guy, just not my cup of tea), that I began to feel deeper and more intimate connection with myself. I started experimenting with a string of spiritual one-night stands. I know you're scratching your head wondering, "WTF is a spiritual one-night stand?"

I started spiritual speed dating, so to speak! New Thought, New Age, Buddhism, Kabbalah, and various forms of Christianity, all became bedmates in the slumber of my life. I hate to admit this, it's going to sound shallow, and may even cause you to throw this book in the trash after I share, but my spiritual one-night stands were all out of my quest for a husband! Not really. Ok, kinda yes, and kinda no, kinda really they were. I was lost. Not because I was gay. That would really make me a hypocrite. I was lost because I believed that spirituality/religion in any form, would land me a man, open me authentically up to receive my passion, and finally, guide me to my life's purpose. Not a bad plan, but the maneuvers weren't working together like a well-oiled machine. Along the way, little enlightened snippets, and nuggets of wisdom came to me when I needed them most. Then, one day as I sat in a mega church in Orange County, California, I realized that I was checking out the guys in the congregation, more than I was partaking of the spiritual nourishment being delivered from the pulpit. Of course, I now know that I was at the wrong mega church to have been fed anything lovingly spiritual...the pastors purpose driven life is to drive homosexuality out of his church... if you get my drift on the "purpose driven." At that moment, I knew it was time to shine a frickin' flashlight on my life, get real, and quit intentionally expecting Church to be the new PlanetOut of my dating expeditions! I immediately went home after church, placed myself in a petri dish under a microscope, and re-examined my spiritual life. That examination led me to finally make room for finding me, the real me, no flashlight necessary!

When Your Calling Finds You, Don't Sidestep or Run From It!

At this point in my post hetero, newbie gay life I took a hiatus as a "spiritual seeker," and (shocking, as it may seem) went on a dating detox. Diving inward to my core essence, I discovered a place that scared the crap out of me. After years as a high flying, globe-trotting executive, "model" husband and father, who'd been playing the game of "pretending to be straight while secretly being gay," I finally executed a triple back flip with a twist into the pool of "Who the FUCK am I, and why can't I just be me?" To begin answering that question, I began dancing to a whole new beat, one that filled my dance card with only the things that mattered most to me.

I spent my days building my small consulting biz, being on Daddy duty every couple of days, keeping one head in my pants, and the other focused on creatively finding ways to cover alimony and child support, while experiencing some level of joy in life. I was done, for the time being, with PlanetOut online dating, and over the thrill-less thrill of hitting the gay bars. I had not one ounce of trust in any guy that said, "You're hot," even if he was being sincere. I teetered precariously on the edge of "bitter party of one." Yet, in reality, I was stepping into "being" with me, in my life, in the present moment; pre-Eckhart Tolle and The Power Of Now.

Better than a Broadway showstopper, with the heavens opening and angels singing moment, I finally saw the brilliant light of truth. I was not destined to

a) be alone,

b) sacrifice my relationship with my kids, nor ex-wife for some piece of ass, and

c) never work for someone again (knock on renewable Bamboo wood).

I'd finally manned up to be my own gay man, and gay father I wanted to be, having an above average relationship with my ex-wife at that time; so step aside world and hear me roar! In the midst of my masculine chest pounding, I considered writing a fabulous Broadway musical entitled, "Losing My Heterosexuality," (still on my bucket list). In reality, at that stage of life I simply didn't have the energy to be fabulous. In fact, I discovered, there was no need for me to be fabulous, ripped, or hot. All I had to do was just be me!

I had a phenomenal revelation of my own that produced the most powerful orgasm of my life (no sacrilege intended). Actually, it wasn't a singular orgasm in my life. Many more powerful orgasms were to follow in this book of revelations were to occur in my life. However, those tales will be shared in my the next book entitled, "The Authentic Road To Orgasmic Living Regardless of Sexual Orientation!" The revelation about not having to be fabulous woke me out of my zombie life slumber. I started paying attention to things that really got me off, and I'm not talking about well-hung, hairy chested men, with handsome good looks. Ok, they did and still do, but let's get back to the point I'm making! I realized that fatherhood excited and fulfilled me; cycling 20 - 50 miles was an euphoric drug like no other; and playing coy and hard to get (yes, we gay men can play that game too) was not fun, but kept my heart from rushing into relationship roulette. The piece de resistance was discovering how being genuine, honest, and not throwing my sexuality in peoples face like a "piss off" grenade, made me feel happy, transparent, and authentic. Little did I know as I ventured into unchartered territories of parenting with purpose, dating with dignity, and creating a business built on a foundation of "service to others," that the elusive destiny, passion, and purpose forthcoming to take their rightful place in my life's journey.

❧

What's Love Got To Do With It... Everything.

Admittedly, I was burnt out on men, other than the occasional, "Let's screw" guys, so it was easy to remain focused on what really mattered to me – my kids, my relationship with my ex-wife, and my business. Can

I be honest? Of course, I can, it's my damn book, and I'll be as honest as I damn well please! (Sorry for that out-burst. Lemon-Odd Pop just woke up!) Nothing was scarier, at least to me at that point of life, than *coming out* of the closet, getting laid off, navigating "single-parenthood," and buying a house solo. All of these crazy maneuvers were happening simultaneously and all I had to rely on as backup and support was a little bit of a golden parachute, and faith. I still scratch my head, amazed and wondering, "How the $%*# did I pull that one off?" Compared to a lot of others who've travelled this post-hetero life, maybe even you, I was having a pretty damn good life, considering the circumstances. With each step, my passion and purpose kept coming closer, closer, and closer, all the while getting clearer, clearer, and clearer.

Even though I thought that my days of knocking on passion and purposes' door were finally leading to the doorway marked, "Here's your answer Mr. Clemons," Ms. Universe kept holding her 'talk to the hand' up, letting me know 'it's not your time yet!'" I'd one more marathon to run at love and Corporate America before my intended life would begin to unfold, just as it should! It was 2001: two years post layoff and *coming out* of the closet, and 6 months into "officially divorced." The monotony of perusing Monster.com, CareerBuilder.com, and TheLadders.com were beginning to take their toll on me, emotionally and financially. When I couldn't escape and leave the world behind by jumping on my bike for a 50-mile ride, I found myself, succumbing to the numbness of random, "I just need to get off," sexual encounters. Of course, this type of behavior awakened the scary patterns of my past, "I'm not gay, I just like having sex with men," syndrome, during my married life. Out of shear fear, loneliness, and avoidance of reality I catapulted myself once again into the hook up scene of

Me: "Want to screw?"

Him: "Yea!"

Me: "Let's do it."

Him: "Thanks. That was great. Hope to see you again soon."

Me: "Not in a million years."

Emptiness prevailed, except for the delicious moments I shared with my two beautiful little princesses.

No longer capable of finding any solace in the arms of building a business, pleasure hunting for a man, or enjoying the spiritual orgasms of getting to know myself, I fell into getting by mode. I sulked and withdrew from life, in every way possible. What few friends I had, were convinced I was going off the deep end. At one point, I felt like saying "Screw It! I'll just stop trying to be a recovering heterosexual, flip the tables and become a recovering homosexual, return to regularly scheduled life programming as a heterosexual to make things better for everyone concerned, even me." Thank God, I didn't drink that Kool-Aid. Instead, I called forth my inner rebel, fighter, and, of course my beautiful Diva – Lemon-Odd Pop – to get me back on track. Oh, and a few hundred rounds of conversations with the big guy upstairs!

Ironically, and as the saying goes, "When you least expect it, love finds you, and so does the right job!" Ok, that's not exactly the way the saying goes, but once again this is my book bitches and I'll create my own sayings! "For crying out Lemon-Odd Pop, please be nice to our readers!" Sorry about that. For me, the man came first, just days after the 9/11 tragedy. Some might see as an Omen, dooming the relationship from the get go. Well screw them. They're wrong we're still together, and he ain't getting rid of me, nor me of him, at least not that I know of since our last coffee chat about 5 minutes ago! Then, within 6 months of meeting Mr. Man, I swallowed. Wait, that's not what I meant. Within six months of Meeting Mr. Man, I graciously swallowed my pride and took a position with a .com that came along as my next employer. So why did I swallow my pride? Because the position I was offered and decided to take, I believed, would never be able to support me financially. Yet, it was more money than I was producing being my own boss, so I took it. At first, I felt I had failed myself by surrendering from entrepreneurship. What I didn't realize at the time was it wasn't meant for me to be my own boss...not quite yet.

Damn it. The transition from single and unemployed to becoming a couple and working for the .com, were both a blessing and a curse. Love and work became the epitome of my daily grind. Of course, I held tightly to my course of children, first. Well, not exactly. I have since admitted and apologized to my daughters, for the times that chasing a piece of ass, even the one that became their step-father, was more important than being a responsible father. God, that's just hard to admit, but it happened. Now back to the love story.

I met a great guy, and gave myself space to allow the relationship to slowly blossom – a first for me. We grew as a couple, in a short-distance relationship (40 miles apart), two guys from similar yet different backgrounds. A lesson that taught me to appreciate a healthy dose of somewhat "opposites attract!" In truth, we weren't complete opposites, just uniquely different enough to make it interesting, fun, challenging, and surprising, all at the same time.

Unconsciously and unaware, I began to open up to possibilities of being with a man in a much, much different way than I had ever allowed myself to be before, of course except for that one night in London that started this whole journey to my truth. With this new man, my passion for life and purpose for being on earth did rapidly begin to unfold. Like any new relationship, it was challenging, but it also delivered nuggets of wisdom and lessons learned, that now empower me to serve others in a straight-forward, no bullshit, life-coach manner where I challenge others to bravely move into living an authentic life. Plus, I now also see the beauty of learning from others at a much deeper level.

Never believing I had all the answers to anything, I stumbled and tripped, as most of us do when we're trying to figure out how to do the dating shuffle. Even in those insane moments of questioning, and second-guessing, "Should I be here?" I allowed myself to trust the experience and to move forward deeper into this relationship. Of course, it always helps when the person on the other side of the equation is willing to trip and fall as well, which my guy did with grace and ease, including one trip to the hospital after a little too much wine tasting. Honestly, had it not been for our mutual vulnerability, flexibility, and mutual determination to walk, "eyes wide open" into our relationship, it probably wouldn't have ever lasted. Underneath the surface, lurking where we neither one could see it, our relationship was playing a significant role in our individual and united journeys towards living passionate and purposeful lives.

We All Do It Our Own Way! Really! We do!

One of the false pretenses I butted my head against, time and time again, was a belief that there's a magic formula we closet dwellers must discover in order to checkout of the closet. After all, with so many gay people being passionate about who they are, there must be a magical elixir they drank right before transitioning out of the closet. On the other hand, I wasn't blind to the reality that for many gay people, their journeys are pure hell, which meant the "magic" wasn't so magical after all. That being said, "How the hell do you come out of the closet, without coming unglued?" The answer:

Uniquely in your own way!

Firstly, I consciously recognized the unique journeys each of us takes out of the closet, when I hit the dating scene. Every guy I dated had different tails (booties) and different tales to share about their journey out of closet. Stories ranged from family disgrace to, "Hot damn! We've got us an honest to goodness homosexual in the family!" Often, I found myself laughing or crying hysterically at the ridiculously funny and heartbreakingly sad, situations these guys each endured coming into their truth. A common recurring theme they shared was about to take center stage in my own life…"We'll always love you, but we can't accept your lifestyle!" Really? Just what the hell does that mean?

The first time my parents uttered those words (and yes those words continue to be muttered, although much less frequently and more quietly), I began to fully understand the depths of what being out of the closet meant. People actually believed, including my parents, that this "gay adventure" could be labeled as a lifestyle, like a healthy eating lifestyle. GIVE ME A FRICKIN' BREAK! No, I'm not choosing to be gay. However, I am choosing to be gay and eat fresh Kale, Spinach, and Beets as part of my HEATHLY EATING LIFESTYLE! This is not a "lifestyle choice!" Read, and re-read this next part carefully, so that you have it in your arsenal of wisdom when dealing with narrow-minded, lifestyle oriented, assumptive assholes! We gays, both men and women, simply have figured out how to show up, express our innate sexuality, and be uniquely who we are, plain and simple. There's no handbook, magic elixir, or tried and true protocol for coming into our authentic self sexually, or otherwise. As Nike says, you "Just Do It'!"

Likewise, to find your passion and live with purpose, you "Just do it!" It may require experimenting and taking numerous inner nosedives into yourself before you discover your true passion. The most surprising discovery I made was that my passion erupted out of 46 years of searching, listening, building, failing, crying, and trusting. Bundled up in my passion package was a bountiful abundance of purpose that I had least expected when I began this journey out of the closet.

My most profound lesson learned came from experiencing the beautiful relationship I share with my husband. He'd been out of the closet for well over 20 years, when we met. His young adult life had been spent in pursuit of a solid, long-term relationship. Active in his adult gay world, he'd experienced love, rejection, companionship, and heartbreak. He'd also lived through a time in gay history where it was still a matter of being out, but not too out. I, on the other hand, came out and had no intention of hiding my sexual orientation. Here's where the opposites attract comes into play. I had no qualms about showing him affection in public, or calling him honey in the midst of a shopping spree at Target. This was somewhat new territory for him, and at times made him uncomfortable. Not because he didn't love or care about me, or because he was ashamed of being gay, but because his reactions emanated from the space that society wasn't ready for this openness between two men or two women in public. The lesson I quickly learned is we all come into our sexuality, through our own *coming out* process, and into our own way of being gay, at different points in the spectrum of life, none of which comes with a blueprint.

The beauty of flying without a flight plan into our authentic selves is that we have a couple of co-pilots onboard to bring us higher levels of peace, happiness, and a smoother flight – passion and purpose. Ironic as it may seem, the power of living authentically, in our sexuality, or otherwise, is a catalyst for uncovering our life's passion. It is virtually impossible to live with passion without being authentic. Once passion is painted on the canvas of our lives, the brush strokes of clarity make their mark, fulfilling our desire to live on purpose. *Coming out* of the closet may seem a roundabout way of uncovering your life's purpose. In reality, your ability to be authentically you without regrets and being confident in your own existence is a brilliant masterpiece depicting a life lived with passion and purpose!

CHAPTER 10

Uncovering the Passionate, Purposeful Gay Standard of Living

For all the intense feelings, emotions, thoughts, stresses, worries, and joys that come along with *coming out* of the closet, I've observed two very rich experiences most people have in common:

1. *Coming out* ignites a new passion for living, which makes life more exciting.

2. Their life purpose, which up until this point has been elusive, suddenly is staring them right in the face, bringing them a deeper sense of clarity.

These experiences of clarity, like kicking the closet door open, are uniquely individual and tremendously empowering; provided you tune into what's actually at that deeper level of your soul searching. If you invite passion and purpose to join you as you march through the closet door, then you'll find they're kick-ass comrades of support. Fair warning: some of you may not immediately encounter your passion and purpose simply because it's not yet your time, or you've already given birth to them in some form. Don't despair. There's no predicting if, when, why, or how your passion and purpose will come alive. Yet, here's what I've discovered that was the game changer for me. As soon as I planted the seed of desire to live with passion and purpose, nurtured that yearning to keep it alive and well, new branches began to bud, and led me to living a richer life, and challenged me to grow to my fullest potential.

During the transition of *coming out*, two questions often get lost in translation:

1. Why am I passionate about living my truth as a homosexual?
2. What is the deeper purpose for my life, by *coming out* and honoring this truth?

Whew! I know it. These are damn big questions and not to be taken lightly. Yet, they're not meant to trip you up, to cause more stress, or to tempt you to go smoke a bowl either. Broken down to their most elementary essence they're simply "Why?" and "What?" questions. So, reframe them if it makes it easier for you to grasp. Go ahead on, reframe them, if it makes sense for you. "Why is living with passion important to me?" "What does knowing my purpose add to my life?" Remove sexuality out of the equation for the moment. Start by working through these basic questions and slowly bring back the sexuality exploration to add additional flavor to your answers.

One of the things I've learned throughout my journey, and observed with my clients, is once you ignite the passion for living your truth, every day in every way, your real purpose for being alive and sharing your beautiful gay self will arise. It's not magic, some mystical spiritual practice, or threat from Lemon-Odd Pop that brings it forth. Nor does it have anything to do with being gay. Passion and purpose naturally arise from your inner spirit because you are now free from the binding shackles of living a lie. Ironically, these two extraordinary feelings of the human experience, passion and purpose, are often held at bay until you give yourself permission to become fully self-expressed in your truth, sexually or otherwise. Once your truth is set free, then there's nothing to hide behind nor any more need to pretend. Honesty ignites the flames of being more truthful with yourself and others, as well as permits you to get real about your deepest passions without regret. Removing remorse, shame, and guilt from the equation, honesty is about kicking clouded judgment, second-guessing, and confusion about following our intended purposeful living, to the curb, to be swept up by the street cleaners of our life. That is unless Lemon-Odd Pop is acting up, then she gets assigned to street cleaning!

❈

Got Passion? Got Purpose? Get Real!

You cover a lot of miles in your journey from the initial scary thoughts of "What's going on with me?" to, "I'm *coming out!*" By now, hopefully your fears and worries have begun to take a back seat on a more regular basis, and the confidence to live your truth is becoming second nature. What may shock and surprise you is you're getting real with yourself, and by bravely *coming out*, you actually opened the door to living with passion and purpose. The irony, so to speak, is your *coming out* actually was born from your desire to live with more passion and purpose. On the flip side, (there is always a flip side) your passion and purpose to be authentic is driving you to come out of the closet! Go ahead! Think about it, while I sit back quietly and strike my Oprah pose letting those last two thoughts wash over you and sink in.

The honesty of who you are, sexually, probably started with a little inner nudge of "Oh. That seems weird, but feels so right." Doesn't matter if it was a stirring in your groin or a flutter of your heart looking at someone of the same sex. The more you progress and grow through those feelings, the sooner you climb out of your confusion, fear, self-hate, anger, and denial by leaving them on the doorstep of "what was." Once you begin this shift, you'll begin to adapt to your own beliefs, thoughts, and feelings about being gay and become more self-accepting, even in the face of other's beliefs, thoughts, and feelings about homosexuality. Filled with self-confidence, determination, and self-love, you've become more passionate about your truth, your life, your sexual orientation, even if you couldn't outwardly express it up until now!

Regardless of what anyone else may say, you've got loads of stunning passion for living your intended life. The unique difference is how you use it, project it, and allow it to come alive in your life. Even the most demure wallflower has seeds of passion waiting to sprout into life. You couldn't live without a little flame of passion in life; at least, that's my perspective. Waking up and getting out of the bed in the morning takes passion, otherwise you'd just lay there listless. Even if you choose to lay in bed listless, it takes passion to pursue being listless, versus being productive. The unique thing about passion is it works with us or against us, if not kept in check. Too much passion, and only pursuing passion, doesn't leave much room for anything else in life.

Here's an exercise you can do over the next week to get real about your passions. I want you to have some options at your disposal, so choose what best works for you. Write, take pictures, rip pictures out of magazines, or put pictures up on Instagram or Pinterest. Doesn't really matter. What matters most is that you take the time to complete the exercise. Each day, for one week, capture 10 things that you're passionate about, by writing them down, clipping, taking, or posting pictures. By week's end, you'll have your passionate 70. If you have more, then bully for you, you're a passionista, and one step closer to giving Lemon-Odd Pop a run for the crown.

Your next step is to write down one (and only one) emotion you experience when you think about each individual thing on the list that you feel passionate about. Try to avoid listing the same emotion over and over again. The goal is to get snuggled up and deeply acquainted with as many emotions as possible. Go ahead! Jump in, wallow around, and lather up in those juicy emotions. Don't hold back, or you'll miss out on the full experience of this exercise.

Moving right along, the next part of the assignment is to review your Passionate 70 by placing a "plus (+)" sign next to each passion that's grown stronger, since you got real with yourself and came out of the closet. Place a "minus (-)" sign next to each passion you feel has diminished, since *coming out* of the closet. If a passion doesn't rank a plus or minus, then don't write anything next to it. Almost done, I promise!

The final step requires a new sheet of paper. Draw a line vertically down the center of the paper to create two columns. At the top of the left column write "Creates Purpose." At the top of the right-hand column write, "Diminishes Purpose." Yes, I know, you're smarter than Lemon-Odd Pop (yes I went there, and I'll be feeling her wrath very soon). Now, go through your list and for all the "plus (+)" sign labeled passions, write one sentence about how this passion "Creates Purpose" in your life. Trust me, every passion contributes greatly to your life's purpose. Next, for each passion labeled with a "minus (-)" sign, determine if it should be playing a pivotal role in your purposeful life or not. If not, cross it off the original list, thank it for showing up and playing a role in your life, and release it from your life. Write a very condensed version of the released passion in the right-hand column entitled, "Diminishes Purpose." Once the "Diminishes Purpose" column is complete, fold the paper in half vertically, so that the right-hand column can't be seen and so that the "Creates Purpose" column is visible. However, there's one little extra caveat. Any passions that you've marked with a "minus (-)" sign, but you're unsure if you really want to release them, create on a new list on a separate piece of paper with the heading, "May Nurture My Purpose - TBD." Admit these passions are in limbo and let them rest in that state of being for now, until they're ready to be addressed.

Now, take a deep breath, and know you're fully supported for the next part of your challenge. Over the next month, at whatever time of day is most productive for you, grab your "Creates Passion" list and read completely through it daily. Don't place any judgments on what you're reading, simply read through the entire list. Once you've read the entire list, say the following words, "I am thankful for my passions, and how they lead me to my purpose!" Halfway through the month, review your, "May Nurture Purpose" list to determine if any of the passions on this list should be added to the "Creates Purpose" or "Diminishes Purpose" lists. If so, move them and cross them off your "May Nurture Purpose" list; therefore, making them a welcome part of the other two lists. If you've moved something to "Creates Purpose" list, make sure it gets incorporated into your daily list review. In a similar manner, if you've moved a passion(s) to the "Diminishes Passion" list, release it/them, and thank it/them for showing up and playing a role in your life.

This exercise is designed to assist you in powerfully embracing that your passion and purpose go hand-in-hand! Constantly flexing and working out your passion and purpose muscles will bring you deeper levels of joy and happiness, simply because you are being you. Just as you are, a wonderful gay individual with unique gifts to share with the world.

❦

Where Do You Go When You Feel Like SHIT?

I'd be blowing smoke in places where the sun don't shine if I told you, "It's going to be a cake walk, and easy to stay focused, passionate, and purposeful as you embark on your journey out of the closet and beyond!" And I'd be remiss if I convinced you otherwise. In fact, I'd ask ya to just rip this book to shreds right now, if I was being that blasphemous. But I'm not, so please my dears don't shred these sacred pages. However, I digress. I believe it's humanly impossible to stay completely focused on your passion and purpose in life. Why? Let's not play games. We all know, life gets in the way, no matter how hard we attempt to keep our happy, happy, joy, joy mojo alive! Versus, turning your focus on "I can't do..." instead open the can of "Can do possibilities!" How do you do that? Read on my dears, read on!

Create a folder either on your computer, or in a filing cabinet, labeled

"Read This When You Feel Like SHIT!" If it's an online file, keep links to supportive, inspiring articles and quotes, pictures, etc. within easy, mouse click reach. Also, add downloads of videos, affirmations, or things you've written that keep your own chin up, without doing chin ups! Anything you find that gives you a kick in the pants and gets you out of your slump when you're at your lowest points *coming out* of the closet or in life in general, is fair game. The other alternative is to start a manila folder that you keep filled with articles you've torn out of magazines, quotes you've read, and again things that you've written that give you a lift and help you remember you have a passionate purpose on this earth. Makes no difference how you build your "Read this When You Feel Like SHIT" folder. The key isn't to just build it, but use it, and use it until the edges of the folder are falling apart and splitting at the seams like Lemon-Odd Pop in an 80's Spandex Jazzercise leotard! Doesn't do you a damn bit of good, other than in the moment, if you don't go back, from time to time, and reflect upon what you've built (kind of like Lemon-Odd Pop building her fake layer-by-layer bosoms. Oh boy am I in trouble with that comment. No visits from my Diva fairy tonight while I sleep! Or maybe there will be and I better sleep with one eye open!) However, there are two other suggestions I'd like to offer that are cousins to "Read This When You Feel Like Shit!" They are, "Go There When I Feel Like Shit," and "Be This When I Feel Like Shit!"

"Go There When You Feel Like Shit" requires a little bit of imagination, and can be quite fun. For starters, you should be used to this by now, grab a piece of paper and the writing implement of your choice (pen, pencil, lipstick, mascara, feather quill), and at the top of the page write, "Go There When I Feel Like Shit!" Sitting down, in a comfortable space, close your eyes, and think back to a place you truly loved in your childhood. The ocean, hiking in the forest, Disneyland, grandma's house; bring the memory forward, and write it down on your piece of paper. Continue to write similar fond memories down about places that made you happy, progressing forward in your memories until you arrive at the present day. Hopefully, you'll have a beautiful list of memorable places that have brought you pure joy and an abundance of happiness. Only list happy places. No need to invite negativity into this exercise. Once the list is completed, return to the beginning of the list and write, "I was and always will be me, a gay man/lesbian woman." Write that EXACT same sentence at the end of the list. Why do this? It's a powerful way of embracing your sexuality around the peaceful memories of places you've been and acknowledging you've never been anyone other than the core person you've always been. Completing this list in your own presence, with our own self, allowing yourself to fully let go and be in happiness, which creates an empowering feeling and connection to your inner spirit. The more powerful and remarkable your experiences were, the easier it will be to anchor yourself to favorite places and situations that brought you joy, without the voice of "Oh my God, I was so much better off in my past!"

When you're feeling angry, upset, hopeless, worthless; whatever emotion you're experiencing that's causing you inner turmoil, worry, and pain, just remember to step fully into the mind's eye of that happy place and time and breath into the memory...not harboring in it! Allow it to come to life as if you're actually there, reliving it, once again. Give yourself a minimum of five minutes to be in this beautiful, inspiring memory. Notice how your negative, stressful, energy will try to shift you from this space. Once you been in this space for 5 minutes, if you haven't begun to experience a shift, keep holding the vision of what was joyful and happy from the past. I've found, typically within 10 minutes of fully allowing yourself to embark on this inner journey to the blissful place of a contented past, you'll experience your negative energy begin to dissipate, if not completely to disappear.

The third technique of the "Do this when I feel like SHIT" trio is to "Be This When I Feel Like SHIT!" Some of you might find this third part of the exercise a little bit of a challenge. If it is, give yourself a break. For now, focus your efforts on using one of the first two techniques already covered. If you're ready for a challenge, it's time to do some slow breath work, focus, and quiet your mind! Yes, it's possible to quiet the mind (not completely, but close), so let's ease into the exercise. To start, write down the "Top 10 Feelings You Like To Experience." Don't be shy, don't hold back, immerse yourself in your feelings and go for it. If you like to experience joy, then write it down. Does the sense of freedom produce a natural high? Then it goes on the list. Love the ecstasy of an orgasm (AMEN to that), then make sure ecstasy is put on the list. Be daring, bold, and honest! Don't let your appreciation for ice cream dripping down your chin, or the first ray of sunshine hitting your skin in the morning be left off your list if they tickle your pickle. The goal is to create a list of 10 feelings you absolutely relish, thus the pickle reference! Once the list is complete, the next step is to pause, read each feeling out loud to yourself, then close your eyes and bring the feeling to life as if it is actually occurring in the moment; in other words, "Be that feeling!" If you're having trouble being that feeling, dig deeper until you're immersed in the feeling. When you successfully experience the feeling, either snap your fingers, touch your nose with your index finger, give one of your ears a little tug, or anything that will work as an anchor to bring the feeling alive again in the future. Use the same anchoring technique for all of your "Top 10 Feelings You Like To Experience." Mastering this technique as well as the "Be This When You Feel Like Shit" technique will enable you to bring forth a warm, positive feeling, which is best for addressing the uncomfortable situation you're currently facing in your *coming out* journey. It's a simple technique that I personally found extremely supportive and helpful through the first two years of *coming out* and navigating my divorce. One of the strongest memories that still gets brought to life, when I touch my nose (my anchor move), is the feeling of whisking down Pacific Coast Highway on my bike, ocean breeze in my face, during my very first 70+ mile ride from Newport Beach, California to San Diego, California. To this day, that experience signifies the freedom to be me and accomplishing a goal I never even would have put on my bucket list, prior to *coming out* of the closet. Now, when I'm confronted with feelings of being trapped or buying into my own bullshit that I'm incapable of surmounting an obstacle in my life, I touch my nose, inhale the ocean breeze, and pedal myself towards freedom. I didn't have to load my bike on my bike rack, get in my car, drive 60 miles, to have that experience. I just touched my nose!

All that lovely anchoring and stuff being shared isn't meant to sugar coat the truth. *Coming out* and stepping into your sexuality can feel like pulling yourself out of quicksand, or as if you're climbing Mt. Everest; both of which, I've never done, but hear are hellish to do! Then, add to the *coming out* experience trying to find your passion and purpose in the midst of chaos, and it's enough to drive anyone to the brink of insanity. Instead, trust me, create your "Read this, Go There, Be This When You Feel Like SHIT" toolkit, so that you can face down your Negative Nellies, Nelsons, Nimrods (whatever you call them), that are standing in the way of you living a passionate, purpose filled life outside of the closet. No reason to wallow in that muddy quagmire unless it's in a nice mud bath designed to make your skin silky smooth and your surrounded by Greek Adonis spa attendants to wash the mud away from every crevice of your body! Then wallowing in mud is well worth the price of admission.

Darkness Is Only Scary Until You Turn On The Light!

As a kid, I hated the dark. Not because I thought someone was lurking in the shadows, peering stealthy through my windows, ready to kill, kidnap, or harm me...no, no, no. That's too melodramatic, even for gay old me! Ok, maybe I did have more than a few of those thoughts. Honestly, I was more afraid of the dark because of what I couldn't see. Creaking walls, about to come crashing down, suffocating me as the house settled. Rustling branches that I believed actually weren't branches, but vicious wild animals scampering over the roof of the house, desperately trying to find a way in to come have me for dinner. Footsteps, unattached to any living, breathing human beings. By now, you get the drift, and I bet have some of your own scared of the dark stories to tell. It's ok sugah, we'll keep that our little secret. Hell, Lemon-Odd Pop's afraid of her own eye shadow, or lack thereof! Thank goodness for the sense and sensibility of adulthood that sets in when we grow up, losing the fear of the dark (for most of us), so we can finally say, "How silly is that!" Can I get an Amen?

For that being said, I find it most interesting that a majority of us don't grow out of our fear of the dark. We're still there, roaming around in the darkness, believing in the dank, dark stuff that doesn't exist, until it does. Call it "creating scripts," or "letting our minds run wild," we go to the dark spaces of needing to know, being in control, and fearing outcomes. Nyoshul Khenpo Rinpoche in his beautiful poem, "Rest In Natural Great Peace," refers to it as "This exhausted mind, beaten helplessly by karma and neurotic thought." We all do it, so don't shake your head as if you're better than the rest of us and never experienced this self-imposed darkness we seem to subject ourselves to for no damn good reason! Quite honestly, it's in our human nature and DNA to see the dark and ignore the light. I never quite understood this phenomenon until during my coach-training, a colleague made the observation, "The dark is only scary until you turn on the light!" BAM! That simple explanation had a huge impact on how I saw things in life and I hope you get that too!

Coming out of the closet can be a dark, dank journey. Hello! The same can be said of growing up, taking on the responsibilities of adulthood, having children, losing someone close to you. A myriad of wretched possibilities can drive us into the darkness of life, if we allow the darkness to engulf us. Ironically, we all possess the ability to flip on the light switch, and make that damn darkness go away. As elementary as it may sound, flipping the switch is a powerful truth that sheds light, pun intended, on everything we believe to be dark in our lives. In that vulnerable moment, we realize there's equally as many light switches as there are dark scary places in our life. Then, in that the magical moment, we each step into our power to live by choice, not by circumstance.

One bright Diva (Lemon-Odd Pop) once asked, "Why the fuck don't we just turn on the light when things get dark?" Great advice Lemon-Odd Pop, yet let's be honest. Fears of the unknown, possibility of failing, and not knowing exactly how to get out of the dark, plus a myriad of other reasons, handcuff us to the chair in the dark. Plus, for those of us of the gay persuasion, there's one more excruciating haunt that we face – WE'RE NOT WORTHY! Mind-numbed by societal beliefs, for a majority of our lives we've been told we're not good enough, a freak, and not worthy of *coming out* of the darkness to live our truth. Our families, friends, faith, all in some way planted a seed that all it takes is flipping a light switch to make the darkness of our gayness skitter away. This is an understandably, normative perspective; if you're blinded by the wrong light. Coming through the closet door, there's one light switch, that once switched on, casts its brilliance on the darkness of being gay in a way that no one can take away from you. That is, provided you keep the switch flipped on to being authentically you. You know the one labeled, passionately, purposefully, living your gay truth.

Well beyond the realm of resetting our self-thoughts; beyond the labor of building confidence; above the acceptance of stepping fully into our truth, is a beautiful brilliant land of passionate, purposeful living as a gay person. This understanding was elusive to me as a gay man, until I grasped the importance of "letting go, so life could flow" work that I continue to buttheads with daily, but not nearly as hard as I thought. I discovered as I let go of the wheel of beliefs, anger, fear, and doubts about my sexuality, I ended up being steered down a peaceful, maturing path to be authentically me. A path that wasn't completely focused on the carnal urges of engaging in sex with men. I'd be lying if I said, "Sex and intimacy with men isn't part of who I am." However, the deeper essence of me being who I am led me to a new friendship with authenticity, which in turn led me to deeper levels of intimate, loving, relationships that really got my rocks off.

In this day and age, the word authenticity is thrown around like a beach ball at a concert. That's ok, there's always some new catchy phrase to learn and use like, "OMG, LMAO, and LOL." I say, "Hallelujah" if authenticity is becoming a popular pastime for the human race! Authenticity, sparked by passion, fueled by purposeful living is one hell of an end goal to achieve when you close your eyes at the trails end of this human experience. Surprise, surprise, surprise (Gomer Pyle intonation included)! Who'd have thought that *coming out* of the closet would lead to living a passionate, authentic, purpose filled life? Actually, it's no surprise given the turmoil, confusion, and pile of crappy beliefs that have been thrown on ya! Without being a trite Diva (I leave that role to Lemon-Odd Pop), do ya best to remember there's light at the end of every tunnel.

Here's a simple exercise to turn the light switch on, and to take you out of the darkness of your *coming out*. Whatever darkness is causing havoc in your life, take a deep breath, slow down and ask yourself these three simple questions:

1. Is what I'm experiencing something in my control? If it's not, then let it go!

2. What is it I would rather experience? Be crystal clear in your answer, in order to bring about quicker change in your life.

3. How have my thoughts influenced what's happening?

If you can only see the darkness, you can only experience darkness. Flip the light switch on the situation and suddenly it's lighter!

The difference between light and dark is light and dark. Which do you choose?

If It Feels Good, Do It Again. Kinda Like Sex!

Rather funny how we sometimes forget to repeat the things that make us feel good. However, it's not unusual in the midst of utter chaos, like *coming out* of the closet, to imagine anything could feel good. Call it the contrarian affect, pure blindness to the truth, or forgetting to see the silver lining. There's no damn reason to hold back. Go ahead and say it, "That's the way, un huh I like it, un huh, un huh!" Admit it! As long as what you're doing doesn't maliciously hurt someone else, then do it again. For instance, if you get a feeling of pure freedom saying, "I'm gay," then say it again. Or, if you love the thrill of knowing you inspired others with your *coming out* advice, then share it, over and over, and over again. Nowhere is it written, "Do not share or repeat your happy moments in life!" In fact, not sharing happiness is a crime. (Almost as much of a crime as the Kardashians having another T.V. Reality Show.)

Your joy, happiness, and feeling good are worth repeating. One of the unique ways you can wash, rinse, and repeat your feel good moments is to give yourself full permission to experience them again, and again. Allowing yourself to feel good and experience joy is extremely important as you maneuver through the initial phases of your *coming out* journey. Often, moments of joy, happiness, and contentment hang around us like ornaments on a holiday tree, to only be enjoyed for a brief season, then put away until next year. Don't allow your joyful, happy, content moments to be boxed up and put away. Wear them around your neck to fight off the negativity vampires that try to suck the very life out of you sacrificing your ability to love, love, love on yourself.

It's interesting when you invite joy, happiness, and contentment to hang around, they will! In fact, when you ask self-love to hang out with you, it will too. Taking the time to intimately date and create a deep marriage with yourself – mind, body, and spirit – will enhance the journey of your gay life. By opening up to the vulnerable space of loving yourself, you'll find it much easier to love others as mere human beings, who need love too. This practice enables us to be vulnerable with others and give them space to be themselves as much as we are being ourselves in our new gay skin. Let's do a little love experiment to help anchor this idea. Think about something, or someone you love, that brings you joy, happiness, peace, laughter, whatever feels right to you. Sink right into those feelings, then touch, then feel, then taste, then hear, then see in this moment that you are meant to immerse yourself in a warm, cuddly, love experience. Feels good doesn't it? Now while you're all snuggled up in this feeling, try to be negative, yet keep focused on love and happiness. Love, happiness. Love, happiness. Negative. Love, happiness. Love, happiness. Negative. What's happening? If you're like most people, the ability to bring something negative into your thoughts is nearly impossible as long as you keep focusing on love and happiness.

Therein lie your challenges and your escape tools from negativity. The next time you're faced with a negative thought, situation, or person, either out loud or quietly in your mind, say these words or your own version of a positive affirmation. The key is to include the words love, happiness, joy, peace, and content to anchor you and take you to a higher plane of being:

I am more than this moment and I am love, happiness, joy, peace, and content.

Repeat.

I am more than this moment and I am love, happiness, joy, peace, and content.

Repeat.

I am more than this moment and I am love, happiness, joy, peace, and content.

Continue repeating this affirmation until you return to a calm, peaceful state of being that enables you too rationally with sensible thought, step out of the negative situation and into loving, happy, joyful, peaceful, contented space. Your assignment is to write a simple mantra, no more than 10 words, that you can easily pull out of your back pocket or clutch when you're drowning in negativity and need a life preserver. Use this new lifeline again, and again, and again because it brings you love, happiness, joy, peace, and contentment!

❧

When "P" Meets "P"

Not sure if you've ever noticed, most people can't talk about passion without talking about purpose, and vice versa. Somewhere in the ages of human language, passion and purpose started dating, and became a couple. Now they're blissfully married, and rarely make an appearance without one another. Much like couples that have been together for long periods of time, finishing each other's sentences, there's very little separation between "passion" and "purpose," even though they have very different meanings.

Passion is defined as "any powerful or compelling emotion or feeling." Purpose is defined as "the reason for which something exists or is done, made, or used." However, look what happens when the two definitions become one. Passion and Purpose: "Any powerful or compelling emotion or feeling that is the reason for which something exists or is done, made, or used." Ok, I took creative liberty and added a few extra words to make it flow fabulously. However, Lemon-Odd Pop and I believed my definition is pretty damn close to how most people would describe living with passion and purpose. Your gay life is no different; it's an integral piece of the ensemble of your passionate and purposeful life. Lemon-Odd Pop has two full sections in her closet just for passion and purpose. I wish I was kidding!

Your journey into gay life wasn't by mistake, nor is it a bad joke; it's here for a passionate, purposeful reason. Not everyone's capable of being gay. That in and of itself is a blessing to be cherished. In fact, there's an extra character in front of your DNA, "G." GDNA (Gay DNA) signifies your calling and purpose for being in the human experience in your way. For each of us, the calling and purpose is different, and no one can do it the way you will do it in this life.

Some of us are authors, coaches, therapists, activists, doctors, teachers, artists, you name it: each of us providing our own unique flair of being gay in the world. It's what I loving refer to as "URU." Yes, it's my own little texting language I made up meaning You Are You! It's also a simple reminder that no matter what, URU. If you're flamboyant and the life of the party, then URU. On the other side of the coin, you might be gay and not really concerned who knows about your sexuality. Congratulations, URU too! URU is a means of

a) Accepting yourself just as you are,

b) Helping your true calling find you, and

c) Seeing at the deepest level what love's got to do with everything.

If you doubt that URU is the truth, then I'm challenging you in opening-up your mind and exploring the following.

Accepting yourself just as you are, you're being real, authentic, and honest. In other words, URU is you being real, authentic, and honest. There's no other way for you to be you. Ok, maybe there is, but real, authentic, and honest is still part of URU. Let's look at this from another angle. URU might mean you're shy, ashamed, and disappointed that you're gay. That's ok. In those feelings, URU, being real, authentic, and honest. Doesn't mean you can't change or feel differently. Every second of every moment, URU. Starting to make more sense now? If not, here's one more way to clear up the fog. URU is all you can be in each moment. As soon as that moment is gone, hello, here's a new moment to be URU, and so on, and so on, and so on! You can't escape from URU, no matter how hard you try to quit being URU. Even when you're growing, learning, failing, to be URU. The bottom line is, URU: Love, Embrace, and Accept IT. Hell, if Lemon-Odd Pop can accept that she's a big, beautiful, black diva, who shouldn't squeeze into a lime green, spandex dress, then you should be able to accept that URU.

URU is the diving board that catapults you into a deeper exploration towards your true calling in this life. The moment you break the surface to love, embrace, and accept URU, you've started the ripples of discovering your inner beauty. As you swim under the surface towards your deeper self, passions will come out, swimming along with you, leading you towards your purpose! UAU (You Aren't You) isn't going to get you there! Honesty, vulnerability, and pretending to be someone you're not, is the only way to discover your passion and purpose; therefore, being URU.

Finally, URU helps you answer Tina Turner's heart wrenching question, "What's Love Got To Do With It?" with a resounding, "Everything!" Love's what kept tugging you to come out, even if someone else pushed you into the closet. There's a piece of self-love that's been aching for URU to come forth, out of the closet, and be the authentic URU. Even in the moments when it feels scary, confusing, and uncomfortable to step fully into being URU, trust the fact that URU is massively more powerful than UAU (You ain't you). URU is you loving you enough to be yourself. URU is challenging you not to settle for mediocre living. URU is begging you to respect, care for yourself, and come out of hiding. URU is simply you being the best you, for yourself, for each and every moment of the day!

Passionately, Purposeful LGBT Living Check-in

Answer these questions and complete these exercises before moving forward My Dear!

1. Why am I passionate about living my truth?
2. What is the deep purpose for my *coming out*?
3. Define what passion means to you.
4. Define what purpose means to you.
5. Who is the most passionate person you know and why?
6. Who do you admire that is living their purpose and why?
7. Complete the "...Feel Like #$%*" exercise.
8. Identify "10 Dark Feelings" and what you could do to turn the light switch on to make those feelings go away.

9. Write a short, 10-word mantra that you can say to yourself when you feel in a rut, scared, or hopeless.

10. Finish this sentence, "I am passionate about being (gay) because..." Write the sentence as many times as you like with as many different endings that fit how you feel!

11. Finish this sentence, "My purpose for being (gay) is..." Write the sentence as many times as you like with as many different endings that fit how you feel!

Frankly my dear it's time to move on and make room for the others in your life, on the other side of closet door.

CHAPTER 11

The Other's Side Of The Closet

Up until this juncture, the focus has been on my thoughts, feelings, emotions, experiences, and me as I came through the closet doors. Another piece of this journey has been the coaching chapters where I provided you with insights, advice, and tips for making your journey a little more manageable. If you choose not to take any of that advice, then no harm no foul, just know that I did my best to guide ya. Now, I feel like you're putting a dagger in my heart by ignoring my good intentions. In fact, that wailing you hear is Lemon-Odd Pop crying because she wanted this book to change your life and of course be so popular that it would become a *New York Times Bestseller*, so that she could experience some little spotlight of fame...but of course that's all about her! It's all good. Even if you don't love this book, me, or Lemon-Odd Pop, it's all part of the journey; learning to suck it up, and keep moving along. (Keep your minds out of the gutter, please).

I'm going to throw a little lemon twist into the story and acknowledge how lucky and blessed I am that my life has turned out the way it has, thus far in my gay journey. Even though, I've knocked on my fabulous circa 1800 wood chest from China for good luck, so many times that my knuckles have bled, it hasn't been a solo endeavor, to have arrived at where I consider I have a fairly balanced life. I've been surrounded by a multitude of people who encouraged me, bitch slapped me, yelled at me, held me, and loved me through the darkness of *coming out*. Each of them, in their own way, brought me bright shiny objects of wisdom, sometimes masked as diamonds in the rough, which contributed to me kicking my heels up and loving myself as a gay man. Without people in our lives, or even those who choose to step out of our lives, we can't fully experience the spiritual side of *coming out*. It's just not possible!

My Bedmate, Soulmate, and Confidant Of 13 Years

Some of you are reading this book, seeking guidance, as you recover from being a married "heterosexual," possibly with children, just like I was before I came out of the closet. If so, brother/sistah, "Bully for you for finding yourself, bravely taking a stand, and *coming out*!" You've got Chutzpah (translated means BALLS)! It takes more courage than Lemon-Odd Pop has room in her steamer trunks for her wigs, to step bravely forward to be yourself, turning everyone's lives in your inner circle into a chaotic tornado. No matter how much it may feel like you just left your family in a path of destruction, in the end, your *coming out* is coming from a place of love and will be a win/win for everyone concerned. In fact, you'll probably find you'd be rich if you had a dollar for every time someone says to you, "I can't believe you're..." or "I can't believe you got married, knowing you were gay!"

Yes, you'll get it from all directions, and you'll be remorseful, living with the guilt and shame of living a lie for however many years you lived that lie. Don't kid yourself into thinking, once you're *out* that those feelings skip away down the "no longer an asshole" brick road. Honestly, guilt and shame take every footstep forward with you beyond the closet door until you take away their power. Even once you believe those feelings are diminished, they still have little tentacles suctioned to your unconscious thoughts to remind you every once in a while, what a lying SOB you were. Hopefully, "were" will be the operative word that will be no more... sooner rather than later. More than likely, the person you shared your bed with for the last (INSERT NUMBER OF YEARS), will remind you at the most inopportune times for you and most opportune times for them, what an ASSWIPE you've been for running his/her life. Surprisingly, in those moments of "you suck," reside beautiful seeds of personal growth and hidden joy.

One of the first things my ex-wife said to me after I said, "Frankly My Dear, I'm Gay," was "You cheating SOB," quickly followed by, "Pack your SHIT and get out!" Hey, who could blame her, right? Even so, she'd never spoken to me like that, nor ever even called me a son of a bitch. In the tornado of emotions that were swirling between us, as the life we knew began to unravel, being called a son of a bitch hit me harder than being thrown out of the house. Likewise, finding out I cheated on her, hit her harder than the fact that I was gay. A little known revelation that came up many years later.

Slapped shamefully into my own chaotic reality, I stared the asshole I'd become straight in the face. "What kind of a man wears the loving husband and father mask as if every day were Halloween; in addition, going and turning tricks and treats in the arms of strange men? Who does that?" In the fog of "I just blew it," I saw my own hypocrisy staring me in the face. Me, Mr. Loving Wonderful Husband, throwing judgments helter-skelter at my macho, hetero, co-workers who constantly banged babes on the side, outside the realms of holy matrimony; how was I any different? I sat there all "holier than thou," calling them slime balls, horny little boys pretending to be real conscious, loving, husbands. Now look at me. I didn't even need Lemon-Odd Pop to kick me upside the head with her stiletto to remind me I was just like them. The only difference was that I was a lying, cheating, horny, little gay boy who didn't have the balls to stand up to his own truth. I was truly the definition of HYPOCRITE!

The hurt, heartache, and shattered confidence in love I'd brought upon my wife was immeasurable. It's difficult enough to calculate the devastating, long-term effects of divorce, let alone the sting of your husband leaving you for a man. Tears, bitter words, and her inability to conceive how she would move on was the song stuck in replay in my mind, but didn't listen to at an intuitive level. I was completely wrapped up in me, making me a bigger asshole than I'd ever been in my life. Thank God, even in her pain, she had the strength to slap me out of my self-absorption and taught me the powerful lesson of accountability. Under no terms was she going to let me skate away, go live my "boys will be boys" gay life, and become a "one night a week, every other weekend" father. Not that any of those thoughts ever even crossed my mind. Hearing the "don't cross me asshole" conviction in her voice, told me I better keep my cock and balls out of arms and kick reach if I for any reason were to screw up and bring any more pain down on her. She was woman and she could roar. Someone had met Lemon-Odd Pop and I had no idea how the two of them had got introduced, nor was I going to find out.

My bedmate, soul mate, confidant of 13 years taught me three valuable lessons through our separation, divorce, and in the years following as we mended, to the best of our ability the fences of our relationship to work as a co-parenting family unit.

Lesson #1
The truth may hurt, but lying can kill any hope for healing.

At first, I actually thought we'd never mend the relationship in any way, shape, or form. My trying to overcompensate, being understanding of what she was feeling, just drove the nails of the coffin deeper. I quickly discovered how no one can understand how anyone else feels, it's simply impossible. Steer clear from saying, "I understand how you feel..." with anyone, especially a spouse scorned by "Frankly My Dear, I'm Gay!"

From the moment you drop the nugget of truth regarding your sexuality, a truth that hurts like hell, you MUST, as much as possible, stay in truth of who you are, respect the feelings of others, and finally, give them space to process their form of healing and mending.

✂

Lesson #2
Divulge Only What Is Necessary. You're Not Lying!

Even when questioned about any myriad of details concerning when, why, how, etc. you "became gay," or if you've acted upon it, provide no more information than is necessary. I realize in Lesson #1, I encouraged truthfulness. Here's the caveat. It's not uncommon for a spouse to want to know, "Who are you messing around with now?" or "Why were you late, did you have somebody to hook-up with?" Sometimes the scorned partner will ask for information that they really don't want to hear, even though they inquire. This happened on numerous occasions until I learned the valuable lesson of asking, "Do you really want to hear the answer?" Too many painful faces, with tears flowing followed those discussions when truth was shared. A pained and hurt spouse really may not want to hear the truthful answers. They just haven't figured out any other way to connect and disconnect, so that they can let go and move on. Breathe easy and "Don't be nice, be real." That's a great book, by the way. Another great one is "Fierce Conversations." Highly suggest getting both of those books, reading them, and taking them out of the closet with ya.

✂

Lesson #3
Responsibility is a two-way street.

The fact that we were parents never left a doubt that even divorced, we would both be responsible for our two precious daughters. Yet, as my little gay boy came out to play, no longer locked in the closet waiting to rock his ass away at the gay club, there were times I forgot to be a responsible adult to and for my ex-wife and kids. I never forget to pick the kids up, or was late paying child support, or alimony. That's just not my style. The lack of responsibility was more a lesson in "zip-it." Enthusiastic and over joyed by the discovery of my newfound self, and newly found freedom, I'd often have diarrhea of the mouth when talking to my ex. Why the hell did I think she cared about where I went with this guy, or who I was seeing on Saturday night? I was not being responsible to be respectful! She was no longer my confidant. Those shoes would have to be filled by someone else in my life. The same would hold true for her in her post-divorce world. I don't need to hear it from her either other than if it is something that affects our children.

Regardless of the financial strife, verbal digs, inner pain, unintentional suffering fear of the future, and wishing it weren't true, that we both experienced as we dismantled a 13 year marriage, my ex-wife gave me a gift that I'm so blessed to have, a relationship with our children. Many gay men and lesbian women sacrifice this part of their lives when they come out, either out of choice or force. Had it not been for our mutual determination, that no way, no how was I going to go skate merrily off into gay la la land, I don't believe we would have mended the fences of our civil relationship as strongly as we have. My intentions were never to let anyone take my kids from me because of my sexual orientation. I was their father, plain and simple. However, nothing says power like a woman hell bent and determined on ensuring her children have a relationship with their father. That was the first sign and glimmer of hope I saw that "Yes," we can heal, even from the darkest moments in the tornados of life. I appreciate my ex for being a stubborn rock, forcing me to keep a level head, and never forgetting the power of family in those early days.

�֎

Spawn Of Their Loins

Parents. We're a supernatural, over-bearing, ever-knowing, loving and well-intentioned breed for the most part. Now that I'm a parent, I get it. Did you hear that Mom and Dad? I get it! I also now see my own shit in brilliant Technicolor playing out on the reality TV show of my life. There's a haunting, cynical laughter, continuously playing on repeat, "I told you that you'd be like your parents, I told you that you'd be like your parents!" AGGGGGHHHHHH! Ok, maybe I'm not exactly like my parents, but close enough to justify my need for a 400 bottle wine collection, which constantly needs replenishing.

Mom and Dad were supportive; in the best way they knew how to be, given what they had to work with in their parent-training course. After all, they'd been through this once when I was 19. Remember they sent me to restorative counseling with the hunky pastor. Every time I say that, I feel like I've committed a sin. It's just that he was so damn hot. Sorry, got off track. Any who. Mom and Dad did what most parents do, stepped into their own values, drawn from their own socialization, and stood their ground because they're the parents. And parents do what's good for their child. God love em! However, what's good for your child is not always what's best for your child. Their ability to stand their ground, draw their line in the sand, also taught me how to stand my ground, draw my own line in the sand, hold my own in arguments, and powerfully defend my values and beliefs about being gay. I'M GAY, PLAIN AND SIMPLY GAY! And boy howdy, did I ever dig into the sand on that one! Thanks, Mom and Dad, for gracing me with the talent to dig in and hold to my values and beliefs, a gift none of us should ever sacrifice.

Many closet busters face a journey with their parents and family members fraught with ugliness, veiled threats, acid words, and even months of no communication. Ironically those experiences taught me the invaluable lessons of how to be better with my parents and to be a better parent:

1. **No one's ever right.** Everyone's entitled to his or her position. Right belongs to recipes, scientific formulas, brain surgery, and directions for getting you from point "A" to point "B." Even then, is anything every 100% right?

2. **Flexibility doesn't cost you your values.** If you flex and give, doesn't mean you're not aligned in your values. It simply means you've added a new dimension to a value.

3. **Fear based beliefs hold no water.** Of course, this lesson came from the almighty, "What the bible says..." discussions. Sorry God, not blaspheming your book. Yet, what I learned in these shouting matches, which in and of themselves were so ridiculous, was that FEAR, even fear of standing up for your FAITH is still FEAR of what you don't know and understand. And, how much are you in your faith if you have to yell and scream it at someone? What's up with that?

4. **I closed "My way, or the highway" thinking permanently.** I regret, even to this day, when my parents and I fall into the trap of "It's my way, or no way." That's a surefire way to ensure nothing gets done and no one gets heard. In fact, frickin' love flies out the damn window when we were in this space. This is no way to live. I said good-bye to this type of thinking, although it still creeps up from time-to-time when Lemon-Odd Pop is alive and well.

5. **Differences may prevail, but at the heart so does love.** We, my parents and I, still struggle with this one from time to time; however, we have moved to a fun little space in the playground of life where gays and heterosexuals play nicely together. Through it all, they never stopped loving my daughters, my ex-wife, my husband, and me. They love the best way they know how to, as do I. The key ingredient to remember here is "the best way they know how." I'm the same as they are. I love them "the best way I know how." At the end of the day, that's all anyone can ask. Well, not really, we could ask them to get over their SHIT and just get that gay is gay, and

even the American Psychology Association can see it as "it is what it is." However, they are who they are and that's just the way some people are!

Regardless of our differences, that still exist today, I honor my parents to the best of my abilities, knowing they're like a spouse, boyfriend, girlfriend, child, etc. If you spend all your time trying to change them, then you'll have no time left to enjoy life, to be with people you don't need to change, and little room left to work on being the best possible you. No matter what may be happening with your parents, family, friends, co-workers, through this monumental coming out journey, realize one thing, and one thing only. Whatever you're experiencing is being given to you because it's what you are meant to experience and grow from. Same goes for those people in your *coming out* journey. Oh, and one other tidbit. If you're lucky enough, one-day your Mom will text and call your partner/husband/spouse more than she does you. That's when she's more his problem than yours. LMAO!

Relating To Relations.

I'm going to be transparent and honest. I'm a family guy, and I'm just not an extended family guy. God, I hope some of my extended family isn't reading this, and Lord, I hope some of my extended family is reading this, so they'll understand why I don't have a damn thing to do with them any longer.

Before we jump into the extended family rhetoric, I want to acknowledge my brother. At my age, it's getting harder and harder to recognize people without my glasses, let alone acknowledge them. LMAO! Seriously, my brother and I went through a phase, right after I came out, that... well let's just say wasn't pretty. We both were contending with our shit lives. Intermingling his crap, with my poop, sprinkled with a touch of brotherly love and rivalry was a true recipe for disaster. No matter how we stirred the pot, it wasn't the right time for either of us to be giving each other advice, or support because we were so screwed up. We were the blind, leading the blind, both searching for life preservers. What a joke we were, but thank God we survived and both woke up!

In the midst of the jokes, that had become our mutually exclusive lives, I sunk into my deepest fear of possibly losing everything I cared about. My relationship with Mom and Dad was temporarily on hiatus. Now, I was also losing what little relationship I had with my brother. All I had left were my "See ya tomorrow!" work relationships; my "I get you because my husband was gay too and came out of the closet" therapist, a few gay friends, and thank goodness a somewhat accepting ex-wife and my loving kids. My worst nightmare had come to life in the light of day. My family had turned their back on me because I was gay. Wait, that isn't exactly true, and it probably won't be for you either, if you fully absorb the next sentence. My family had chosen not to embrace my "lifestyle" (God, I hate that word when referring to being gay).

It's an ironic "Wake the Fuck Up" moment when you understand that people accept your sexuality on their terms. And guess what? You get to do the same! You get to accept their response, to your sexuality, on your terms. Why? Because every moment of every blessed day that we've been given to live on this earth as our authentic self, we get to choose how we react to everything we've been handed, including how people accept our sexuality. Can I get an AMEN? By drinking this thought process into your being, in the same way, you do a loving glass full of 2010 St. Clement Chardonnay, all forms of judgment begin to dissipate. And, if the judgments don't run away, drink more wine! What's interesting is when you just accept others on their terms and let it be, there's no need for stress, angst, and worry. It's just what is and nothing more.

Now, back to the extended family, and why my *coming out* had nothing to do with any of them. The biggest reason my *coming out* didn't go into the family history books under "shocking tales," was because I hadn't interacted with most of the extended family with any regularity for the last 20 years of my life. In fact, if you were to ask me where most of my aunts, uncles, and cousins live, I couldn't tell you. I'd be guessing where they were on the planet, based on tuned out conversations I've had with my parents about the rest of the family. Call me an asshole for being this way with extended family, but I am who I am. For me, I've found that extended families fall into one of three buckets.

Bucket #1 - They stay connected, have big reunions, and look forward to going to them and are glad when they're over.

Bucket #2 - They stay connected, have big reunions, and dread going to them.

Bucket #3 – They stay connected while the kids are growing up, and then everyone goes their separate ways only to get back together to have awkward conversations at weddings and funerals.

Kind of funny how the buckets somewhat parallel my life. Bucket #1 was kind of like trying to play it straight. I tried to connect to it, looked forward to making everyone feel comfortable, but was always glad when I could retreat back to the quiet of my dual life, just me, the wife, and kids. Bucket #2 is when things began to unravel. I dreaded being around family, showed up, but began to show up more and more as a miserable, unhappy, bitter guy, spoiling the fun for everyone. I hated going to the family stuff, and dreaded returning to my hidden secret life. Now, I'm kind of in, kind of out, of Bucket #3. Still connected to some family, mostly parents and brother, and my husband's family, love showing up for some of the events, but still at times have awkward moments of "How do I do this now that I'm out?" Actually, I know how I did this, they don't, and that's where it gets wonky. However, it's just part of the journey, so climb on board and take the ride.

Regardless of my connections to family, the one thing I've learned, and continue to learn, is family will surprise the shit out of you when you least expect it, especially when you're gay. Each time they blow me away, I learn more about them, the human condition, and myself. When we're in our human state of being, tremendous opportunities to discover others, and our self abound, if we just open our eyes to the beauty of inner exploration.

Everyone in my life, from Mom and Dad, my brother, extended family, my late grandparents, and especially my gay uncle Wil had a huge impact on me, as a guide to being the man I am today. However, the four relationships that have taught me the most about being a gay man, gay father, husband, partner, and human being are my nuclear family – my daughters, my husband, and my ex-wife. Each of them, for the most part, takes me just as I am and kicks me in the ass when I need it, just like Lemon-Odd Pop. Without them, I wouldn't experience emotions that stop me in my tracks. Without them I wouldn't question if I could do better. Without them, I wouldn't stretch to push myself beyond the self-imposed limits I place on myself. You see without them, I wouldn't be here today, sharing my insights, advice, trials, challenges, and learning's that I've been blessed to experience as I came out of the closet and said, "Frankly My Dear, I'm Gay!"

In your own world, inner circle, nuclear, and extended family, you're going to encounter some of your biggest fans. On the flip side (and there's always a flip side), you're going to go head to head with some real assholes. That's a fair warning. I encourage you, in your best possible way, to see the beauty in the experience you've been given, even if it feels like a crock of shit wrapped up in glittery wrapping paper. Don't be detoured or distracted by the challenges. Instead, jump right in and ask one question, "What am I supposed to be learning from this experience that will enhance my life for the future?" It's there sugah, just waiting for you to see it in all its brilliance. Once discovered, wear that lesson like a drag queen dons her wig – head held high, not a hair out of place, the crowning touch on a fabulous outfit that even Michelle Bachmann wishes she could pull off! LOL.

Coming out is your spiritual moment to be you. Those who challenge your spirit are simply there to ensure you dig deeper, and embrace the spiritual wonder of being gay as only you can be!

CHAPTER 12

Wash, Rinse, And Repeat

Ironically, a funny thing happens on the way to *coming out*. You trip out of the closet, all excited and ready to be yourself, ready to wave the rainbow flag like nobody's business; ok, some of us do, others don't, and suddenly find you're *coming out* seems to be more other people's business than your own. Now don't get frightened, or defensive. That kind of behavior simply isn't becoming to someone *coming out* of the closet. The reality of this *coming out* process is, you ready for this, a life-long journey! Um hum!

It starts with you. The fact that you've picked up this book and are reading it means you've gotten to, pretty darn close to, or are just beyond the juncture of *coming out* to yourself! If you haven't yet come out to yourself, then just keep exploring, finish the book, and start reading it again, if necessary. It's kind of like sex. The more you practice being your gay self, the easier it becomes to be your authentic self. The orgasm of the whole *coming out* process is being you in your own skin! I know that may not sound like an earth shattering mind-blowing orgasm, but trust me it will be. The moment you actually say to yourself, "I'm gay," you'll tingle, shudder, smile, and feel ecstatic. Immediately following those feelings, you'll wish you'd worn a diaper because you might have just messed your pants out of fear. Perfectly normal; totally understandable. Joy and fear often rendezvous in a weird way because they can, and that's how they really screw with us.

In this state of mind you're encouraged to fully trust yourself to be yourself, sooner rather than later. Sooner because once you trust yourself that URU (remember that lesson), then it takes the edge off of telling someone else URU. Here's a few recommendations to get comfy making URU a part of the wash, rinse, and repeat cycle of your life:

1. Practice saying to yourself, "I am _____ and this makes me unique and worth loving even more." Practice this in various forms – gay, homosexual, and me - and start to add "Why it makes you unique" to the dialogue. Take as much time and practice with this as needed.

2. Make a list of 10 people you feel you can trust beyond a shadow of a doubt. These people can be, but may not be your family, or closest friends. They could be casual acquaintances.

3. Once the list is complete, determine why it is important for you to share the truth about your sexual orientation with these individuals. How would sharing with them make you feel? What would you experience by sharing your truth with them? Why is it important that they know about this aspect of your life?

4. Drawing from your "I am _____ and this makes me unique and worth loving statements," try to find the right statements that make it easier for you to share with the list of people in task #2.

5. In addition to task #3, also write down why you are sharing this part of yourself with each of these individuals in task #2. You will want to share this piece of information with them as well, so that they have a deeper understanding of why it's important to you to share this intimate side of yourself with them.

6. When the time is right, and you'll know when it is, share your truth with each person. Also, add anything else to the formula that makes sense for you, and that might make your share more meaningful to the person that you are opening up to.

There you have it. 6 little tasks to get you out of the closet. Wait! Hold your horses! This is only the beginning of wash, rinse, and repeat cycle! So, let's move on!

Let's Start From The Very Beginning...
It's A Very Good Place To Start!

Julie Andrews was quite right when she doled out her characters "start from the very beginning" and "spoonful of sugar" wisdoms as Maria and Mary Poppins. It makes sense to add a little sugar to each step of your *coming out* process, and to start at the very beginning too. Let me explain.

The "spoonful of sugar" concept is simply changing your negative thoughts regarding what you anticipate might happen each time you come out to someone. Instead, swallow a sugary pill of positive thinking, reset your mindset about *coming out*, and go boldly forward. Here's an example: imagine putting a big ol' smile on your face before you tell someone, "Hey, I have something I want to share with you... I'm gay!" Now, imagine the same scenario, only with a frown on your face and a "woe is me attitude." What's the difference between the two scenarios? How did each make you feel? Which one gave you the most confidence? Try it one more time, with the smile, the positive attitude, and a nice tall stance. "Hey. I've something I want to share with you... I'm gay!" Notice a difference? Feel your power? Typically your positive attitude, strong stature, and belief in yourself are the real game changer in having powerful, authentic conversations about your sexuality, or anything else for that matter.

Now let's talk about that "starting at the very beginning" piece. In the first few chapters of this book, a lot was shared about changing your thoughts, re-tweaking your own perspective of what it means to be gay, and embracing what is for what is! The same stuff is going to be coming up for whomever you're sharing your truth. They're going to need time to examine their own thoughts about you, how they feel about being a part of your life now that they've been given new information to work with. Probably the biggest part of their exploration will be examining their own value and belief systems to see where everything fits together under the headlines of gay, homosexual, and relationships. Like you, they'll need time, space, and patience, so give it to them. And, no it wouldn't be a good idea to hand them a rainbow flag the moment you smile and tell them "I'm Gay," unless they're gay. If they are, they might hand you a rainbow flag, bracelet, necklace, or t-shirt to welcome you to the family.

The really cool part about mastering the wash, rinse, and repeat process is it's like knowing grandma's secret recipe for her rum butter, chocolate cake, with raspberry vanilla frosting. Once you know the secret, you can use it over and over again in so many situations. Of course, I'd never share my grandma's recipe, that'd be a BIATCH slap to her legacy. However, I will share a five-step formula for helping anyone "come out," even if they are not *coming out* the closet. Yes, even heterosexuals have their own funky closets to come out of too. The formulas very simple, and you'll start to recognize some of what you've already learned.

» **Step 1:** Reset the mindset

» **Step 2:** Build courageous confidence

» **Step 3:** Embrace the truth

» **Step 4:** Uncover the passion

» **Step 5:** Live with purpose

That's it, 5 straight forward steps. Regardless of who they are, or whatever their *coming out* journey, everyone will go through these stages. For example, let's talk about your parents because it's always fun (most the time) to talk about Mumsie and Poopsie! Let's say, they aren't crazy about your "I'm gay," revelation. Most parents aren't, even if they eventually become supportive. Let's go through the steps using Mumsie and Poopsie, as an example, shall we?

1. **Reset the mindset**. For starters, they'll be examining their own belief systems, feelings, fears, etc. Like you, they're probably going to go deep into themselves to figure out on the bell curve of their belief system is where the new you lands for them. Once they begin to unravel and repackage their thoughts, feeling, emotions, beliefs, they will start to show their true self. For some, this inner delving happens in a Nano second and they know exactly where they stand. For others, it will take time.

2. **Build courageous confidence.** Whether they agree with you or not, they're stepping into their own version of building courageous confidence to share their opinions and beliefs with you, as well as gaining confidence to say they have a gay family member. This often leads to disagreements, arguments, and words that kill. At this juncture, you also have the great opportunity to stand solidly in your own courageous confidence, as will they. This is a great place to start uncovering middle ground where you can work together, be a family unit with new terms of agreement, or agree to disagree like respectful adults. Hurtful as it may be to stand in separate corners for now, and maybe for the rest of your life, this may be as good as it gets. Accept it, roll forward to the best of your ability, and keep leaning into your own courageous confidence.

3. **Embrace the truth**. At this pinnacle, on both sides of the equation, each of you is starting to embrace a new truth. You're accepting your gay truth; your family and friends are accepting their gay truth as being someone intimately connected to someone gay. The truth that you each face is identical, in so many ways. It's the intricacies of the "what" that truth is, and "how" that truth is embraced that becomes the key differentiator. Here's the powerful piece about truth

that often gets missed, leading to strife, fights, and things being said that may be regretted later. "Each person is doing the best they can, with the abilities they have, in each and every moment they've been given." All any of us can do is to be our best, with the knowledge we have, in the moment we have. This is such a powerful little tidbit, even Lemon-Odd Pop says, "Hallelujah!" Don't forget, there are many shades of truth that can blossom once we give others and ourselves the space to be in truth.

4. **Uncover the passion.** Passion is one of those funky words that we all seem to seek, yet is often elusive. I challenge you, and those around you, to find your passion in the journey "out of the closet," and let it inspire you and support you from a position of love. You, your family, and friends are each going to be passionate about their individual views toward sexual orientation! Embrace your passion, and recognize that your parents and anyone else that you've shared your truth with, will be passionate about their unique position as well. Passion inspires all of us to live our best lives, even if it means we don't always agree with others perspectives; that's part of the passion driver, allowing others to be passionate about their lives, while we're being passionate about ours. Passion is just one more log on the fire of life that keeps life exciting and enables each of us to stay motivated to live our truth!

5. **Live with purpose.** The amazing thing about passion is it's a sibling of purpose, as we've already discussed. I've yet to see anyone who's discovered their purpose without first having passion, and vice versa. The two hold hands every step of the way. In this moment as you're feeling deeply passionate about who you are, you will also discover your purpose begins to come alive and clear as well, in ways that you've never thought possible. This is happening for your parents, or anyone else you've come clean with about your sexual orientation. Good or bad, there's a purpose to their reaction and the stance that they've taken regarding your sexual truth –

for you and for them. Embrace the fact that there is a purpose in everything that comes into your life. Instead of saying "There's a reason for everything," change the dialogue to "There's a purpose for everything!"

From this simple and quick run through of wash, rinse, and repeat principles shared thus far, hopefully, you can begin to see the parallels between you're journey out of the closet, and the journey others in your inner circle are also taking right alongside you out of the closet.

⚜

Wash Cycle Revisited

Laundry is a weekly task, (unless you're a college student, then it's a monthly) or when you go home, so mom can do it. We all wear clothes (even nudists). Clothes get dirty, need to be cleaned, and we wash them. In fact, we wash, rinse, dry, wear, and repeat. I know; "Why am I telling you this?" It's not that I think you're stupid, so please take no offense. I'm metaphorically driving the point that *coming out* is similar to doing the laundry! Hiding the truth of your sexuality is your dirty laundry until you wash it out. Scrubbing, treating stains, letting it soak, it's all the same in laundry and *coming out*!

For starters, at some point, maybe even now, you felt that being gay is dirty, yucky, and wrong; whatever the feeling that made you hide yourself from your truth, and that truth, from everyone else! Trust me, you're not the first, nor will you be the last to have those feelings and want to hide. Quite honestly, you view yourself as dirty laundry, which means it's time to begin the cleanup. Before you can step into the "wash cycle," you've got to find all the dirty parts of being you in your gay self. In other words, find the stains. There's no way to get the stain out until you find it, know what it is, and figure out the right way to remove it. Right? Think of it as Tide for the soul! Let's revisit some of the most common stains about *coming out* and being gay:

» Your sexuality is a sickness

» Homosexuality conflicts with your religious beliefs

» Being gay will lead to rejection by family and friends

» You'll never be accepted in the gay community

» Shame and guilt will be with you for the rest of your life

A whole book could be written entitled "The Stains Of Being Gay and Home Remedies to remove them!" What's most important to realize, the stains about being gay can be removed. Patience, perseverance, and self-love are just a few of the stain treatments utilized to remove the ugly spots that tarnish your beliefs about your sexual orientation. You can also rub out the gay blemishes with confidence, acceptance, honesty, integrity, and respect. Regardless of the annoying stain that's making you feel dirty because you're gay, there's always a gay hotshot spot remover, you can use. You've just got to get curious and uncover the stain remover that fits for you!

Once the spots are treated, it's time to wash up! Go ahead. Jump into the wash cycle, allow the waters of new beliefs to wash over those stains, and rinse them away and out of your thoughts. Continue to scrub and scour each time those ugly stains creep up on the authentic, unique essence of you being you. Remember, there's nothing that has to stain you for life, unless you allow it to.

The wash cycle also provides deep inner cleansing that impacts other areas of your life. For instance, if you wash away the belief that no one will accept you as a gay individual in your work environment, then you'll probably relax more at work and just let it be without trying so hard to hide it. Now, don't take that last sentence the wrong way. I'm not advocating you come out or don't come out at work. As of the writing of this book, in a majority of states in the United States, you can still be fired for being gay. My little secret stain removal about being out at work is meant to support and relax you about your sexual orientation and being out at work in a way that works for you! Be yourself, and know that you are fine just as you are, even at work. Releasing the stress around your "outness" can help you be more productive, which in turn could lead to a potential promotion, and possibly making more money. Just sayin'! Anything is possible when we allow the truth of who we are to wash over us, scrubbing and removing all the stains of false thoughts and beliefs we've created about being gay!

One of the core super soaps to add to the "wash cycle revisited" is to continually Reset Your Mindset! No, this doesn't require a magical key, or using a special phone app, although both would be handy; it simply requires having an open mind to carry you forward through the various stains ahead. The journey out beyond the closet doors always presents opportunities to re-think your thoughts. Each time your thoughts get scrubbed clean of stains, your mindset is reset and you can move forward in monumental ways, using your gay super powers... no cape required!

�֎

Rinse Cycle Revisited

Wash. Rinse. Similar, yet different, as they both involve water... or do they? It's both. Realistically, water is the common wet thread in both washing and rinsing. However, in the *coming out* journey, I'm throwing down the bedazzled, bejeweled gauntlet to say that rinsing can take on any form that cleanses away the doubts, fears, and anxieties of being yourself in your gay skin. Mediation, self-help, working with a life coach, opening up to a therapist; each in its own way is part of the rinse cycle. The moments of self-discovery enable you to identify the stains, treat as needed, scrub and wash to loosen them up, and rinse away.

For the purpose of Frankly My Dear, I'm Gay, rinsing is about creating courageous confidence to be yourself and embrace your sexual truth. Allowing yourself to constantly rinse your thoughts and beliefs with confidence and truth, it's helps to prevent stains from creating long-lasting blemishes on your perception of self. If that thinking is to airy-fairy for you, then try this angle. If you're filled with self-confidence and truth, how can you possibly get stained? You can't unless you allow other people to tarnish you with the stains of false beliefs about yourself. Stains only blemish your character, and Lemon-Odd Pop's face after too much sugar, if we buy into others B.S. (Bogus Scripts) about us!

The *coming out* rinse cycle is specifically designed to rid any remnants of stains from your new way of being in the world. Powerful rinse additives of confidence and truth prevents B.S. from infiltrating your thoughts, provided that you add them to the "dirty laundry" of our *coming out*! To overcome the belief that *coming out* is a dirty journey, fraught (big word for filled) with lifelong stains, we just need to douse ourselves in the cool rinse waters of confidence and truth.

The rinse cycle, like the wash cycle, will be repeated over, and over and over again throughout our lives, whether we're *coming out,* or in other areas of everyday life. Surprise, surprise, while we never stop *coming out,* and we also never stop being challenged by other aspects of life that are completely unrelated to our sexual orientation or *coming out.* I'm sure you grasp this concept. And yet, I felt compelled to throw in the reminder that *coming out* and living life are not mutually exclusive because they're both integral pieces of the master plan! You can't have one without the other! Like passion and purpose (hint, hint).

In addition to confidence and truth, there are unlimited other possibilities to rinse out during your *coming out* journey and life. The entire purpose of the wash, rinse, and repeat cycle is to ensure you stay on course, through life, *coming out,* and being authentically you utilizing the insights, tips, and tricks you've learned in this book and through other powerful resources, in order to be at peace and comfortable in your own skin.

Repeat Cycle Revisited

Quite honestly, not that I think this needs repeating, once you got the goods on wash and rinse, then it's an "in your face" no-brainer, to

"Repeat." Right? After all, why wouldn't you "repeat" a process or formula that's working? If it's not working, go back to washing and rinsing until you feel fresh as a sunray on a spring morning. Sorry, just had to wax eloquently for the moment. Now, back to our regularly scheduled discussion about "The Repeat Cycle."

One of the simplest reasons to repeat things that work are to (ready for it) have passion embrace the purpose that they serve in your life, and the life of others. Passion and purpose can be funky words that can get in the way of accomplishing what you set out to achieve. "I don't feel passionate about..." or "I don't see the purpose in..." Regardless of which of the "P" word gets in your way, both either propel you forward, or get you stuck in the mud. Unless, you realize that passion and purpose are the driving inspirations that keep you washing, rinsing, and repeating.

Passion and purpose for being you, as only you can be in this world, as a gay individual, keeps you focused, and spiritually alive. It's your spirit that guides you to be passionate about a career that's exciting. The same applies to living without shame for being gay. Your spirit guides you to love, accept, and wrap yourself up in self-love as a gay person. Likewise, purpose grounds you, building a firm foundation of knowing, "Yep, this feels right and all signs point to this being my intended life path." You've probably heard it said numerous times, "No one would choose to be gay." I tend to agree and disagree. If the choice around being gay had no quantifiable purpose, then I agree, why would I choose to be gay? Yet, when I twist the thought, and look at it from a different perspective that I have a purpose for being gay, then there's a good possibility I would choose to be gay. I know being gay is not a choice, and I feel blessed to view my sexuality from this vantage point because I know it serves a purpose.

From my perspective, the purpose of being gay is to be another reflection of humanity. I know, it's kind of hard to think in those terms, isn't it? We've been conditioned to see homosexuality as "Right vs. Wrong," and to step outside of those bounds is like walking out of the house naked in a snowstorm. Blinding and chilling! However, I believe our purpose is to be a beacon of diversity. A healing ointment on the wounds of human bigotry, a solace in the storm of hatred for those who have yet to find their own strength to be themselves just as they are in their sexual orientation. I'd invite you to also become that same type of beacon once you are out of the closet.

Passion and purpose have an innate ability to kick the crap out of 'self-doubts,' and "What if's..." provided we're not blinded by the lights of "not good enough!" You're good enough, if you have passion. You're good enough, if you have purpose. Besides, who dictates whether you're good enough? Nobody, unless you let them reset your mindset, burst your courageous confidence, and you stop embracing your truth, prevent your passions from coming alive, and let them convince you that your life has no purpose!

It's your spirit that guides a passionate career that's satisfying, and an ability to live without shame as a member of the LGBT community. Likewise, purpose is grounding you and providing the foundation for knowing, "Yep, this feels right and all signs point to this is my path." You've probably heard it said numerous times, "No one would choose to be LGBT." Like I said before, if the choice around being LGBT had no quantifiable purpose, then I agree, why would I choose to be LGBT? Yet, when I twist the thought and look at it from the perspective that I have a purpose as an LGBT individual, I would choose to be LGBT. I know it's not a choice, and I feel blessed to believe I'm here for a purpose.

I believe the purpose of being an LGBT individual is to be a reflective mirror of the human condition, no right or wrong. I know it's kind of hard to think that way isn't it? We've been so conditioned to see "Right vs. Wrong," to step outside those bounds is like walking out of the house naked in a snowstorm. Blinding and chilling! However, what if our purpose is to be a beacon of diversity, a healing ointment on the wounds of human bigotry, and a solace in the storm for those who have yet to find their strength to be themselves just as they are regardless of sexual orientation.

Go ahead! Get out that unique brand "You" detergent, start spraying the "Get Rid Of Those Thoughts," spot remover on the stains of false beliefs, and start scrubbing. Even though doing laundry isn't the funest chore, having dirty laundry ain't no picnic in the park either! Of course, a picnic in the park with Lemon-Odd Pop is like preparing for a two-week vacation, but again I digress! Wash, rinse, and repeat for a lifetime of *coming out*, being you, and living your truth with passion and powerful purpose.

CHAPTER 13

Awake, Aware, Alive

N o more snoozing. There's more than enough living to make up for now that you've come out of the haze that was your life. All was not for naught along your journey thus far, even though, at times, you may have felt you wasted a lifetime hiding behind a mask, living a dual existence. Without the living you've done, there'd be no lessons to be learned; lessons that will serve you well, as you venture forth into the next chapter of your life, beyond the closet door.

The unknown of what lies ahead, varies for each of us, on our own particular journeys. Yet, many similarities will be uncovered as you begin to explore the new gay circles with others who share your experience. In fact, having your own gay inner circle is an invaluable asset, and one you shouldn't do without, provided you step out and let yourself be found by a gay inner circle. As crazy as it may sound, some people avoid or feel they can't find their gay posse, so to speak. For some, maybe even you, seeking a gay group for support, could bring up lingering fears of rejection, preventing or slowing down the ability to move forward into your new gay life. On the flip side, you might be one who will immediately be welcomed into a new gay crew, and reject them because they don't fit your mold of "gayness." Caution: Be wary of harsh, judgments in either direction about adopting a gay support system and allow the experiences to unfold. One of the keys to moving forward is to surround yourself with a solid support group that keeps you focused on the important stuff like looking fabulous, drinking the proper gay cocktails, and knowing all the "A-List" places to see and be seen. I'm Kidding! That's Lemon-Odd Pop speaking and once again doling out her Diva wisdom about being gay. Nothing wrong with any of those things, just not necessarily the most important stuff to focus on right out of the closet. Honestly, without the right focus and support you may find yourself, "Out, but not proud!" One of the best ways to step fully into you, once you've *come out*, is to be fully awake in your truth, swearing never to fall asleep again behind the wheel of mediocre living.

✂

Awake Behind The Wheel of Your Gay Life.

If you've ever been driving a car and unexpectedly found yourself a block, two, or three down the road with no conscious memory of how you got there, then you've been awake behind the wheel without judgments as to what you've been doing. It's a pretty cool state of being, even if it seems scary to be driving unconsciously, so to speak. Yet, for years, you have been driving unconsciously through life consciously knowing you weren't being your true self, like most of us who've hidden in the closet. The *coming out* alarm clock awakens you from an unconscious deep nightmare of who you think you are by shaking you out the slumber of avoiding your authentic gay self, and awakening you into your gay skin, which is just another aspect of who you are, not your entire being.

You'll know you're wholly awake in your sexual energy, when simply being who you are requires no apologies, shame, or justification. You may be scratching your head and wondering, "How long does this take to get that comfortable and awake in your sexual self?" Honestly, it happens at a different pace for everyone, and a lot depends on your own outlook regarding your sexuality. To be a fully-awakened individual who's comfortable in his or her own sexual identity first requires identifying what being fully comfortable in your own sexual identity means to you, and only you. Dialing into that clarity enables you to put the plays in motion to reach the end goal. How you get there, and the amount of time it takes is up to you, and the circumstances you face! There's one other factor more powerful than any other for kicking your butt into this awakened state of being your most authentic self. **CHANGE YOUR THOUGHTS.**

If you BELIEVE your thoughts, you BEHAVE your thoughts. Every time you buy into your thoughts, you manifest your thoughts into reality. This trifecta - thoughts, feelings, behaviors – are the chauffers driving your destiny for living a fulfilled, rich life. Of the 70,000+ thoughts we have a day (shocking, isn't it?), we actually have the capacity to change them as they show up, with practice. Ok, maybe not every thought can be changed, nor needs to be changed. Yet, think of the immense power you harness by merely changing thoughts that cause you to believe "you're not good enough, you can't do something, or shouldn't do something because it's not what someone else would do." Egads! Those three thoughts alone take more energy than pulling Lemon-Odd Pop away from the lunch buffet at Hometown Buffet! Your awakened state of you being you is adorned in honesty, truth, acceptance, empowerment, motivation, and freedom.

Stepping beyond the state of numbness that was your life, and into a gay awakened state of being you, can have the powerful effect of inspiring you to stay on course, expand your thinking, and re-engineer your beliefs about being gay! You can use the wash, rinse, and repeat cycle lessons to create an awakened state of living your gay life your way. Each time you masterfully change a thought, experience a new feeling, and create a new behavior, you catapult yourself into a delicious state of inner peace and happiness! Now that you're awake, continue to repeat the pattern, moving effortlessly towards a fabulously decorated room of "trusting yourself to be yourself."

�֍

Aware of the Past, Present, Future!

If you've got one foot in the past, one in the future, you're going to miss the priceless here and now, happening right in front of you in the present. This isn't new age talky talk, it's real life knock, knock, knocking on your head, begging you to listen. If you're not hearing the knocks, then you're not awake and you're not fully aware. No worries! Awareness is like getting Lemon-Odd Pop into her "falsies." It takes practice too. Most of us who've just *come out* are often either aware of what we're doing yet not fully awake to it, or not aware of it and blind to what affect it is having on our present or future. Others are awake now that they're out of the closet, yet not completely aware of how living in an aware state of being will enhance their lives – gay or otherwise. Sound confusing? Let's straighten everything out and get ya out of that confused state of being.

Awake, but not aware. You're completely awake when you're "out of the closet." Well, except when you're asleep, but you get my drift. You're FINALLY awake from your hiding. It's no longer scary, or at least starting to be not as scary, to be who you are now that you're on the other side of the closet doors. You're settling into being gay on your terms, you know, being gay your way. BEWARE! The awareness could sting you when you least expect it. You're out and proud; yet unconsciously unaware that you sometimes may hide who you are unintentionally! Don't worry, it's not a character defect, nor a criticism. You're simply breaking down the old habits of hiding your truth, getting used to purposefully taking big bold steps to be yourself without regrets. It's all brand new territory, so be gentle with yourself. Awareness is a little crosscheck of self-introspection that helps you focus and ask the question, "Am I being who, what, and how I want to be in my authentic self?"

Aware, but not awake. You may believe you're fully aware that you're gay, yet you may not be awake to exactly that what means for you. All around you are examples of gay life – media, prime time TV, in your community, your circle of gay friends, maybe even in your own neighborhood or at work. On the other polar opposite extreme, you may feel isolated from gay life and highly aware that you have nowhere to turn other than headlines news, prime time TV, and the occasional weekend trip to a more highly populated gay corner of the earth. Your *highly-aware state of being gay* is awaiting your *awakened state of self* to catch up. The awakened state often surprises many newbie gays. It's a "holy crap" moment when you realize being gay means (FILL IN THE BLANK), and you're ready to be (FILL IN THE BLANK); however, that is to your fullest extent. In that moment, awareness holds hands powerfully with the awakened you and doesn't allow anyone else to tell you how to be so that you can be (FILL IN THE BLANK). It may take a little practice and patience, but you will get used to taking these steps.

On the surface, it may seem that awake and aware are interchangeable, which they are to some degree. Releasing yourself fully into being your sexual self causes an awakening that leads to deeper levels of mindfulness and awareness of who you truly are at your core. Your awakened state is a lovely "wake up to your truth" moment, whereas awareness is, I believe, the "embrace your truth and live it" moment. A playful interchange between awake and aware helps bring balance to what lays ahead, a life-long journey of *coming out.* Giving yourself permission to be awake in the reality of who you are and who you are becoming ignites higher levels of awareness. Once powered up, awareness begins to open your thoughts, feelings, and behaviors to the unending spectrum of what it means to be alive and gay your way!

Alive And Pulsating To a New Beat.

I'm going to be completely honest, not that I haven't been up to this point, about my desire for you to be ecstatically alive outside the confines of the closet. For too many years you've hidden, not being yourself nor being fully alive. You've been breathing, eating, drinking, and participating in a wide variety of forms of living yet, something's been missing; the real you. Before you read further in this chapter, I want you to read the next paragraph, and please do the actual exercise before continuing.

Imagine you are standing in the back of a giant movie theater. No one else is there. It's you, the empty seats, and the movie screen, surrounded by stillness. It's cool, dark, and comfortable. Soft light emanates from the wall sconces and overhead lights. Your focus is drawn to the screen as the curtains slowly pull back. A subtle image begins to appear on the screen, and the lights slowly dim followed by your name in simple bold white letters against a cool sky blue background. Your name fades out and the next words that appear are "What was!" Those two words and the background fade away, replaced with images of your past life. As you watch these images on the screen, reflect in your mind upon memories of when you weren't truthfully being yourself. For the next 5 – 10 minutes, close your eyes and focus on the movie screen, in your mind's eye, transporting yourself into the movie experience of your past. As you focus on the past, let feelings of honesty, shame, integrity, guilt, and truth rise to the surface. Also allow happiness, joy, sadness, and peace to show up as well. When done, answer the following questions:

1. How did it make you feel to go back to the past and play in those feelings?

2. What did you discover that surprised you? Inspired you? Caused doubts?

3. What would you have liked to change?

4. Who might you need to fix things with?

5. How would you like to be different moving forward?

6. What do you need to do to let go and heal?

This visioning exercise is not about opening old wounds, nor bringing up old shame or guilt. It's designed to help you see how to step away from the past and come alive. Let go and be in your new skin by moving forward and away from the state of numbness and hiding. Identifying people, situations, behaviors, feelings, thoughts, and emotions that caused you to retreat into hiding your truth, you're becoming more alive and able to catch yourself when you're starting to fall into the old patterns of hiding and pretending to be someone you're not. It doesn't matter if it's about your sexuality, the kind of places you like to hang out, or the type of guys/gals you like to date. Opportunities are equally abundant to be who you are as they are to hide who you are, in all aspects of life.

Your ability to be fully alive in your life, without the puppet strings of others' expectations is one the inspirations that led you out of the closet. Yet, more often than not, the desire to be accepted and loved by a whole new group of others (the gay community), can drive us back into another closet that keeps us from being alive in our own way. Once back in the closet we diminish our ability to feel authentic and to be ourselves at our core. There's a fine balance of being *for others* and *staying true* to one's self. One step too far to the right, and you're back to living to make others more comfortable. A little shimmy too far to the left, and you're a selfish, conceited, all about me asshole.

Releasing yourself from the complications of *always living for others* takes practice, as does keeping the egotistic self in check. Most of us were never taught how to do this and to maintain balance. Our parents, teachers, religious leaders, family, and friends have always, in some way, encouraged us to do things for others – a very noble way to be in life. However, there's a huge difference between being of service and sacrificing one's self. When done in a healthy manner, being of service to yourself first enables you to be even more present, of service, and able to take care of others. Done correctly, it becomes a win/win scenario for all concerned. Of course, that leads to the question, "How do you know the difference between the two ways of being?" Easy! If you don't feel jealous, jilted, overextended, angry, sad, and frustrated by doing something for someone else, then you're being of service in a balanced way. The moment those catabolic emotions flare up, your being of service to others is out of balance, and you're doing it for all the wrong reasons. That's a sure-fire way to find yourself not feeling alive and feeling victimized. The numbness in those moments quickly leads to a spiral of despair and feeling as if there isn't anything you can do to rectify the situation. Yet, you can.

❧

Change Your Thoughts!

There's an art to being fully alive as a person, especially as a gay person. Your life is the canvas waiting for brilliant brush strokes of joy, happiness, and peace to color the picture. In turn, as you emanate joy, happiness, and peace, others will have the opportunity to capture the brilliance of you as you bring your authentic self to the world. While *coming out* may be a challenging, emotional, frustrating, exciting, scary, and joyful experience, we often forget to look in the mirror to see what we are projecting outward into the world. Projecting a challenged state of being, leads to a defensive reaction in return. In this state, you're portraying an image of *boxing gloves up!* Likewise, by emanating a state of joy, you're more likely to receive happiness and joy in return. In this state, you're portraying an image of *arms wide open!*

One of the greatest strengths gays and lesbians have is an innate ability and a determination to step beyond *what was* and to allow ourselves to come alive in *what is.* Yes, you do and don't fight it or question it. You have this innate power. The quickest route to live in this manner on a regular basis is to give yourself the nod of approval to come alive in a very positive, loving, supportive, and respectful manner towards yourself and others. If others reject the upbeat, authentic you, then embrace and realize their feelings and reactions are all about them, not about you. Your new state of being alive and authentic in yourself is pushing some buttons within them that they need to come to terms with, and it has nothing to do with you! If you decide to own the responsibility for healing their buttons, there's a high likelihood of finding yourself back in a closet of living to make others feel comfortable about who you are for their sake, not yours. You will either be bending too far for them, or trying too hard to fix them. Before you know it you're miserable. Instead, mirror passion and compassion to them. If they can't get on that train, then it has nothing to do with you.

Personally, being awake, aware, and alive in my sexual truth has enhanced my life, beyond my wildest dreams. If I'd known that coming to terms with my sexuality, and cuddling up with my sexual energy would have led me to...

» Experience deeper levels of happiness in myself

» Challenge myself professionally

» Explore the essence of my spirituality and discover peace

» Focus on relationships that inspired me, dumping those that don't

» Live a healthier life that works for me

I probably would've come out sooner then at age 38, given what I know now. However, I believe whole-heartedly had I come out sooner, I would have never learned the valuable lessons of being awake, aware, and alive. Lessons that opened up the viewfinder to how numb, dead, and asleep I'd become in life. Without these insights to guide me to my truth, my deepest desires, and my version of living authentically, I would have never risked it all to finally say, "Frankly My Dear, I'm Gay!"

Even though chaos, heartache, fear, pain, and turmoil followed those five spoken words to my now ex-wife, the act of those words have jolted me awake, opened my mind to higher levels of awareness, and ignited the fires for me to live my intended life. My intuition tells me that once YOU realize your under the influence of the *fictitious me* drug, you'll also want to break the habit of living without purpose, and step into the bright world of your own freedom. It's a world that empowers you to be awake, aware, and alive in your truest essence without regrets or shame, provided you release yourself to be free. One aspect of true freedom is discovering the loving balance between doing what's best for you, while being of service to others in a healthy manner. Once this balance is achieved, you'll no longer feel as lost, confused, or afraid of saying, "Frankly My Dear, I'm Gay!" You'll grab hold of the powerful energy of authentic living, catapulting yourself into your intended life of truth on the other side of the closet door. You'll be living your own version of "It's a Wonderful Life," and rockin' your own style of the "Emperor's New Clothes."

✖

Awake, Aware, Alive Check-in

Answer these questions and complete these exercises before moving forward My Dear!

1. When in your life have you felt most disconnected to living?

2. What led to this feeling of "disconnect?"

3. How did you "reconnect" to life in this situation?

4. In terms of living as a gay/lesbian, what does being "awake" look, feel, and mean to you?

5. In terms of living as a gay/lesbian, what would being "aware" look, feel, and mean to you?

6. In terms of living as a gay/lesbian, what would being "alive" look, feel, and mean to you?

7. After having done the movie theater visioning exercise, how might you use this exercise in the future? How might you use this experience to catch yourself when you start falling prey to living more for others than for yourself?

8. What makes you most uncomfortable when you hear the statement, "Live for yourself first, so you can live better for others?"

9. Who taught you to always live for others and not for yourself? Once you've identified the person/people, write the following sentence for each person:

(Persons Name) I forgive you for teaching me it was (Whatever they taught you) rather than doing things out of love for myself first. I thank you for teaching me (Whatever they taught you). I now know and accept that I can (Whatever it is you know you can do for yourself) which will enable me to be better for others in my life. You are now released from any future responsibility in these areas of my life.

10. Describe what BEING alive means to you. In your description, incorporate all the senses – sight, touch, hearing, taste, smell. Also include what emotions and feelings you experience as well as how you behave when you feel fully alive.

Frankly my dear, you're now ready to manifest. Manifesta standard for living your life your way as a gay individual. Please watch your step and move proudly forward!

CHAPTER 14

Gay Manifesto For Living

Ironically, there's still life happening beyond the closet door even though you're now on the other side of those doors. Well, it's not all that ironic now, is it? Family and friend obligations, work, bills to be paid, studying for school; any number of things were alive and well beyond the closet door, before you ever stepped out of the closet and they are still there waiting to be attended to regardless of your newly-found sexual orientation. Nothing and everything's changed now that you're on the other side of the closet doors. Take an honest look at what's really changed in your life. Depending on your situation, either everything's been turned upside down and inside out, or maybe only a few minor shifts have been made. No matter how monumental or insignificant the changes to your life, the core of who you are has not changed. You still wake up, eat (hopefully), go to work or school, talk with friends (or at least those that still love ya), and do whatever else is part of your *normal life*. Whatever isn't part of your norm is simply your *new normal* after *coming out*, and being out, without coming unglued. It's just your new normal, normal, normal. Don't ya hate hearing that? I know. I did too. Here's another zinger that you'll probably get tired of hearing too, "It gets better!" It does, it really does. (TRUST ME!)

Honestly, it doesn't matter if you're 20, 30, 50, or 80 when you *come out*, there are pieces of your life that will change drastically, and others that only budge a bit. Once you start the process towards *coming out* of the closet, common first thoughts are, "Is this normal? Am I different? What's wrong with me?" These questions signal the new adventure of life shifts ahead. Your inner explorer is raising warning flags that something is amiss (and it isn't one of Lemon-Odd Pop's false eyelashes) like your sanity, and it also indicates an extraordinary shift is happening. Depending on how you conduct your soul search, coming into your truth will either be a deep, enlightening discovery, or a nerve-wracking plunge into an abyss of confusion. Either way, you'll grow. Hidden aspects of you that have lain sequestered, finally step forward into the commanding spotlight of authenticity. A deeper level than you, you've never ever experienced before in your life emerges.

One of the most profound awareness that arises is how coming into your sexual identity touches all aspects of your life, not just the ones you worried over. Don't worry you're not alone. Myself and others have been down this road too, and it's all about keeping your head on straight and not losing sight of the goal...*being authentically yourself, your way.* Detractors, pessimists, and internal little gremlin voices will do their best to throw you off course. Let them. I know that sounds crazy, but let them give it their best shot to cause you to lose faith in yourself. Why? Each time you encounter naysayers, the uneducated, and your internal "Are you serious?" voices, you'll grow stronger, smarter, and more comfortable in your own skin. Of course, you can't let them get under your skin either. A pivotal point to starting your "gay" life on the right foot, even if your not right-footed, is knowing who you are, which is exactly who you're supposed to be, regardless of what others may think. That's why I love Lemon-Odd Pop so much. I know who she is because she's real and doesn't care what others or I think of her. Ok, she's a figment of my Diva imagination, but that doesn't bother her or me, either!

Having the confidence to step into your rightful self, comes from within, not from outside of yourself. Confidence, self-esteem, and faith in self knows no gender, nor sexual orientation. This powerful triad only recognizes the beauty and gifts each of us has to share with the world, and share we should, without second-guessing, remorse or shame. However, confidence, self-esteem, and faith recoil faster than Lemon-Odd Pop's girdle when loosened, in disappointment each time we don't acknowledge ourselves, which includes our gay selves, as a beautiful gift to the world. We are who we are, so celebrate baby. Celebrate! Our gifts are our gifts, and no one else contributes to the world the way we uniquely do! To believe otherwise is as shameful as hiding our sexual orientation in the closet. Not sharing ourselves fully with the world, in our own way, impacts every aspect of our lives. Some of us, in fact most of us, have hidden our true selves for so long that we've become blinded by fiction versus truth of who we are; whether we're looking in the mirror, buying into expectations of others, or listening to the voices in our own head. To break free of this devastating habit of not sharing our authentic self with the world first and foremost requires full acceptance of self, flaws and all. Yes, we all have flaws (even Lemon-Odd Pop)! To vault over this hump of self-acceptance, it's time to create your own *Manifesto For Living*, which includes your *Gay Manifesto For Living!*

To get started, bring someone to mind you deeply admire. Maybe it's their fashion sense, their ability to make friends easily, or possibly their career success. Someone who seems to have balanced in both their life and their gay life, making it all integrate together. Stay focused on things you admire about them, placing no judgments on them or your thoughts. Write down things that pop into your conscious stream of thought, listing at least 10 admirable traits you appreciate about this person. If need be, pick two or three people and compile a list drawing out things you admire about each of them. Once your list is complete, using a scale of 1 – 10 (with 1 being least important, and 10 being most important) rank the importance of having each of these traits/characteristics in your own life. Be completely honest with yourself as you do this exploratory exercise. There's no right or wrong. Once you've completed and ranked your list, draw a line through anything with a score of 4 or below. Next, look at your list, for everything ranked 8 or above, and ask yourself this question, "How happy, fulfilled and joyful would this (insert trait/characteristic) make me feel?" If you find yourself second-guessing any item on the list, draw a line through those items too. Finally, look at the items that are left, specifically those ranked 5 – 7. What's left on the list are the things you know deep down inside you'd really like to improve upon or bring into your life. However, upon closer review, if they don't resonate, draw a line through them as well. Now that you've drawn lines and eliminated, *items, traits, characteristics that aren't your 'must haves,* look at the remaining items on the list, and ask yourself one final question:

"Is this something I truly need, want, and desire in my life?"

If it's a need, cross it off the list. Needs are things that are required to survive – food, water, shelter, etc. Unless it helps you survive, it doesn't need to be on the list. Now let's work with what's left – wants and desires. I've defined "wants" as things that once we achieve or receive them, help us experience a positive emotion – fulfilled, accomplished, happy, etc. "Desires" by my definition, while similar to "wants," are things that we're driven to do whatever it takes to make them happen or bring them into our lives. Nothing will get in the way of a deep seeded desire. That's my perspective on *wants vs. desires,* a perspective which is the foundation for finishing the exercise. Use these two definitions as a guide, review the items that are left on your list, and determine which of the remaining items, traits, characteristics are most important for you to develop in yourself. Rank them least important to most using a numbered scale (1 being least important and 10 being most important). Starting with your least important item, and moving to the most important, answer the following questions for each item on your list:

1. What am I willing to do to achieve this change in my life?

2. Who do I need support from to bring about this change?

3. Why is this change important to me?

4. What needs to change physically and emotionally to make this change?

5. When would I like to have this accomplished in my life?

6. How can I best make this change a reality?

Allowing yourself to explore, rank, and then to create an action plan about what you admire in others that you'd like to have in your life, is a great beginning for unraveling the beautiful mystery of your *Gay Manifesto For Living*.

❈

Defining and Crafting Your Gay Manifesto

Before we get too far along, let's talk about this word "Manifesto." According to Dictionary.com, manifesto is a "public declaration explaining past actions and announcing the motive for forthcoming ones." I couldn't have said it better myself, except Dictionary.com's version sounds much more dignified than mine.

What I love about this definition is that it mirrors the journey and experiences many of us have had hiding our sexual truth, only to then bravely declare, "This is me. I'm gay." It's an intimate dance where in one step, we acknowledge the past actions that crippled us from living as our truth, and then with the next dance step, we boldly forgive ourselves and embrace being authentically who we are in our sexuality.

I personally love the word "manifesto." It's an energetic word that's empowering, affirming, and moving as it slips off the tongue. The act of creating your own manifesto for living your life, in your own skin/your way, is an invigorating and liberating experience. I'm so enamored by the word "Manifesto," that I've created a "Manifesto For Living" exercise that is non-negotiable part of my coaching programs. All clients – gay or straight - must complete a life manifesto to help guide them out of whatever closet they're *coming out* of in their lives. The intention of creating a manifesto is to develop a deeper sense of inner intimacy with yourself that ignites the fires of freedom within, burning away any chances that you'll ever return to pretending to be someone that you're not.

Before plunging headlong into the process of creating your *Gay Manifesto For Living,* please follow these guidelines for optimal results:

1. Accept that there's no right or wrong way to create your *Gay Manifesto For Living.*

2. Permit yourself to be fluid, without judgments as you create.

3. Acknowledge your past without regrets, and embrace the experiences as fuel for where you are, and where you're headed.

4. Release feelings of anger, shame, resentment, and guilt towards yourself and others.

5. Be deeply honest and forthright with yourself regarding how you want to live your life.

6. Take nothing for granted during this exploration. Remember, your "Manifesto" will morph and change over time.

7. Be true to you, which isn't being selfish.

8. Take it slow and don't rush.

9. Push your limits and commit to be brave, bold, and raw.

20 key areas will be incorporated into your *Gay Manifesto For Living.* Initially, some of these areas may not resonate with you, so leave them blank and move on to those that make most sense to you. If you get stuck in an area, ask yourself the following questions to awaken the creative juices:

» How does my sexuality impact this area of life?

» Why does this area of life impact my sexuality?

» What big bold statement can I make about this area of life and my sexuality that I would like to live by?

Though this may be a challenging exercise, there is a very specific purpose for creating your *Gay Manifesto For Living*. For some, this exercise will enable you to be more open and vulnerable with yourself. For others, you may discover you've never considered the deep impact of your sexuality on some of these areas of life. Either way, you'll discover interesting, challenging, and beautiful insights about yourself by the end of this journey. Before unveiling the 20 areas of life to be incorporated into your *Gay Manifesto For Living*, here's an example of a *Gay Manifesto For Living* statement:

Area of Life:

Financial Success

Manifesto:

I seize financial opportunities to live an abundant life, which enables me to support myself, my family, and contribute a portion of my earnings back to the greater good of mankind and my LGBT community.

I commit to utilize my abundance to celebrate my family, my friends, my LBGT community, and myself.

I will do my best in the moments I've been given, and with the talents and gifts that have been bestowed upon me to ensure that I do not squander my financial blessings in manners that cause me to lose myself or to hurt others.

Your *Gay Manifesto For Living* can be shorter, longer, simpler, or more complex. It's yours, not mine, nor is it someone else's. Let it flow from your heart and from your truth. Whatever appears on paper is exactly what's meant to be for you in this moment. Enjoy and have fun with this exploration. Feel free to add other areas of life to create a uniquely *Gay Manifesto For Living*, as you see fit!

20 Areas Of Life Exploration For Creating Your
Gay Manifesto For Living

1. Financial Success
2. Intimate Relationships
3. Sexual Energy
4. Family Relationships
5. Leadership
6. Time Management
7. Creative Energy
8. Spirituality
9. Career
10. Personal Freedom
11. Fun and Enjoyment
12. Purpose
13. Work Relationships
14. Friendships
15. Passion
16. Communication
17. Health and Wellness
18. Work Life Balance
19. Values and Beliefs
20. Contribution to society

Before embarking on, defining, and crafting your *Gay Manifesto For Living,* here are a couple more suggestions to make the process even more effective. First, do not use a computer to do the initial work. It's been shown that most people are more creative, spontaneous, and open when they write freehand versus using a computer. Second, find or create a "solitude place" that stimulates you to relax and settle deeply into the exploration. As much as possible, conduct all your exploration in your solitude place, and at the same time each day. Finally, be brave, bold, and raw as you explore. You'll be amazed at what shows up to support you from this day forward in your continuing journey beyond the closet doors.

✖

Implementing Your Gay Manifesto For Living

Raw truth time. If you're going to invest the time in creating a *Gay Manifesto For Living*, don't stick it away in some closet or file, never to be seen again once completed. What's the point of doing the work if it's not going to be put into action? Before you wig out and think, "Damn, how am I supposed to make my '*Gay Manifesto For Living*' a reality," slow down and breathe deep. Similar to your *coming out* process, getting comfy with yourself in your own skin, stepping into your *Gay Manifesto For Living* may take some getting used to. Perfectly understandable, totally expected, so don't be too harsh on yourself. And, for the doubters, or those of you that are still feeling a little unsure about the benefits of having a *Gay Manifesto For Living*, play along with me for just a moment, so that you can see the significance your *Gay Manifesto For Living* will play in your life.

Imagine you've been given an all-expenses paid trip around the world to celebrate your *coming out*. Pretty cool, right? Hong Kong, Sydney, Moscow, London, Paris, anywhere you desire to visit is included. All your meals, hotels, sightseeing, transportation completely "on the house!" Oh wait, Lemon-Odd Pop just reminded me, there's one caveat. There's no itinerary or time tables available to get you from place to place, and no one can assist you with figuring out this critical piece of your round the world trip. You're literally left to fly blind, no pun intended. Maybe you'll take a chance and start at your nearest airport, and hop on the first plane to anywhere. Or, maybe you'll hitchhike to the nearest train station and catch the first train that pulls into the station. How excited are you now about this trip? You're free to go wherever you want!

The adventurous few of you are grinning ear-to-ear, excited by this new twist in your adventure. And of course, those of you that are the logical, solution-minded ones in the group are already calculating strategies for beating the system. No matter which seems to best fit you, each of you is creating a plan/manifesto for moving forward. Remember, the definition of Manifesto is, "public declaration explaining past actions and announcing the motive for forthcoming ones."

Whether you publically declare your intentions to move forward or not with the trip, you've internally declared a manifesto to yourself regarding what you're going to do about this situation. Your "Manifesto" is a combination of the decisions and actions you've taken in the past, and how you're going to make decisions, and take actions for the future of this trip. The same holds true for creating your *Gay Manifesto For Living*.

Based on your beliefs, thoughts, feelings, emotions, actions, and behaviors from closet dwelling all those years, you'll either view the journey on the other side of the closet door as: a) a grand adventure, or b) a "screw this moment," and cope through the *coming out* later in life journey. My hope is that you'll create a *Gay Manifesto For Living by,* operating from the *grand adventure* perspective, with just a little smidgen of coping mixed in, so that you can experience a rich, life long journey of *coming out*, and living your truth.

Explore and incorporate what's worked for you in the past when you're faced with difficult situations. Allow moments of coping as necessary to get by in the short term, and use your logical head to create a strategy for living that serves you, makes you feel comfortable, and creates your own version of Tim Gunn, "Make It Work!"

�֎

Staying The Course

No one ever said life was going to be easy, not that you didn't already know that. On the other hand, suffering and playing the victim card through life is a choice. Even when the worst calamities knock us to our knees, and not in a pleasurable way, we have a choice. We can either suffer and brood, or suck it up and move on with life. That's precisely the reason I suggest creating a *Gay Manifesto For Living* – so you can operate from choice versus from lack of choice. Plus, a *Gay Manifesto For* Living comes in really handy when Ketchup from your fries drips on your shirt, you wake up late for work and find your car has a flat tire, or the first guy or gal you meet after *coming out* of the closet drops you after a week, you'll have a solid blueprint for getting through the humps, bumps, and dumps of living your gay life.

Your *Gay Manifesto For Living* may, and will, present challenges as you try to walk the walk and talk the talk. That's ok. Be extremely gentle on yourself, trust the process, and know that flexibility is the key, in any aspect of life. You designed your *Gay Manifesto For Living* as a guide to help you create focus, better understand yourself as a gay individual, and to allow for alterations along the journey of life where you'll never quit *coming out*.

I've personally found my *Gay Manifesto For Living* serves me best when I'm simply being present, not forcing things, and allowing the *Manifesto* to simply be a guide and a reminder of my intentions. At times, if you're a "do it, want it, have it now" person like me, you'll need to surrender and accept that not every moment of your life will fit snuggly into your *Gay Manifesto For Living*, and vice versa. Patience, persistence, trusting yourself, and allowing your *Gay Manifesto For Living* to be flexible in accordance to life's ebbs and flows, will ensure your *Gay Manifesto For Living* is serving you in the best possible manner – as it's meant to be. Here are three final thoughts for embracing your *Gay Manifesto For Living*:

1. Be flexible.
2. Be vulnerable.
3. Be authentic.

CHAPTER 15

The Others...It's Now All About Them!

What I'm about to share is a painful, yet powerful piece of my journey. Ignoring this aspect of the expedition would mean I've left the wound of not living authentically open and vulnerable for infection. Without addressing this aspect of healing, there can be no healing in the *coming out* process. While recovery and final healing may lead to "agreeing to disagree," it's vitally important to allow the restorative process to take its course for all concerned in the journey out of the closet.

I'm inviting you, the person who's *coming out*, to step off center stage for the remainder of this chapter, and allow "the others" in your life to become the leading players in the journey out of the closet. By no means am I implying you should crawl back in the closet, or diminish the strides you've made thus far in the journey as less than triumphant. However, one of the greatest dangers that throws our family, friends, co-workers, and intimate relations off course in this challenging time of *coming out* is to make it all about ourselves, with no room or consideration for their feelings, emotions, and beliefs. Please don't skip this chapter; thinking it's not for you. No, no, no! This chapter is possibly the strongest tie that binds everyone together in the *coming out* journey. Relax, take a few deep breaths, and know the forthcoming lessons are being presented to bring as much harmony as possible to your *coming out* journey and the *coming out* journey your family, friends, and co-workers have now embarked upon too.

❈

It's Not Only About Them!

If you're a parent, brother, sister, friend, co-worker who's taken the opportunity to read *Frankly My Dear, I'm Gay*, then I want you to know this chapter is fully devoted to you. It's designed to provide you with tools and tips for coming through the closet door in your own way. Often, and I speak from experience as the poster child for this during my own *coming out* journey, the person who's *coming out* forgets that the others in their lives weren't prepared to hear the words, "Frankly My Dear, I'm Gay!" It makes no difference if you're a parent, spouse, child, friend, or co-worker of the person who's *coming out*, you weren't given the internal memo that this person you love was *coming out*! Maybe you suspected something was different about your child, parent, spouse, or friend. Yet, it still comes as a shocking blow to the system when they say, "I'm gay."

In my case, I realized on the surface, and from a heart-centered pain level, that my *coming out* was going to inflict pain and invoke chaos for those around me. I also knew that I was in pain and chaos internally and could no longer live this way or I'd crack. While I value and live by the practice that self-care enables better care for others, I made a fool out of myself by placing way too much emphasis on the "me" part, and not enough emphasis on the "we" part of the equation. I expected everyone to instantly embrace me, my bright future in my gay life, a feeling that's not abnormal for many who are *coming out* of the closet. I overlooked the reality that I'd been preparing for this moment for 38 years, while my wife and children hadn't even been given a Cliff Notes version to help them prepare. Of course, at the time, my daughters would have appreciated a story about Clifford or the Teletubbies vs. Cliff Notes about their dad being gay! After kicking down the closet doors, I was a self-serving, arrogant, downright asshole who showed up quite frequently in my interactions with almost everyone in my life. At times, this behavior was typical for me, but not the core of my character. What I discovered, and what I observe in many of my clients as they go through the *coming out* journey, is that this type of behavior takes center stage out of fear, uncertainty, and mostly during moments of conflict. It is a blatant defense mechanism that comes alive when the story of our *coming out*, that we created on the big screen of our mind, doesn't play out exactly as scripted. By no means does this justify the behavior, I'm simply stating what often is the truth as to why this behavior manifests. Hopefully, that will explain a little bit of the Jekyll and Hyde behavior.

Fear, angst, and "When You Grow Up..."

Regardless of your role in someone's *coming out* story – spouse, parent, child, friend – you've created an award winning script in your mind about who this person is and the future you had planned with them before they had the audacity to f#$% everything up by *coming out* of the closet. Everything you knew just got flushed down the toilet. Thoughts of "When she grows up..." or, "When we retire into our golden years, he and I will..." are now shattered pieces of life, fueled by false hopes. Truths you believed in, dreamed of, and bought into, now laugh in your face tauntingly calling you "SUCKER!" You're betrayed, shocked, and embarrassed. Completely understandable and anyone in your shoes feels exactly the same way.

Ironically, the bomb dropper (aka the jerk, or jerkoff) actually feels the same way; however, the only difference is that they knew the bomb was going to be dropped at some point. Whether they thought this consciously or unconsciously is irrelevant. However, at some point, in the course of their life, they dropped the bomb on themselves, "I'm gay. Holy crap, I'm gay!" Even though the light bulb of truth came on, their darkness didn't magically disappear. They, too, stood in the shattered truth of themselves, alone, fear and confusion swirling around them as if their whole being had been sucked down the drain into the sewer. Unsure of what to do, they waged an inner battle, a war between "what they knew themselves to be," versus "what they know now themselves to be." Conflict, despair hopelessness quickly became their bedfellows. Unfortunately, these same bedfellows stand waiting for you in their pajamas, unless you're 100% OK with your spouse, child, parent or friend being gay. Even if you are cool as a cucumber, beware because you'll have your own inner demon moments to come to terms with this news, and little creepy emotional monsters will strike when you least expect!

A first step towards healing, understanding, and meeting each other on some common ground is to realize the feelings and experiences you're encountering within yourself are almost identical to what they're experiencing or have experienced. Whatever metaphor you wish to use, two-way street, parallel universe, reflection in the mirror, you're both having a *coming out* experience, and would be well served to respect each other in this chaotic, shaky space. If all parties concerned, for the moment, realize this isn't about right or wrong, sacrificing core beliefs and values, or expecting anyone to act as if everything is coming up gay rainbows, then there is room for acceptance on both sides of the fence. It's simply a request for all concerned to be respectful to the best of their mutual abilities, so that the situation can unfold in the best way possible. Meeting this one request can ensure everyone is heard and equally listened to.

✁

FMDIG Principle #1

Everyone Speaks and Everyone Gets Heard

Ok, ok, ok, I know! I'm one of those people who lied, hid, and wasn't strong enough to be authentically who I was; however, I'm not your enemy on this journey as you're walking through your own trials around *coming out* with someone you care about. In fact, the ideas I'm sharing I hope will be a catalyst that helps you as well as whomever in your life has just come out of the closet to both heal with grace, deep understanding, and unrequited compassion. As much as the closet dwellers wanted to be heard and understood, so do you, as you should! Often, whether its conflicted views over someone *coming out*, or another life challenge, we humans have the annoying habit of only seeing our version of a story, and hearing what we want to hear. We forget to allow and make space for everyone to speak and be heard. I can assure you, the person who just came out may have bucketful's of "It's all about me," that they may be throwing on, and at you. "Why?" They've been storing up their feelings, holding back their emotions, and hiding who they are for years out of fear of what you and others will think of them. They're afraid of the consequences they will face, if they have the audacity to be real. Now that they've been brave enough to share their truth, any questions, comments, or even your body language can signal that you're not embracing them in any manner, which may cause the floodgates of confrontational emotions to come out. Their boxing gloves are up and ready to go into the ring when the bell sounds. Here's a little secret, like it or not, you'll probably be prone to do the same yourself. Gigantic, life-changing moments are not something any of our families were trained for, nor their families. Generation upon generation have been trained in the nuances of what, and how gay people are supposed to be based on the stereotypes, and now here you are, facing this journey. It's happening to you, right in front of your own eyes, with your person, your family, or your peeps!

The principle of "let everyone speak and be heard," is meant to lay a foundation for keeping communication open. The moment they, or you, shut down, nothing will be healed or resolved. You're in shock and so is the person who just came out of the closet. I know it sounds crazy, but it's true. Even though the person who just came out had the inside scoop on their thoughts, feelings, and emotions, they didn't really know what to expect once they finally admitted, "Frankly My Dear, I'm Gay!" More than likely they've prepared little sound bites, justification speeches, and pleas for understanding as to why they didn't come out and come clean sooner. It's no big surprise actually; they've had years to mull this over in their heads. You on the other hand have just been blind-sided. That's why, out of respect for you, I'm adamantly encourage those who've come out of the closet to, "Let everyone speak and to be heard." After all, that's what they expect, so they should expect to give the same in return. Fair is fair in love, war, and *coming out*. Likewise, if you, the one who's been dealt the "WTF moment," can graciously return the favor by listening, letting them speak, and opening your mind to understanding, then you might find that raw, bold, honestly will prevail and the truth of this entire situation may set all free to a richer life.

FMDIG Principle #1 – Let Everyone Speak and Be Heard

✄

FMDIG Principle #2
You Didn't Do a Damn Thing To Cause Their Sexual Orientation!

Crazy human nature insists when crisis raises its ugly head in our lives, someone, or something has to be blamed. Honestly, if you didn't feel blame needed to be placed somewhere after being told by someone you least expected, "I'm gay," then I'd say "Bless you my child. Can I bottle your wisdom and sell it? Profits will be shared, 75/25 in your favor!" Honestly, to feel someone is to blame, for this revelation out of left field showing up in life, is like holding someone responsible for you not winning the lottery. Without being flippant, you're going to seek someone to blame – plain and simple. Here's a little secret? The person who came out to you, wanted to do the same thing – blame someone for them being gay. They so desperately wanted to blame someone, or something for the "gay feelings" they're experiencing. His or her conflict, worry, fear, and self-flagellation stemmed from a need to blame someone for them being this way – the freak, the weirdo, or the sexual anomaly. Starting to sound somewhat similar? Of course, it is. Here's the thing. No one is here to blame. Of course, some of you at this juncture are going to take the path of "It's a choice they're making!" I'm not here to debate that time worn argument and I won't. As I said, I'm here to support and help you through this transition.

For a minute, let's consider, maybe it is a choice. Really? This person you know, that you care about deeply, has chosen to subject him or herself to societal ridicule and potential physical harm because they simply want to have sex with someone of the same sex. They've made the choice and they're to blame. Now, you've got your answer on where the blame falls. Fine! Here's a question for you. Now that you've got someone to blame, do you feel any better? If they take on the full responsibility for their sexuality as a choice, then aren't you off the hook? Ponder that thought deeply for just a moment!

Even if you do believe homosexuality is abnormal, wrong, a sin, not in alignment with your beliefs, or that it is a choice, at least go easy on yourself, and know you had nothing to do with your loved one or friend "choosing" to be gay. Their "choice" wasn't caused by something you've done, that made them wake up and say, "I'll show you. I'm going to be gay out of spite and see how much you like that!" The choice they're making is to be who they are, some one no longer hiding behind a mask of false truth. Likewise, they aren't responsible for your reaction to their announcement that they're gay.

We're all responsible for our own thoughts, feelings, emotions, and behaviors. The person who has come out has shared the facts about their sexual orientation, which became a catalyst for your thoughts, feelings, emotions, and behaviors. However beyond that, they can't be held responsible for what your choice is as how YOU choose to think, feel, emote, and behave. They are not your thoughts, feelings, emotions, or behaviors. Only you control your thoughts, feelings, emotions, and behaviors. The same applies to them. Each of us owns our own thoughts, feelings, emotions, behaviors, and destinies.

Regardless of where you stand in the realm that "homosexuality is a choice," your perspective starts with a thought and triggers the rest of the chain of events. If you glean nothing more from this chapter than the concept that thoughts lead to feelings/emotions, which lead to behaviors, then it'll be worth the price you paid for the book. Learning to master our 70,000 +/- thoughts per day, will lead us all to live more, love more, and be more in life. Even though it sounds easier said than done, let's start with a baby step as an example:

Initial Thought: I did something to make him/her gay.

New Thought: I'm not responsible for him/her being gay.

Say those two thoughts out loud, paying close attention to how your senses and body react to each. Most people will experience differing sensations in their bodies based on the spoken these thoughts. Where did you feel it? What did it feel like? How were the feelings different?

Regardless of your perspective of "choice" vs. "born this way," give yourself the option to, if even only for a moment, to trust that "you didn't do anything" to bring gay into play for the person you care about!

FMDIG Principle #2 - You Didn't Do a Damn
Thing To Cause Their Sexual Orientation!

FMDIG Principle #3
Your Beliefs Are Your Beliefs. Honor Them.

No matter who you are, some piece of someone's *coming out of the closet* is going to rub up against one of your own core beliefs, and get under your skin, which may cause you to do a double-take. Especially, if you're a pride flag waving ally. Second-guessing can't be avoided. We've all been raised, and conditioned, with a certain set of unique core beliefs that are ours and ours alone. Granted, we've got beliefs we share with others, like Democrat versus Republican political views; Christian versus Buddhist religious practices; it's the diversity of beliefs that makes the world a delicious melting pot of experiences for all of us to grow in and learn from in the human experience we call life.

In the midst of this unexpected *coming out* journey you now find yourself on, be ready to have your innate beliefs, life views, and core values tested. How you face this test, work through it, and score on it, is completely up to you. Doesn't mean you're left out to dry! Oh no. There are plenty of powerful reasons for you to need support as there are for the person who came out. They've been through and continue to go through the test, finding resources to guide their process. Oops we did it again, paralleling the experiences between what they've gone through and what you're going through. They've placed their core beliefs under the microscope, analyzing them against a newfound strain of knowledge and sexuality that they're coming to terms with now that they're on the other side of the closet.

You'd have to have been sleeping at the wheel of life, out of touch, hands over your ears, to not know one of the most controversial beliefs surrounding someone being homosexual are their religious convictions. Again, I'm not here to debate, or convince you that the Bible or your religious beliefs regarding homosexuality are wrong. In my belief book and view of the world, there are very few things that fit snugly into neat little drawers of right or wrong. Most things in life have beautiful shades of gray!

The invitation I'm extending to you is to lovingly honor yourself and stand firm in your beliefs and convictions, without hatred, bitterness, or condemnation towards your newly out family member, or friend. Before you jump to conclusions, and accuse me of talking out of both sides of my mouth, I want you to understand that for you to be authentically you, me to be authentically me, and whomever just came out of the closet to be authentically who they are, we can all stand firmly in our beliefs and convictions, until we and only we as unique individuals choose to change our beliefs and convictions through our own free will, not because it makes others comfortable.

In other words, "everyone is entitled to their own unique opinion, just don't try to make your opinion theirs, without their permission!" Only a true narcissist creates no space for differences of opinions, and my gut feeling says none of us wants to be considered a narcissistic jerk. Thus, the reason I encourage everyone in the *coming out* journey to honor their beliefs and core values by sticking to them, out of self-respect, with one caveat... that you give that same levity to others. In fact, I think this statement sums it all up best – "Let's all refuse to tolerate intolerance!"

FMDIG Principle #3 - Your Beliefs Are Your Beliefs. Honor Them.

✖

FMDIG Principle #4

"I Understand" Only Goes Skin Deep.

Let's step back to the asshole I was when I came out of the closet. On numerous occasions, whether in heated debates or in tearful quiet pleadings with friends and family to accept me, I often said, "I understand..." Bullshit! I didn't understand; therefore, I couldn't because I wasn't them, no more than they were me. This hallelujah moment took me an incredible amount of time to discover and embrace that "no one is every fully capable of understanding someone else," and I'm not referring to talking with your mouthful not being able to understand someone else. I'm pointing a Lemon-Odd Pop "don't mess with me" finger at flippantly throwing around words we've all been conditioned to blindly regurgitate when life's repeat performances show up – births, deaths, job losses, graduations, etc.

"You must be so proud."

"So sorry to hear of your loss."

"I understand how you feel."

"Now that you have your own kid, you'll understand how I felt."

Ok! We get it. All of us have rehearsed diarrhea of the mouth that unconsciously shows up appropriately and inappropriately, no harm, no foul.

Take head and caution! First, I'm referring to the person who has come out. Do not, for any reason, pretend to know or understand how those you've shared your secret with feel. I know you're still going through a baptism by *coming out*. It happens to all of us in very unique ways, and is an integral lane on the lovely little road of *coming out*. Nevertheless, even though you've experienced your own mind-fuck about being gay, and don't shake your head and say you didn't, there's no way you can "understand" what the people in your inner circle are feeling or experiencing because of your revelation.

Second, as for you, the person who got slammed upside the head with the gay wrecking ball of truth from someone you love and care about deeply, stand your ground, and don't let Mr. or Mrs. "I understand" get away with pretending he/she understands your pain, confusion, anger or worry completely. He or she, depending on who swung that badass wrecking ball into your life, can't get off that easy by saying "I understand what you're going through!" Pieces of the puzzle may fit because they've had their own earth shattering, "come to gay talk" with themselves. Yet, it's no substitute for the feelings and pain that are racking your logical mind, heart, and physical body. Ironically, you both battle the "I understand" demons. You might find yourself saying, "I understand you think that you're attracted to guys, but you're the captain of the football team. How can you be gay?" Or maybe you'll get caught saying, "I understand you find Joan attractive. I do too. But, I'm your husband. We've made babies together." Guess what? You don't understand. You can't, won't, and never will fully understand, no matter how you try.

This pendulum of "understand, don't understand," takes on a wide-reaching life of its own, if you allow it to. Don't! Don't let the temptation to *understand* make matters worse. Remove *understand* from the dialogue. Instead, lovingly interject new dialogues of understanding. "I think I understand some of what you're..." or "Help me understand..." will make room for understanding. A deeper, richer level of understanding will enable you to kick the "doing it because it's what you do" habit, and open the closet door to authentic communication.

FMDIG Principle #4 - "I Understand" Only Goes Skin Deep.

✼

FMDIG Principle #5
Yes, You're The Only Person Who's Ever Been Through This Experience. WRONG!

Crass as this principle sounds, it's necessary to get raw and real and quit bullshitting yourself. Trust me, everyone who's been in the closet and come out felt "I'm the only one." For a greater part of my life, far longer than I want to admit, I was convinced I was the only heterosexual, married guy, who was attracted to guys, having sex with other men, but I wasn't gay! Of the millions of men and women who walked on earth, I was the only one like me, even though all those other married guys that I was having sex with were just like me. Of course, the moment I came out of the closet, stepped into the gay community, boy was I shocked to become surrounded by a whole gaggle of out gay men and women, just like me who'd been married in a heterosexual life. They'd taken the road less traveled, living a closeted homosexual life, in a heterosexual marriage, some even with kids. It wasn't a quiet little country lane that I was traveling. It was a frickin' rush hour jammed freeway filled with drivers from all walks of life, driving cars of hidden homosexuality. Similarly, you will discover you're not the only parent, spouse, child, brother, sister, cousin, boss, friend, etc. of someone who's come out of the closet.

Let's once again revisit, me, the post *coming out* asshole. I used this little tidbit of "first, nor last" to my advantage, slinging it at people in my life when heated debates ensued over my sexuality. "Yeah Mom and Dad, you're not the first nor last parents with a gay son. For crying out loud Dad, your own older brother was gay, even though no one wanted to admit it, so get over it." Even writing those words gets me fired up, pounding the keys of my keyboard with a vengeance. Breathe in, and exhale. Breathe in, and exhale. Yep, that's the best damn way to release stress for everyone on the merry-go-round of *coming out*. Deep breathing through your nose, and exhaling through your mouth, for 4 counts. Works like a charm every time to release the stress. And, don't forget to get down on your bad self, look yourself straight in the eyes and admit you're not the only one who's traveled, or will travel this journey. Sorry to rip that tiara off your head, but Lemon-Odd Pop doesn't like it when others steal the spotlight away from her. Especially when the spotlight is a bunch of made up bullshit! YOU ARE NOT THE ONLY ONE WHO HAS EVER BEEN ON THIS JOURNEY! GET OVER IT ALREADY!

No doubt, you're traveling a unique journey out of the closet that will make you feel like a lone wolf at times whether you're the one *coming out* or the one on the other side of the closet door being come out to. Take comfort in knowing you're not alone. Whether you're the person *coming out*, or the person(s) who's been pulled into this crazy *coming out* tilt-a-whirl ride, neither of you are alone unless you choose to isolate yourself from people who can and will support you.

Give yourself a gift. Take time, do research, and you'll find there are beautiful support groups for every *coming out* situation; Straight Spouses Network for the spouses being left behind; Parents, Families, and Friends of Lesbians, and Gays (PFLAG), with chapters across the globe to support everyone caught up in the *coming out* process; Gay and Lesbians Centers around the world, offer layer upon layer of support – before, during, and after the transition out of the closet. Even if you feel at risk to reveal the pain you're going through, there are numerous anonymous means for being supported from afar. You, simply have to be willing to ask for the support you need, no fear, shame or guilt!

FMDIG Principle #5 - Yes, You're The Only Person Who's Ever Been Through This Experience. WRONG!

FMDIG Additional Principles

There are numerous other principles to assist you as you take baby steps and big, bold, brave strides walking through the *coming out* journey as the "others." Instead of going into elaborate detail, I'm going to provide the remainder of the concepts short statement form. Hopefully, you will find additional support and wisdom for your journey now that you have someone in your life that has come out.

FMDIG Principle #6:

Space to process is a gift. A gift for everyone to be given and received during any monumental life changes; especially during the *coming out* process!

FMDIG Principle #7:

Patience is a two-way street. You both deserve it.

FMDIG Principle #8:

Fears are love and concern, masked behind, "I'm not in control" and "I need help gaining clarity."

FMDIG Principle #9:

It's perfectly ok to agree to disagree provided there's still plenty of room left to love each other in the conflict and accept each other just as you are.

FMDIG Principle #10:

Being right can be detrimentally wrong. So, is it worth it to be right?

FMDIG Principle #11:

If you don't know the answer, ask. If you ask, make sure you're ready for the answer you're about to receive.

FMDIG Principle #12:

Often the most loving things show up in the guise of pain because it's in our best interest to thrive through the pain.

FMDIG Principle #13:

What may be perceived as an act of intentional hurt towards someone else, may simply have been the universe saying, "It's not time for the truth of who you are to live – for you, or others."

FMDIG Principle #14:

One's inability to see, understand, and embrace their own truth may take years. It doesn't mean they've been hiding it from you. They simply hadn't discovered it for themselves yet.

FMDIG Principle #15:

Unconditional love has no constraints. None, none, none!

FMDIG Principle #16:

Coming out is everybody's journey. It's not a solo adventure.

FMDIG Principle #17:

The fear of being alone, never finding loving allies who support your position, and being uncertain are all part of starting a new chapter in life. It simply shows we're all just human on the other side of the closet doors!

FMDIG Principle #18:

Truth, integrity, and authenticity are cornerstones for getting raw with your bad self and with others.

FMDIG Principle #19:

The rate at which we heal from pain is directly proportionate to the amount of love we give others and ourselves.

FMDIG Principle #20:

Admitting what is starts the ball rolling towards what can be.

FMDIG Principle #21:

Life is a fun house of mirrors constantly reflecting back the truth of who we think we are and who we might want to be. The problem is that we avoid looking in the mirror for our truth and we don't encourage others to do the same.

FMDIG Principle #22:

Closets where people hide, pretending to be someone they're not, aren't just filled with gays and lesbians.

FMDIG Principle #23:

There's nothing selfish about doing what's best for ourselves, except in the eyes of those looking at us from the outside.

FMDIG Principle #24:

Your truth is your truth, when you finally get it! Not when someone else tells you "this is your truth!"

FMDIG Principle #25:

There's only one way through the fire, going straight through it.

FMDIG Principle #26:

When someone says, "You can't be," you should smile because you know in your heart and soul that you can.

FMDIG Principle #27:

The art of *coming out* isn't an art at all. It's a masterpiece for all concerned.

FMDIG Principle #28:

The ability to be yourself is directly proportionate to your ability to allow others to be themselves.

FMDIG Principle #29:

Accepting "what was" enables you to open up and embrace what will be.

FMDIG Principle #30:

No one does anything alone, unless they choose to isolate.

CHAPTER 16

Life Long Journey

A very wise pastor once said something that I will never forget, "*Coming out* is the most spiritual journey anyone can experience." In that moment, waves of emotions welled up within me and tears of joy puddled my eyes. I'd been out of the closet for almost 10 years, at that time. The fear, angst, worries of what would happen to me, my children, and my ex-wife had become distant memories tucked into a rainbow colored filing folder, filed under, "See I Told You It'd Be Fine." As he spoke those words, I also realized that *coming out* is a spiritual quest for truth. Not unlike the first time you're challenged with the question, "Is there a God?" and if so, "Why do bad things happen to good people?" Similarly, you find yourself questioning, at a very deep level, "Am I gay, and if so why?"

For me, the answer to that question came when I could no longer drown myself in false expectations of who I thought I was, nor who others thought I should be. I recall a distinct memory of waking up, dead of night, and the electricity had gone off in my small, studio apartment in Laguna Beach. It was only months after I'd *come out* to live my truth. My daughters were with my ex-wife, and I was alone. I now know what occurred next was divine intervention, uniting me with my spiritual, authentic self. I suddenly blurted out "Why me?" The words echoed, bouncing off the four walls of my bedroom, for what seemed an eternity. Lost in a rapturous state of confused wonder as to why those words had escaped my lips, and intrigued by the resounding echo, I at first was naïve to the warmth and suffocating pressure overtaking my body. I immediately assumed a heart attack was assaulting my body: sensible assumption, given the overwhelming stress that had overtaken my life, the past months. Yet, my breathing was normal, no numbness in the arms, and no chest pains to be felt. I quickly did an inventory of the past 8 hours of my life, recalling foods and drinks consumed, encounters with people that may have caused delayed stress reactions; I even recounted my work out for the day to see if possibility I had over done it. Nothing seemed amiss or out of the ordinary, except for the fact that I hadn't consumed any alcohol that day. A decision made out of choice to quell an alcoholic habit I'd realized was potentially leading me to a destiny I'd prefer not to confront.

Lying there in the still pitch dark of night, I surrendered to my spirit, allowing my thoughts to slow, watching each one pass through the window of my mind's eye. The pressure and warmth continued to engulf my body, as I began drifting rapidly towards the beckoning doorway of sweet slumber, an experience which had become foreign to me over the last six months. Reaching the threshold of blissful inertia, my thoughts awakened for a brief moment, intercepting the answer to the still unanswered question, "Why me?" Little did I know in that moment in the dark of night, all alone, that the answer I was about to receive would catapult me forward to be a better man: a father, ex-husband, partner, son, friend, and citizen of the human race. The answer I received was simple:

SO, YOU CAN BE YOU AND GROW!

Deep within me, the answer bubbled forth from the core of my being. In that moment, it did and didn't make sense. Now it makes perfect sense.

The years of denial, hiding behind masks of infidelity, being someone I wasn't meant to be, came into my life in order for me to have the time to grow into my skin, my way as a gay man. I know deep within my essence, had I stepped out any sooner from that closet, I wouldn't be sharing this story, nor these insights regarding my truth with you. I wasn't mature enough in my own gay spirit, my life, my gay body, to handle the wonders and challenges of being gay, let alone gay my way.

By no means am I pretending, nor insinuating that being gay in this day and age is a walk in the park. Yet, I clearly see the challenges and trials that seem ginormous in our lives at the moment are simply textbooks being written and filled with wonderful lessons to be learned. As I've said before and I'll say it again, I'm not proud of the life I hid behind for 38 years. And as I've said before and I'll say it again, without having lived that life, having experienced those experiences, and embraced the people who showed up in my life to love, influence, and guide me, I wouldn't have been able to take the scariest step of my life and admit:

FRANKLY MY DEAR, I'M GAY!

Blessings, strength, and love for your journey out of the closet and beyond. After all, we never stop *coming out* to be our authentic selves – regardless of our sexuality. Life is a beautiful tapestry of *coming out* moments. Never ever forget to cherish each and every one of them. Never!

—Namaste

CPSIA information can be obtained
at www.ICGtesting.com
Printed in the USA
LVOW03s1929210817
545811LV00015B/1895/P